Movement and Music

Developing Activities for Young Children

Movement and Music

Developing Activities for Young Children

Jere Gallagher
Associate Dean, School of Education,
University of Pittsburgh

Nancy Sayre
Emeritus Professor, College of Education and Human Services,
Clarion University

PEARSON

Boston   Columbus   Indianapolis   New York   San Francisco   Upper Saddle River
Amsterdam   Cape Town   Dubai   London   Madrid   Milan   Munich   Paris   Montreal   Toronto
Delhi   Mexico City   São Paulo   Sydney   Hong Kong   Seoul   Singapore   Taipei   Tokyo

Vice President and Editorial Director:
Jeffery W. Johnston
Senior Acquisitions Editor: Julie Peters
Editorial Assistant: Andrea Hall
Vice President, Director of Marketing:
Margaret Waples
Senior Marketing Manager: Krista Clark
Production Project Manager: Jennifer Gessner
Procurement Specialist: Michelle Klein
Senior Art Director: Jayne Conte

Cover Designer: Jennifer Hart
Cover Photo: Sbego/Fotolia; KidStock/Blend Images/
Getty Images
Media Project Manager: Noelle Chun
Full-Service Project Management: Aptara®, Inc.
Composition: Aptara®, Inc.
Printer/Binder: LSC Communications
Cover Printer: LSC Communications
Text Font: Meridien LT Std Roman 11/15

Credits and acknowledgments for material borrowed from other sources and reproduced, with permission, in this textbook appear on the appropriate page within the text.

Every effort has been made to provide accurate and current Internet information in this book. However, the Internet and information posted on it are constantly changing, so it is inevitable that some of the Internet addresses listed in this textbook will change.

Photo Credits: Dave King/DK Images, ribbon image; Videographer: Ryan Noblet, Songwriter: Stacey Steele, p. 2; Ryan Noblet, p. 3; JackF/Fotolia, p. 17; Nancy Sayre, p. 35; Karelnoppe/Fotolia, p. 52; Jere Gallagher, p. 72; Sumnersgraphicsinc/Fotolia, p. 77; Videographer: Ryan Noblet, Songwriter: Stacey Steele, p. 90; Videographer: Sandy Grissom, p. 93; Kimberly Reinick/Fotolia, p. 108; Switlana/Fotolia, p. 114; Nancy Sayre, p. 141; Videographer: Sandy Grissom, p. 146; Katelyn Metzger/Merrill Education/Pearson Education, p. 159; Jere Gallagher, p. 174; Katelyn Metzer/Merrill Education/Pearson Education, p. 191; Jere Gallagher, p. 198; Joanna Zielinska/Fotolia, p. 202; Jere Gallagher, p. 223; Laura Bolesta/Merrill Education/Pearson Education, p. 231; Glen Jones/Fotolia, p. 267; Anson/Fotolia, p. 269; Hui U/Fotolia, p. 297; Andres Rodriguez/Fotolia, p. 303.

Library of Congress Cataloging-in-Publication Data

Gallagher, Jere Dee.
   Movement and music: developing activities for young children/Jere D. Gallagher, Ph.D., Associate Dean, University of Pittsburgh, Nancy E. Sayre, Ph.D. Emeritus Professor, Clarion University.
      pages cm
   Includes bibliographical references and index.
   ISBN 978-0-13-306568-8—ISBN 0-13-306568-5   1. Movement education—Study and teaching (Early childhood)—Activity programs.   2. Movement education—Curricula—United States.   3. Music—Instruction and study—Activity programs.   4. Physical education for children—Study and teaching (Early childhood)— Activity programs.   5. Dance for children—Study and teaching.   I. Title.
   GV452.G33 2015
   372.86—dc23
                                                                                    2014000475

ISBN 13: 978-0-13-306568-8
ISBN 10:   0-13-306568-5

To all the wonderful children who have inspired and enriched our lives by being creative and original individuals and to the education students who have remembered the joy of being a child. Thank you—it has been a wonderful journey.

preface

M ovement and music are important in the lives of children for a variety of reasons. Children love to move, and they love to sing. This book is about developing the love of movement and music so it continues for a lifetime. We see children engaged in movement and music when they are young; however, that intrinsic love and need for movement and music somehow disappears as children make the transition into adolescence and adulthood. One of our main goals is to discuss how to continue that love of and need for movement and music.

A second goal of the book is to understand the growing obesity epidemic and how movement and music can assist children in engaging in physical activity to develop healthy lifestyles. In the past 30 years, childhood obesity has more than tripled (CDC, 2012); in 2008, more than one-third of children and adolescents were considered overweight or obese (National Center for Health Statistics, 2011; Ogden, Carroll, Curtin, Lamb, & Flegal, 2010). In addition to long-term health problems such as diabetes and heart disease, obesity is also related to problems that include decreased academic performance and social exclusion (Castetbon & Andreyeva, 2012).

We know that physical activity is important for the health of the child, but it is also just one component of the lifestyle of children who are not obese. The question is whether children who have better movement skills engage in higher levels of physical activity compared with children who are less skilled. The research has demonstrated that children who have good motor skills are more physically active than children who are not. Not only is there a relationship between gross motor skill performance and obesity in children, but surprisingly there also appears to be a relationship between fine motor skill performance and obesity: Children who are obese have poorer motor skills, and motor skills are critical to maintaining weight control. Movement and music can improve both gross and fine motor skills. This book will assist the educator in helping the children develop the concepts and skills to successfully participate in physical activity. In "M^2 Fun" segments throughout the book, we give examples of ways to get children engaged in movement and music.

Both movement and music enhance academic performance in most cases, but they have never caused a detriment in academic performance, even when including movement and music in the curriculum reduced the time spent in academic learning. We discuss the research on the relationships among physical activity, music, and academic performance and address the factors that affect brain development. Physical activity and music provide children with a release of energy and assist focusing on the content of their academic studies. We provide a variety of examples of how to integrate both movement and music into the day to reduce behavioral problems and increase attention to academic performance.

Movement and music are important in the learning and developmental processes of infants, toddlers, and young children. This book strives to present this information to future educators so they can understand the benefits of movement and music and learn how to motivate and engage children in movement and music. We are not only preparing the educator to teach young children today, but we also have to teach the child the skills that will be needed in 2025. Today we do not know the exact skills that will be required to live in 2025; therefore, we must be able to provide children with the abilities and skills they will need to adjust to and make decisions in the world of the future.

Guiding Principles of the Book

The book is founded on the following guiding principles based on the National Association for the Education of Young Children's (NAEYC's) framework of Developmentally Appropriate Practices:

❶ Individual Needs Met

❷ Environment and Curriculum Reciprocated

❸ Movement and Music Integrated

❹ Family and Community Involved

❺ Standards and Assessment Provide Guidance

The child is at the center of education and learning. We need to understand the child at his or her own level and match the environment and curriculum to the child's level. Movement and music are integrated throughout the curriculum to bring joy to the child and assist in engaging the child in the curriculum. Family and community are part of the learning process and need to be involved in schooling. Standards are required to determine the developmentally appropriate curriculum, and assessment assists in modifying the curriculum to determine the next level of performance. Each chapter is built on a combination of these five guiding principles—and the final chapter assists the learner in evaluating the application of the guiding principles.

Application of Movement and Music

An important component of the book is application. We provide examples of application of the knowledge, concepts and skills throughout each chapter. We start each chapter with **Chapter Learning Outcomes and Guiding Principles**, followed by **Making Connections.** The learning outcomes are objectives that we have linked to guiding principles. Each of these learning outcomes navigates the student to the main headings throughout the body of the text. Following the learning outcomes, we present a true scenario that demonstrates the main concepts of the chapter.

Interspersed throughout the chapter are Movement and Music Fun (**M^2 Fun**) suggestions. These assist the reader in having fun with children while engaging in movement and music learning. Also woven through the chapters in the Pearson eText are hyperlinked videos illustrating key concepts and applications to enhance the course content.

We conclude the chapter with a general chapter summary, but we also include a summary for each learning outcome. To assist students in applying the information, we give them the chance to practice the concepts in the **Demonstrate Your Knowledge, Skills, and Dispositions** section. These assignments can be done for classwork or homework.

To conclude each chapter, we present a section titled **Planning for Engaging.** This provides the student with a simple example of teaching to a standard. We select an M^2 movement, music, or dance standard and develop three learning activities that can be used to develop the content standard. An example of an evaluation for each of the learning possibilities is included. A second Planning for Engaging example is provided, called **Now You Try It**; however, in this case, only the first learning possibility is provided. Following the first example, the children can develop two of their own learning possibilities.

Instructor Resources

An instructor's resource manual provides additional ideas for the teacher educator in engaging the student in the content. We begin with a suggested course outline for a 15-week class that meets two days per week. For each class session, we provide suggested class activities and "new to the text" ideas for class breaks. Additional explanations and class assignments are included. A test bank includes test questions. PowerPoint Slides are also available.

Chapter Summaries

Chapter 1: Movement and Music Working Together to Create a Healthy Child

In this chapter, we focus first on understanding the importance of movement and music in the lives of young children. Movement and music are part of an individual's life prenatally and remain so throughout life, into old age. Information gathered from the various sensory systems enhances learning, whereas movement and music are used to express emotions. The child's environment influences his or her engagement in movement and music—either encouraging or discouraging it. Children initially engage in movement and music through exposure, followed by instructional engagement and, finally, mastery. Howard Gardner's multiple intelligence theory is examined and related to movement and music. The concept of developmentally appropriate practice is emphasized. Theories advanced by John Dewey, Jean Piaget, Lev Vygotsky, Urie Bronfenbrenner, Karl Newell, and Émile Jaques-Dalcroze are discussed in relation to designing learning activities in later chapters.

Chapter 2: Developing Curriculum and Environments for Music and Movement

A well-developed curriculum is critical for school success. In this chapter, we discuss both a competence model and a performance model of curriculum development, and support the competence model. When developing the curriculum, it is important to involve the children in making curriculum decisions—this will enhance engagement of the children, as they will have a decision in what they are doing. We provide a guide that will assist you when selecting or developing your early childhood curriculum. As examples of well-developed curricula, High Scope, Creative Curriculum, the Bank Street Developmental–Interaction Approach, and the Waldorf curriculum are discussed. We conclude with the steps in developing your own curriculum, including goals and objectives, learning possibilities, and standards and assessments.

Chapter 3: Music Provides the Rhythm for Movement and Healthy Lifestyle

The importance of including music in the early childhood curriculum sets the stage for a discussion of developmentally appropriate music experiences for young children and a review of national and state music standards. The Jaques-Dalcroze, Kodaly, Orff, and Suzuki methods of teaching music are reviewed, followed by suggestions on how to teach music. The chapter concludes with music suggestions for inclusion in the early childhood classroom.

Chapter 4: Matching the Individual, Task and Environment to Enhance Learning

A focus on understanding the growth and developmental and maturational changes in the child is used to determine developmentally appropriate tasks and skills for the child and setting the environment to ensure success. An important concept that is discussed here and in some of the following chapters is performance constraints, which can help or hinder performance. An example of a constraint that hinders performance is strength and balance. Children cannot stand if they do not have sufficient strength and balance. A constraint that helps performance is ball size. A child can catch a large, soft ball but may fail to catch a small rubber playground ball, turning his head and closing his eyes because he is afraid the ball will hit his face. We discuss how to match the task and the environment to the child to ensure success. An understanding of culturally relevant activities is provided.

Chapter 5: Movement Content During the Early Childhood Years

Movement and music are integrally related and are important throughout life. In this chapter we discuss movement concepts and the language of movement. In addition, we review the development of fine motor skills and ways to enhance development. The role family, community, and culture play in planning movement and music activities is addressed.

Chapter 6: Dance and Music: A Healthy Lifestyle Partnership

An easy way to increase physical activity in children is to incorporate dance. We start by reviewing national and state dance standards and explore ways to teach dance. Creative dance and critical thinking are linked and the teaching of dance is discussed.

Chapter 7: Development of Gross Motor Skills for a Lifetime of Movement

Coordination and balance underlie the development of gross motor skills and is therefore discussed first to provide the foundation for examining the development of gross motor skills. We provide a developmental sequence for gross motor skills and apply that knowledge to lesson planning. National standards for physical education are important to select content for lesson planning. The learning environment must be conducive to decision making and building confidence.

Chapter 8: Fitness and Nutrition Create a Healthy Lifestyle

Because of the increasing obesity epidemic, we feel it is critical to address the importance of physical activity and of healthy eating. We first discuss the definition of a physically educated individual and the benefits of physical activity. Skill-related and health-related fitness are explained, with the emphasis on the development of health-related fitness. In addition to engaging in physical activity, the child needs to eat a healthy diet. We define healthy eating and discuss how to create an environment and culture to develop healthy eating.

Chapter 9: Movement and Music Broaden Learning

The mind–body connection is discussed initially, followed by a discussion on the relationships among physical activity, exercise, fitness, music, and academic performance—all the given factors increase academic performance. In addition, both movement and music should be part of interdisciplinary lesson planning. It is important to include physical activity breaks throughout the day.

Chapter 10: Assessment, Evaluation, and Engagement

For learning to occur, we must evaluate performance. We first discuss the purpose of assessment, followed by a review of the NAEYC and NAAECS/SDE Position Statement on Assessment. We discuss ethical conduct in assessment of children and examine how to create different types of assessment for movement and music. We conclude the book with a review of how early childhood educators can evaluate whether their classrooms incorporate the Guiding Principles.

References

Castetbon, K. & Andreyeva, T. (2012). Obesity and motor skills among 4- to 6-year-old children in the United States: Nationally representative surveys. *BMC Pediatrics*, 12(28), 1–9.

Centers for Disease Control and Prevention. (2012). Childhood obesity facts. http://www.cdc.gov/healthyyouth/obesity/facts.htm.

National Center for Health Statistics. (2011). Health, United States, 2010: With special features on death and dying. Hyattsville, MD: U.S. Department of Health and Human Services.

Ogden, C., Carroll, M., Curtin, L., Lamb, M., & Flegal, K. (2010). Prevalence of high body mass index in US children and adolescents, 2007–2008. *Journal of the American Medical Association,* 303(3), 242–249.

Acknowledgments

Writing a book becomes a time for organization and reflection—organization of all the knowledge and skills gathered in the content area, and a time to remember and thank the individuals who have helped us gather and develop our knowledge and skills.

We would like to thank all the children who we have had the privilege of working with over the years, especial Cassandra, Natalie, Madeline, Henry, Barrett, Chip, Rachel, Hannah, Daniel, and Emma. You have certainly made our lives richer, and we have enjoyed being part of your lives. You have contributed enormously to our understanding of motor development and the enjoyment of music. The stories used in the book are the stories you have given to us over the years.

We would also like to thank Stacey Graham Steele, Assistant Professor of Music at Slippery Rock University of Pennsylvania. Stacey Steele has dedicated her professional career to enriching the lives of children through the enjoyment of music combined with movement. She has been an inspiration to many children and university students. Her assistance in the development of this textbook has been extremely valuable and greatly appreciated.

The Slippery Rock University students who contributed their time and skills in singing the M^2 song were brilliant. We would also like to thank all the university students with whom we have had the privilege of working over the years. You have helped us to organize our knowledge and skills. We know you will brighten the lives of the children you teach and ensure that they are actively engaged in movement and music.

Finally, we would like to thank those who reviewed our book along the way, providing helpful and constructive feedback: Myra Classen at Clackamas Community College, Kelly L. Jennings at University of Central Florida, Cassandra Keller at Lynn University, and Paul H. Rheaume at Kellogg Community College.

Jere Gallagher and Nancy Sayre

brief contents

contents

Movement and Music

Developing Activities for Young Children

chapter 1

Movement and Music Working Together to Create a Healthy Child

LEARNING OUTCOMES AND GUIDING PRINCIPLES

Students reading this text will be able to demonstrate Learning Outcomes linked to Guiding Principles based on the National Association for the Education of Young Children's *Developmentally Appropriate Practice in Early Childhood Programs Serving Children from Birth through Age 8.*

Learning Outcomes	Guiding Principles
1.1 Develop an understanding of the importance of music and movement in the lives of young children	Movement and Music Integrated
1.2 Explain the role of environment systems	Environment and Curriculum Reciprocated
1.3 Understand inherited culture and musical and movement choices	Environment and Curriculum Reciprocated
1.4 Recognize that the National Association for the Education of Young Children provides a framework for early childhood programs	Environment and Curriculum Reciprocated
1.5 Distinguish how Guiding Principles address individual developmental and learning differences	Individual Needs Met
1.6 Value the importance of play in engaging children	Individual Needs Met
1.7 Discuss how theorists provide guidance in understanding the role that movement and music have in child development	Individual Needs Met

Making Connections
Gonna M² Video

I'm gonna move my body every day!
I'm gonna move my body every day!
Moving gives me energy to work and to play!
I'm gonna move my body every day!

I'm gonna eat good food every day!
I'm gonna eat good food every day!
Food makes me healthy in every way!
I'm gonna eat good food every day!

I'm gonna make some music every day!
I'm gonna make some music every day!
Singing makes me happy I could sing all day!
I'm gonna make some music every day!

(Steele, 2013)

L isten to the song, "Gonna M²," by viewing the **video**. This song, by Stacey Graham Steele (Steele, 2013), Assistant Professor of Music at Slippery Rock University of Pennsylvania, and sung by Slippery Rock University music education students, expresses the importance of exposing young children to movement and music while they enjoy a healthy diet. Individually, movement and music are important, but when in combination, they form a dynamic duo. Dynamic M² enhances development, learning, and enjoyment. To help the reader of this book appreciate the pleasure of movement and music activities and understand basic concepts, **M² Fun** ideas are inserted throughout the book.

1.1 Develop an Understanding of the Importance of Music and Movement in the Lives of Young Children

Music and movement have been present and enjoyed by every culture in the world for centuries. Children throughout the world have an instant connection to music, and their way of showing this connection is

▲ Future music educators singing about the importance of movement and music.

to move. They move their bodies, their hands, and their feet when listening to music. We all have stopped to watch a very young child who, while listening to a musical selection, moves her hips, shoulders, and arms up and down to the rhythm of the music. This child is feeling true uninhibited joy. The pleasure in music and movement is something we want all children to experience because by moving and experiencing happiness, children will develop into healthy individuals, both physically and mentally.

Movement and music are excellent partners because they enhance each other and provide great enjoyment to the participants and to the observer. Mothers and caregivers intuitively understand the advantages of this partnership. They know that by combining singing and rhythmic movements, such as rocking and caressing, children are soothed (Levitin, 2006). It is understood that the two are tightly coupled.

In premodern cultures, most members of a society were involved in listening to and moving to music. Gradually, society has become divided into two separate groups: music performers and music listeners (Levitin, 2006). Early childhood educators and parents want children to be both performers and movers. There are many benefits to being both a listener and a performer because M^2 will stimulate the senses.

M² FUN   **Space Awareness**

Divide the children into two groups, A and B. Each child in Group A will be given a hula hoop and will hold the hoop in various positions. Children in Group B will move, one by one, through the hoops using a variety of movement styles, such as crawling, dancing, wiggling, robot walking, and hopping. Play a musical selection while the children are moving through the hoops.

Senses Enhance the Learning Domains

Children learn through their senses; all domains—cognitive, socioemotional, and physical—should be integrated in the learning process. Music plays a vital role in the sensory development of infants (Whitwell, 2012) and provides a connection to all four lobes of the brain—frontal, temporal, parietal, and occipital—in addition to the cerebellum (Levitin, 2006). When children hear a sound, a beat, a rhythm, or a song, their brains are stimulated to make important connections to the developing nervous system (Hannaford, 2008). The first sound a fetus hears in the uterus is the beat of the mother's heart. This beat or rhythm becomes an organizer for music and movement and, later, for language and mathematics. Music helps infants prepare for later language development (Levitin, 2006). In addition, appropriately designed music and movement activities can enhance cognitive and emotional development, help remediate or prevent learning problems, and reduce stress (Healy, 2012).

When children *hear* a beat of a rhythm or a song, they move—even when seated or lying down. Their arms, fingers, legs, or toes move, increasing stimulation to the developing brain and strengthening muscles. As the child moves, air molecules move, and the nerves located on the skin are stimulated by the flow of the air over the body—the sense of *touch* is stimulated. Moving air becoming a carrier for smells—the sense of *smell* is stimulated. Movements—up, down, and around—cause the eyes to constantly adjust to the surroundings; this stimulates the sense of *sight* and all the brain receptors connected to seeing. The senses of hearing, touching, smelling, and seeing are heightened, helping to enliven and to integrate the learning domains. Learning is enjoyable for the child.

Music and Emotions

Music plays a powerful role in encouraging movement because it has such a compelling effect on our emotions and our intellect. To listen to music without moving is difficult for many people to imagine. To listen to music without feeling some emotional response is also difficult. Imagine going to a rock concert and neither moving nor feeling some type of emotion. Compare this to going to the symphony, where standing in the aisle and dancing are not acceptable, but the emotional component and the urge to move are still present. We must value movement with all types of music and respect the emotional effect music has on the state of mind.

Music can both provide excitement and stimulation and be calming. It is played at every major political, educational, and community event because it can affect the way we think and feel (Bales, 1998). Advertisers, film directors, politicians, and military leaders use music to stimulate emotions and to move entire groups toward a desired goal, such as buying a product or going into battle. Across cultures, music can make us feel happy, sad, angry, scared, or peaceful, and is linked to an internal locomotor or movement system (Sievers, Polansky, Casey, & Wheatley, 2012). The way the music is structured (melody, rhythm) by the composer and manipulated by the musicians influences our emotions. Listen to some of the following selections of music in Table 1.1 and notice if you or the children feel happy, angry, sad, scared, or peaceful.

The examples given in Table 1.1 are general examples for the broad American culture, but there are variances due to cultural influence and personal experience. Cultural variance between children and among groups of children will have an influence on what and how children learn music and movement.

Table 1.1 Emotion and Music Examples

Emotion	Music Selection	Artist or Composer
Happy	"What a Wonderful World"	Louis Armstrong
	"You've Got a Friend"	James Taylor
	"Here Comes the Sun"	Beatles
	Serenade for Strings in E minor (2nd movement)	Sir Edward Elgar
Sad	"Nothing Compares 2 U"	Sinead O'Connor
	"Hallelujah"	Jeff Buckley
	Violin Concerto (2nd movement)	Samuel Barber
Angry	"Irreplaceable"	Beyoncé
	"I Will Survive"	Gloria Gaynor
	Night on Bald Mountain	Modest Mussorgsky
Peaceful	"Angel"	Sarah McLachlan
	"Don't Panic"	Coldplay
	Canon in D	Johann Pachelbel
Scared	"Fear of the Dark"	Iron Maiden
	"Thriller"	Michael Jackson
	Peter and the Wolf	Sergei Prokofiev

1.2 *Explain the Role of Environment Systems*

Urie Bronfenbrenner's (1979) "ecological theory" provides awareness that children do not live in isolation. The child affects the surrounding environment, and, in turn, the environment has an influence on the child. The child may have an active role in the immediate environment (family, teachers, neighborhood), even though he or she may have no active role in the expanded environment (culture and socioeconomic) (see Figure 1.1).

The child will have a direct impact on family, school, teachers, and peers, but not as much of an influence on socioeconomic levels, political, and religious systems, and culture. In contrast, the culture and socioeconomic level of the child, as well as political and religious systems, may have a huge impact on the child.

Families, schools, religious affiliations, and culture can influence a child's perspective on movement and music. The child's inherited culture can have a bearing on music and movement preferences of infants, toddlers, and young children; their emotional reactions to music and movement activities; and musical and motor memory. The child's family and the surrounding teachers, peers, school, and religious affiliations can further encourage appreciation and use of the cultural music and movement.

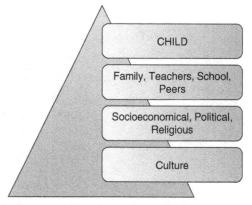

Figure 1.1 Impact of child's environmental relationships.

1.3 *Understand Inherited Culture and Music and Movement Choices*

From birth, children are exposed to the music selected by their families and the neighborhoods where their families congregate and shop. Gradually, teachers, peers, and perhaps religious institutions will have more of an influence on the types of music appreciated by the individual. This is also true of movement activities. The child's movement choices will depend on the family's and school's choices and, later, on games such as soccer, football, or cricket, often seen through television and video games. The overall umbrella is culture.

Mary Falto has just begun as a movement teacher at an elementary school. In reviewing the previous teacher's curriculum choices, she was surprised to see that the children were exposed to only two sports: football and basketball. When she asked the administration about these sport choices, she was told that these were the interests of the families in the school. She decided to develop a new movement program, with an emphasis on catching, throwing, running, and kicking. These fundamental skills areas could be used in football and basketball, but could also provide a basis for other sport areas, such as soccer. Her plan expanded the interests of the children while continuing to follow the traditional practices of the school and the families.

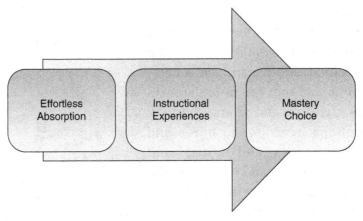

Figure 1.2 Stages of music and movement learning.

A child may progress through three stages to learn about music and learning (Campbell & Scott-Kassner, 1995)(see Figure 1.2).

■ *Stage one, effortless absorption:* The child is immersed in his or her imme-diate surroundings (family, peers, teachers). The child absorbs music and movement with little effort. The inherited culture of the child will dictate the types of music and movement present in the environment.

■ *Stage two, instructional experiences:* The child will begin to experience the conscious thinking and learning process. Families and teachers will have a direct effect on this stage of learning. The child will be exposed to learning experiences through planned instructional periods. The child is actively involved in the learning process and will want to strive to be competent in the practice. At this stage, an adult observer will see the child toil to accomplish fundamental motor patterns and to sing and to play rhythm instruments.

■ *Stage three, mastery choice:* The child may work to become proficient at a sport, skill, and/or singing or playing an instrument. Not all children will want to progress to stage three, however; some will be content to remain in stage two.

The child's inherited culture will frame the music and movement that the child will absorb and learn. Children will learn by observation of peers, adults, and events in their surrounding culture through play, pictures, technology, and sporting events. Throughout the entire process the culture, community, school, family, and peers must value music and movement as much as they value traditional academic intelligences. Studies have shown that culture and socioeconomic levels may influence how families view and value different kinds of intelligence.

Multiple Intelligences

Howard Gardner, a Harvard University psychologist and neuroscience professor, developed the multiple intelligence (MI) theory, which placed value on a group of intelligences that captures the abilities valued by human cultures. He was not pleased with the narrow definition of intelligence that has typically revolved around mathematics and language. Instead, Gardner's MI theory acknowledges a variety of components of the human abilities that are independent but complement each other (Gardner, 2011). The multiple intelligences are:

- Bodily-kinesthetic intelligence
- Musical intelligence
- Linguistic intelligence
- Logical-mathematical intelligence
- Spatial intelligence
- Intrapersonal intelligence
- Interpersonal intelligence

Gardner's list of intelligences demonstrates to educators that a variety of knowledge and skills is valuable, and that children learn differently. Therefore, educators should vary how they teach to accommodate individual differences.

Gardner has placed value on musical intelligence and bodily-kinesthetic intelligence. Today's educational programs for young children, however, encourage development in the traditional intelligences of logical-mathematical intelligence and linguistic intelligence.

We need to re-examine our concept of intelligence and value other intelligences, such as musical and bodily-kinesthetic intelligences. It is certainly important for a surgeon to have the linguistic and logical-mathematic knowledge and skills to know how to remove and/or repair a body part, but it is also important for the same surgeon to have the fine motor skills to perform the surgery. All children possess most of the intelligences listed in the MI theory, but they do not process them in the same manner (Gardner, 2011). Individual differences are present; therefore, parents and educators must appreciate and emphasize all intelligences when working with children (see **video** Multiple Intelligences).

This concept was expressed by Loris Malaguzzi, the founder of the internationally acclaimed early childhood program in Reggio Emilia, Italy, in his famous poem, "No Way. The Hundred Is There." The poem describes how a child uses a hundred languages to learn and to communicate. Furthermore, Malaguzzi states that the child's head should not be separated from the body (Wurm, 2005). Movement and music are languages— and an excellent way to stimulate learning and to communicate knowledge and skills.

Movement and music are universal to every child in every culture. M^2 must be introduced and enforced in the curriculum for young children appropriately for the individual and developmental needs of each child. A

M^2 FUN   Space Awareness

Demonstrate blowing up a balloon to the children. Once the concept of an empty and a full balloon is shown and understood, bounce the balloon around to display the lightness of the filled balloon. Tell the children they are going to be balloons and the air opening is in their hand. The children will crouch on the floor in the smallest position possible and begin to fill the balloon with deep breaths. With each breath the children will gradually rise from a low to a higher level. The process can be started and stopped periodically, causing the children to fall back to the floor and to rise again. Once the balloons are filled, the children can "float" around the room.

framework is necessary to provide appropriate guidance to families, child care providers, teachers, and administrators.

1.4 *Recognize That the National Association for the Education of Young Children Provides a Framework for Early Childhood Programs*

The National Association for the Education of Young Children (NAEYC) developed a framework, grounded in child development and learning research, for the early childhood community to use when planning learning experiences for young children. Although specifically designed for early childhood education, it applies to learning across all ages. It has been referred to as *Developmentally Appropriate Practice* (DAP) since its initial development in 1986. The framework was revised and adopted in 2009 by NAEYC and is referred to as *Developmentally Appropriate Practice in Early Childhood Programs Serving Children from Birth through Age 8* (Copple & Bredekamp, 2009).

NAEYC recognizes that many schools are limiting learning experiences in play, outdoor/physical activity, social interaction, problem solving, and the arts (music and visual) (NAEYC, 2009). Intervention is needed to ensure that children are healthy and developing an enjoyment of learning and a strong sense of their own competence in learning based on their individual levels of abilities (see **video** Developmentally Appropriate Early Childhood Education).

DAP presents a variety of important points to consider when developing programs for young children. It is vital for individuals working with children to be aware of the following points and use them to structure learning experiences for young children:

- Interrelationship between the developmental domains (physical, socioemotional, cognitive) and play is a self-motivated learning strategy.
- Development and learning are predictable and sequential, with each level building on the preceding level.
- Development and learning are an interactive process between the child's genetic code and cultural and personal experiences in the child's immediate and extended environment.

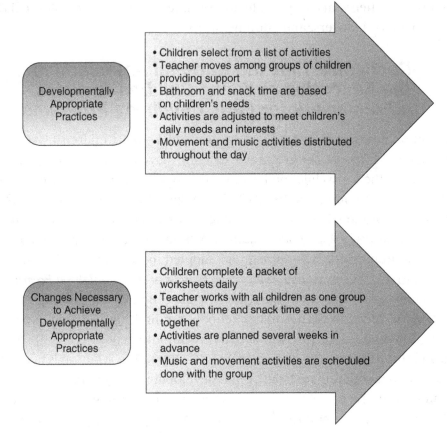

Figure 1.3 Early childhood learning environment examples of progress toward achieving DAP.

Figure 1.3 is an example of an early childhood learning environment that has achieved DAP, and another learning environment that is working on improving DAP practices. Both programs are licensed by their state's early childhood licensing agency.

The DAP essential ideas are very important when designing curricular learning experiences for young children because they serve as the structure for the design of the curriculum and environment. DAP also plays an important role in the development of Learning Outcomes related to the five Guiding Principles used in this book to provide organization for students (see Table 1.2):

Table 1.2 Guiding Principles and Corresponding DAP Essential Ideas

Guiding Principles and Corresponding DAP Essential Ideas	
Guiding Principle	**DAP Essential Ideas**
Individual Needs Met	Development and learning tend to be predictable and sequential.
	Rate of learning and development will vary with each child and tends to proceed from simple to complex.
	Depending on developmental levels and experiences, a child may be more open to learning a skill, a level of knowledge, and/or self-regulation dispositions.
Environment and Curriculum Reciprocated	Development and learning constitute an interactive process between the child's genetic code and the child immediate and extended environment.
	The child has a strong influence on the surrounding physical and social environment.
	Experiences have an effect on a child's learning and development.
Movement and Music Integrated	Development and learning are enhanced through the use of a variety of interactive activities and learning strategies.
	Interrelation between the developmental domains (physical, social/emotional, cognitive) are important for learning.
	Domain areas have an active sphere of influence over each other.
	Play is an excellent self-motivated learning strategy for all domains.
Family and Community Involvement	Social and cultural experiences surrounding the child have an influence on development and learning.
	Development and learning are enhanced when children have secure, positive, and consistent relationships with adults and peers.
Standards and Assessment Provide Guidance	Learning and development are enhanced when children are encouraged to engage in activity levels just beyond their current mastery level.
	Knowledge and skills are improved by interesting and self-motivated practice.
	Each level of knowledge and skills builds upon the preceding level.

❶ An early education program must meet children's cultural, socioeconomic, and individual needs (**Individual Needs Met**).

❷ Learning is an active process between the explorations of the environment and the curriculum-planned activities (**Environment and Curriculum Reciprocated**).

❸ Movement and music learning activities should be integrated and developed to enhance the development of a healthy child who is ready to learn (**Movement and Music Integrated**).

❹ Family and community involvement is important in the design of the learning environment and implementation of the curriculum to enhance learning (**Family and Community Involved**).

❺ Formal and informal standards and assessment should document the child's growth in developmental areas and assist in curriculum design (**Standards and Assessment Provide Guidance**).

1.5 Distinguish How Guiding Principles Address Individual Developmental and Learning Differences

It is important to understand how the Guiding Principles will help teachers and parents to assist with growth and development in an appropriate manner.

Principle One: Individual Needs Met

Child development is sequential and predictable to a degree but varies because of the child's distinctive genetic makeup and environmental (physical, socioeconomic, and cultural) influences. The first movement of the fetus in utero excites every mother. These simple reflexive movements contribute to the development of the brain and to later complex voluntary movements that are major factors in the child's well-being. Movement increases the connections between neurons and also increases the insulation or myelin surrounding the neuronal connectors, called *dendrites*. Music provides sensory input to assist with the development of these connections. This developmental process is enhanced with appropriate opportunities and varied experiences for movement and music in a quality environment.

During the first year of life, the child develops basic movement skills (reaching, grasping, holding, crawling, sitting, and standing). During the toddler years, the child improves fundamental movement skills (walking, running, jumping, throwing, catching, kicking, and bouncing). These fundamental movements are the basis for sport, fitness, and dance activities used in the following years of the child's life. As the child moves into fitness and sport activities, health-related components—such as aerobic fitness, muscular fitness, flexibility, and body composition—become important. Children must have movement experiences under varied conditions and without gender bias to enjoy exploration and play.

Children's musical development follows the same sequential development as language (see **video** The Stages of Music Development by Eric Rasmussen). The infant will engage in music babble by experimenting with speaking sounds, followed later by rhythm babble. During this latter stage, the infant will babble using an erratic tempo (Gordon Institute for Music Learning, 2012). The maturing infant will engage in informal guidance that will be unstructured (birth to 3 years) in the beginning, but then will become structured (3 to 5 years) (Gordon Institute for Music Learning, 2012). Formal musical learning follows the informal guidance stage. Exposing infants, toddlers, and young children to a variety of music in their culture is critical to providing a foundation for music enjoyment.

It is helpful for educators to be familiar with the ages and stages of movement and music development as well as the cognitive, socioemotional, and physical levels of each child. This will help to meet the developmental needs of each child and to provide appropriate learning experiences.

Principle Two: Environment and Curriculum Reciprocated

All children are genetically unique and will experience the learning environment in different ways. The learning environment dictates the success of the learning activity through play and/or guidance by a teacher. Although there are basic guidelines or milestones for each age, how and when each child succeeds at the developmental task vary based on genetic makeup, personality, physical and mental needs, and the larger environment and inherited culture.

For example, 18-month-old Mary enjoys climbing and jumping off objects, whereas her twin, Martha, is far more timid. Martha climbs and jumps but wants to hold an adult's hand while accomplishing these skills. Both movement processes are acceptable and should be valued. The teacher of their early learning and educational program must address the needs of both twins. A soft and flexible environment suitable for jumping should be made available for Mary, and adult support should be provided for Martha.

The example of Mary and Martha shows how important the environment is in the learning process. The environment should stimulate learning that is appropriate for each child, and should match the developmental level for the age range using the learning environment. If the learning is developmentally appropriate for the age and ability of the children it will not only be stimulating, but it will also provide security in the form of mental comfort while keeping the children safe from physical harm.

Principle Three: Movement and Music Integrated

Movement and music are very important to the long-term health of children and their enjoyment of life. These two areas can and should be integrated into the entire day's activities, not just provided at specific time periods determined by the administration. Although it is indeed beneficial to have a music class or a physical education class, it is desirable to use music and movement to emphasize points of knowledge because they provide entryways into all the developmental and learning domains—and they help to remove or diminish stress.

> Ms. Tracy is a first-grade teacher who is leading her class through the end-of-year mandated testing in language arts. The lengthy time periods of reading a story, answering comprehension questions by filling in bubbles, and writing a story are stressful to the 7-year-olds and to Ms. Tracy. She relieves tension by having the children stand, move, and sing a song. In another school district, Mr. Clark uses movement while his second graders work on their mathematic combinations. The children must skip to the board, work the problem, and skip back to their seats. Both Ms. Tracy and Mr. Clark truly understand how important it is to integrate movement and music into the daily lives of children.

Principle Four: Family and Community Involved

Ensuring that children are healthy and ready to learn is important and should involve the entire community. A child needs to feel secure and

▲ Involvement of many generations enhances family activities.

have positive relationships with peers and adults. An example can be seen in a small Maine coastal community of about a thousand residents. This town rallied to call attention to the overweight and obesity crises afflicting the children. Families in the area were invited to an event highlighting movement with balls and ropes, as well as appropriate nutrition. A citizens' group—including an executive chef at a local inn, the staff of the town's museum, the head librarian, a medical doctor, and various organizations—donated time, money, and expertise to the project. To build interest in the day, a retired minister and an investment counselor wrote articles for the local newspaper about the health problems associated with not moving and not eating a healthy diet. In addition, the speaker donated her airfare, and the town donated use of the town hall for the event. Finally, a woman made beanbags for each child. What a community effort!

The community surrounded the children and had an influence on their development and learning. Responsibility for physical and mental support of each child should be the role of the entire community:

Family	Media
Teachers	School administrators
Health professionals	Political institutions

Children depend on their immediate and larger environments to help them mature and grow into healthy and productive members of society.

Principle Five: Standards and Assessment Provide Guidance

As the teachers approach the design of learning activities for young children, they are guided by state and national standards. These standards should be in all developmental areas (cognitive-linguistic, socioemotional, and motor-physical), and provide guidance when developing learning activities in all the major academic areas, including arts, mathematics and problem solving, literacy, scientific inquiry, social studies/communities, and health and physical activity.

All 50 states have established standards to be used to provide guidelines for curriculum and learning activity development appropriate for the cognitive, socioemotional, and physical levels of each child. Professional organizations such as the National Association for Music Education (music) and National Association for Sport and Physical Education (dance and physical education/movement) have produced standards to provide guidance at the national level.

In addition, standards are used to give guidance in assessing how children are progressing in the developmental domains. It is important to have regular formal and informal assessments to determine the direction that should be taken in the design of learning activities appropriate for each child. By doing this, the learning activities will meet each child's developmental needs.

Designing a daily curriculum without knowing each child's developmental level is not appropriate. Teachers are often asked to present to an administrator their lesson plans for an entire year or month, including daily activities. This is not desirable, because learning must be guided by the use of constructive formal and informal assessment methods each day to determine the direction of the next day's learning activities.

Assessment should be completed daily to determine the structure of the learning activities just beyond each child's mastery level. A higher-level learner, parent, teacher, or older child can give guidance and assist the learner in problem solving. Play gives children the opportunity to practice what they are learning, and occurs at the actual developmental level of the learner.

1.6 *Value the Importance of Play in Engaging Children*

Play provides children with the best way to practice at their developmental level of knowledge and skills, with the added benefit of providing opportunities for physical movement. It is a self-motivated way to integrate all the learning domains into the daily activities for the optimal development of each child. Play accomplishes the following:

- Stimulates mental activity through problem solving
- Provides opportunities to master cognitive, physical, and socio-emotional issues
- Builds muscles and increases physical activity
- Develops imagination and creativity

As a child plays alone or with others, problems arise that require resolution by the child and other children. Although adults resolve the majority of problems a child faces, play provides the opportunity for the child to practice problem solving in a nonthreatening way. For example, Dahlia is building a block tower with a smaller block on the bottom, making the tower unstable. She must decide how to correct the problem. Dahlia uses manipulation of three-dimensional objects—the blocks—to decide how to correct the tower. Throughout this experience, Dahlia's brain activity is stimulated by three-dimensional play that enhances brain connections (Brown, S., 2008).

In another example, Sean wants to be the superhero in a game with Francis and Hazel. Once Sean has persuaded Francis and Hazel to let him play the role of hero, he can organize the play and direct the action. Finally, once the actual play has begun, Sean and the other players run, jump and chase each other.

The play examples provided here show how the important imagination and creativity are to the entire process. Creative people regularly solve problems, develop new products, or initiate new questions in domains that were at first viewed as novel but have become culturally acceptable (Gardner, 2011). In other words, the creative person is one who can take knowledge, couple it with skills, and create a new result, such as a product or thought.

M² FUN   Fine Motor Skills

Give each child a piece of paper with five circles drawn on the paper (O O O O O). Ask the children to draw something different in each circle. There is no right or wrong—just an opportunity to express creativity and to use fine motor skills.

It is interesting that when adults speak about creativity, they generally speak about being creative like children. Tim Brown, chief operating officer of IDEO, a design company, has reported that his company uses materials generally associated with early childhood programs, such as paper, glue, and modeling clay, to encourage constructive play and role-playing to stimulate creativity and thinking in different ways with different results (Brown, T., 2008) (see **video** Creative Brain).

To be creative, adults and children must feel secure in their environment. Children are less self-conscious than many adults and will make what adults would call "mistakes." Children really do not have an awareness of what mistakes are and the affect they may have. It is an adult-defined word, ruled by adult judgments. Mistakes, however, are important in learning.

Play is important and vital to children's development. The United Nations High Commission for Human Rights has recognized play as the right of every child (Ginsburg, 2007). Play must be understood, valued, and encouraged by parents and educators.

Play has been studied over the years. Mildred Parten (1932) has provided us with six stages of play related to individuals' relationships, which are still used today.

In the unoccupied stage, the child is not engaged in any behavior related to play. Children engaged in the solitary independent stage may play by themselves and do not need stimulation from other children or adults. In the next stage, onlooker behavior, the child observes how other children are playing but does not participate. When children are in parallel play, they play next to each other but do not interact verbally. The associative play stage marks the beginnings of verbal interactions between the children. In the final stage, cooperative play, the children now take an active role, and the play scenarios are intense in issues related to the lives of the children. Children may exhibit all stages in an observable time period, but it is more likely the stages will be related to the developmental level of a child and the child's comfort in the play environment (Parten, 1932).

A different way to examine play is by type of play. Sara Smilansky (1968) has identified four types of play:

- Functional play
- Constructive play
- Dramatic play
- Games with rules

Functional play involves the senses and muscles. For instance, Jermaine has tied ribbons to his arms and is running around the lawn, trying to make the streams of ribbon fly behind his racing body. In constructive play the child begins to plan and build a structure. Blocks will be placed on each other to make a tower like a building the child sees on the way to school. When the children take on a role, such as mother, father or baby, and build a story around the characters, the play has moved into the dramatic play area. Older children participate in games with rules, in which the participants can exercise more control.

Both Parten and Smilansky understood the importance of play in the lives of children. It is developmentally appropriate for every child to play, but play is not always present in the lives of young children. Free-play time is being reduced as a result of the following:

- National emphasis on the No Child Left Behind Act of 2001
- Reduction in recess time
- Specialized enrichment programs in academics and sports
- Transportation time to adult-arranged events.

Changes need to be made in the way we view childhood and what is important. We must provide children with opportunities to develop all domains. To help make changes, it is important to understand the theories that have been related by guiding theorists who have helped to develop our understanding of children and their role in society. Music and movement provide wonderful opportunities to encourage play and brain stimulation.

1.7 Discuss How Theorists Provide Guidance in Understanding the Role That Movement and Music Have in Child Development

Theorists John Dewey, Jean Piaget, Lev Vygotsky, Urie Bronfenbrenner, and Karl Newell have provided valuable insight on how children learn by exploration of their environment and how to design the environment to facilitate learning, and Emile Jaques-Dalcroze recognized the importance of learning music through movement.

Although these theorists lived at different times, their message is similar: Children learn through movement in a three-dimensional world, and they learn best when they are provided with opportunities to be supported by mature learners and to practice in self-directed and self-regulated play. A timeline of the theorists' periods of influence is important to see to appreciate the scope and depth of the research in child development (see Figure 1.4).

John Dewey (1859–1952). An American psychologist, educator, and activist, John Dewey received his PhD from John Hopkins University and taught at the University of Michigan, University of Minnesota, University of Chicago, and Columbia University. He had a major effect on trends in education built on the ideas of Jean-Jacques Rousseau, Johann Pestalozzi, and Friedrich Froebel. These ideas revolved around the concept that a child is an individual with strong personal rights. The school is the place where the child carries on the educational process guided by the teacher, but it should

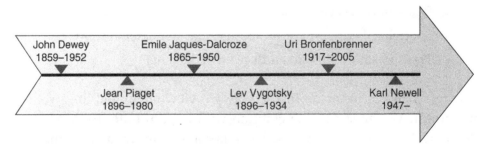

Figure 1.4 Guiding theorists' timeline of influence.

not be a place with an authoritarian teacher instructing a preset curriculum in a sterile, unchanging environment. Dewey promoted the concept that a child learns best through direct personal experience. A child should be provided vast opportunities to practice learning through play. The resulting curricular direction is the project method in which children learn by doing and experimenting. Dewey was the founder of the progressive method.

Jean Piaget (1859–1952). Another theorist who was a strong advocate of learning by doing is Jean Piaget. A Swiss developmental psychologist, Piaget is known for his studies with children. Upon completing his university studies and receiving a doctorate, he worked at a boys' school in Paris, and later at the Binet Institute. Through observation of children, he began to gain understanding of how children develop cognitively. He felt that the thought process of children is different from adults and thus developed the theory of cognitive development. Piaget's theory revolves around the development of *schemas*, defined as categories of knowledge that help a child to understand the world. There are four stages to Piaget's theory of cognitive development (see Table 1.3) (Phillips, 1969).

T a b l e 1 . 3 Piaget's Stages of Cognitive Development

Stage	Ages	Description
Sensorimotor	Birth to 18–24 months	Children experiment with surrounding environment. Infants and toddlers should be given safe, sound toys and musical instruments to manipulate and to use for experimentation.
Preoperational	18–24 months to 7 years	Children begin to think symbolically. Language becomes more mature. Children chant and rhyme and perform simple movement activities with few actions.
Concrete	7 years to 11 years	Reasoning begins to play a role in children's thinking. Children enjoy working with songs, playing instruments, and reading musical notation.
Formal	11 years to 16 years	Thinking becomes more abstract, and children will focus more on knowledge and skills.

Piaget felt that children learn best through discovery and that experiences enhance the cognitive development of the child.

Piaget also believed learning was linked to development that preceded learning (Wink & Putney, 2002). A child had to be of a certain developmental age to be able to learn a particular concept.

Lev Vygotsky (1896–1934). An advocate of the cognitive learning theory, Lev Vygotsky was in agreement with Piaget on many points. Vygotsky felt that children learn in a social context through social interaction. He suggested that a child's chronological age is not a reliable criterion for determining a child's developmental level. He gave instruction a larger role in learning than Piaget and believed that learning can precede development. The "zone of proximal development" was Vygotsky's way of explaining how children can learn concepts beyond their developmental level by having the support of an adult during the learning process (Hedegaard, 2007).

Urie Bronfenbrenner (1917–2005). A notable educator and theorist in the field of developmental psychology, Urie Bronfenbrenner understood the importance that family and society had on the development of the child. Bronfenbrenner's ecological theory places the child, with his or her unique biological predispositions, at the center of all environmental interactions. The interactions between the biological makeup of the child and the environmental influences affect the child's physical development and behavior (Bronfenbrenner, 1979). The child, with his or her unique deoxyribonucleic acid (DNA) makeup, has influence on the surroundings or environment. In return, the child's substantive environment, family, peers, school, and neighborhood, as well as socioeconomic factors and cultural environmental factors, influence the developmental domains: social/emotional, physical/motor, and cognitive/language.

Bronfenbrenner's theory emphasizes the influence parents, and the entire social network—schools, peers, neighborhoods, social services, church, mass media, extended family and culture—have on the child. Whereas educators may be dedicated and committed to providing an educational environment that will enhance the health and fitness of the children in their care, the ecological theory makes one painfully aware this cannot be accomplished without the family and society. In fact, if the family is not involved in the plan, the result will not be effective (Bronfenbrenner, 1974). The entire developmental process is in flux. Neither genetics nor environment plays a singular role in the growth process; it is the interaction between internal and external influences that contribute to the development of the child (see Figure 1.5). It is extremely important for educators to realize how impor-

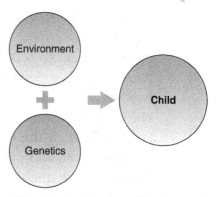

Figure 1.5 Internal and external influences on the child.

tant the family is in this entire learning process when working with young children.

Karl Newell (1947–). As a professor of kinesiology and biobehavioral health and a department chair at Pennsylvania State University in University Park, Karl Newell has helped to refine the current study of motor learning and development by taking into account the role of the environment and the individual's experience. He has built on the ecological theory and a related branch, the dynamical system approach, to explain the development of motor control and learning. These two related theories provide a framework of various principles that can describe and predict the changes observed in motor development, taking into consideration constraints (limits) existing within the body (e.g., cardiovascular endurance and muscular strength) and outside the body (e.g., social and cultural and task contexts) (Aparo, 2009). Movement emerges from the interaction between the constraints (individual, environment, task); if one of the constraints changes, so does the emerging movement (Clark, 1995).

Émile Jaques-Dalcroze (1865–1950). A Swiss professor of music, Émile Jaques-Dalcroze had a strong effect on music education. His work was based on the concept that rhythm is the primary element of music (Choksy, Abramson, Gillespie, Woods, & York, 2001). He felt that many students had a mechanical understanding of music but did not feel and express music. The result was a career spent finding a way for people to use movement to feel and understand music. Jaques-Dalcroze realized that of the three elements of music (pitch, rhythm, and dynamic energy), two—rhythm and energy—depended on movement (Choksy et al., 2001). The result was *eurhythmics*, a way to stimulate musical learning. He postulated that when the body moves, it stimulates the mind and enforces learning. In addition to his work with movement, Jaques-Dalcroze also worked on ear training and sight singing. He developed *solfège* exercises, using syllables (do, re, mi, fa, sol, la, ti) to teach pitch (Choksy et al., 2001). His work is important because he understood the importance of movement in learning.

The research and work of these theorists are important in developing an understanding of how parents and educators should stimulate learning, particularly in movement and music:

- Dewey gave credibility to the concept of building knowledge based on experiences.
- Piaget's stages of development, from birth through adolescence, have become the basis for DAPs (Copple & Bredekamp, 2009) by providing general and sequential steps of child development.
- Vygotsky emphasized the role of the mature learner in the child's learning process.
- Bronfenbrenner provided an understanding of the important role of the environment in the development of the child.
- Newell recognized the importance of the environment in the development and the refinement of a movement concept and/or task.
- Jaques-Dalcroze provided knowledge and appreciation for the role movement plays in feeling and understanding music.

As we work on designing learning activities for children, it is important to review the thoughts and theories of Dewey, Piaget, Vygotsky, Bronfenbrenner, Newell, and Jaques-Dalcroze.

Summary

Movement and music play an important role in the development of children. The two can be considered the "dynamic duo" of M^2 because, when used together, they stimulate the senses and the domains to increase learning. The inherited culture of each child has an effect on music and movement choices. Howard Gardner's multiple intelligence theory recognizes music and bodily-kinesthetic intelligences equally with the other intelligences: linguistic, logical-mathematical, spatial, and personal.

The National Association for the Education of Young Children's *Developmentally Appropriate Practice in Early Childhood Programs Serving Children from Birth through Age 8* (DAP) provides a framework for designing and guiding programs for young children. The important points of DAP are to provide structure to the Guiding Principles and Learning Outcomes.

Play is important to the development of children because it stimulates the brain, integrates the learning domains, increases physical activity, and develops creativity. Music and movement can be involved in play and are important components of learning and the development of a healthy lifestyle for children.

Various theorists—Dewey, Piaget, Vygotsky, Bronfenbrenner, Newell, and Jaques-Dalcroze—have emphasized the role of hands-on-experiences, play, and support of a mature learner in the development and learning of children.

Summary Related to Outcomes

Learning Outcomes	Guiding Principles
1.1 Develop an understanding of the importance of music and movement in the lives of young children	Movement and Music Integrated
Movement and music are dynamic together and enhance each other. This partnership is enjoyed by every culture in the world. Movement and music stimulate the senses, heighten emotional awareness, and touch a variety of intelligences. They should be encouraged in programs for young children.	

Learning Outcomes	Guiding Principles
1.2 Explain the role of environment systems	Environment and Curriculum Reciprocated

The environment surrounding the child—culture, schools, teachers, and families—has an influence on the developmental interest and progress of each child.

| 1.3 Understand inherited culture and musical and movement choices | Environment and Curriculum Reciprocated |

Culture has an effect on the music and movement choices of each child.

| 1.4 Recognize that the NAEYC provides a framework for early childhood programs | Environment and Curriculum Reciprocated |

NAEYC has provided a framework, grounded in child development and research, which should be used to guide programs for young children. *Developmentally Appropriate Practices in Early Childhood Programs Serving Children from Birth through Age 8* (DAP) encourages play, physical activity, social interactions, problem solving, and the arts.

| 1.5 Distinguish how Guiding Principles meet individual developmental and learning differences | Individual Needs Met |

DAP provides essential ideas to be used in designing curriculum for young children. Learning Outcomes can be structured around DAP ideas summarized in this text's Guiding Principles (Individual Needs Met, Environment and Curriculum Reciprocated, Movement and Music Integrated, Family and Community Involved, and Standards and Assessment Provide Guidance).

| 1.6 Value the importance of play in engaging children | Individual Needs Met |

Play is extremely important to early childhood programs. It provides a way for children to practice knowledge and skills at their developmental level and to adjust to emotional situations. The United Nations High Commission for Human Rights has recognized play as a right of every child. There are various stages and types of play.

| 1.7 Discuss how theorists provide guidance in understanding the role of movement and music in child development | Individual Needs Met |

John Dewey, Jean Piaget, Lev Vygotsky, Urie Bronfenbrenner, Karl Newell, and Émile Jaques-Dalcroze, are theorists who provide strong guidance on how children learn, the value of play, and the child's exploration of the environment.

Demonstrate Your Knowledge, Skills, and Dispositions

Students will demonstrate knowledge, comprehension, analysis, and evaluation of Learning Outcomes related to Guiding Principles.

Learning Outcomes	Guiding Principles
1.1 Develop an understanding of the importance of music and movement in lives of young children	Movement and Music Integrated
• Make a stick puppet and demonstrate how the puppet would move to various types of music (possible choices: march, waltz, rap). Discuss how music has impact on the way the puppet moves.	
1.2 Explain the role of environment systems	Environment and Curriculum Reciprocated
• A child from Japan has joined your classroom. How would you make the child feel more comfortable?	
1.3 Understand inherited culture and music and movement choices	Environment and Curriculum Reciprocated
• Make a list of music from various cultures that you can use when working with children.	
1.4 Recognize that the NAEYC provides a framework for early childhood programs	Environment and Curriculum Reciprocated
• Read *Developmentally Appropriate Practice in Early Childhood Programs Serving Children from Birth through Age 8* (NAEYC, 2009). Describe one way your future interactions with children will be different based on DAP.	
1.5 Distinguish how Guiding Principles meet individual developmental and learning differences	Individual Needs Met
• Pick one of the Guiding Principles. Describe how this Guiding Principle could have enhanced your learning as a young child.	
1.6 Value the importance of play in engaging children	Individual Needs Met
• Describe how play meets the needs of a shy child and an aggressive child.	
1.7 Discuss how theorists provide guidance in understanding the role of movement and music in child development	Individual Needs Met
• Your newspaper has hired you to interview Piaget. What would he answer to the question: What is the value of play for young children?	

Planning for Engaging

Complete the following M^2 standard–based learning activity designed to meet various interests and developmental levels by designing two possibilities/learning activities in movement and music.

M² Movement Standard: Children will apply an understanding of movement concepts and principles to performing locomotor skills (walk, run, hop, slide, and gallop).

Possibility One	Possibility Two	Possibility Three
Children will demonstrate hopping skills by taking a beanbag from a container, hopping on one foot to another container and depositing the beanbag in the container. Note: There should be one beanbag and two containers per child.	Children will demonstrate hopping skills and imagination by showing how various animals will move by hopping. Animal suggestions: elephant, tiger, snake, grasshopper *Note:* Pictures should be used to stimulate creativity.	Children will hop at different speeds using music for rhythmic models. Play different types of music with different tempos such as: Slow (lento) Walking pace (andante) Moderate (moderato) Fast (allegretto) Very fast (allegro)
Assessment Children should be able to hop on one foot for the majority of the time.	**Assessment** Note the various imaginative ways the children demonstrate how the different animals hop. Observe if they consistently have their weight on one foot.	**Assessment** Observe whether children change their speed when hopping to the various tempos.

Now You Try It

Complete the following M² standard-based learning activity designed to meet various interests and developmental levels by designing two possibilities/learning activities in movement and music.

M² Movement Standard: Children will use movement to produce elements of music: high/low, fast/slow, and loud/soft.

Possibility One	Possibility Two	Possibility Three
Learning Activity Each child will create a puppet from a lunch bag using markers, paper, and other items. Play various types of music and have children move the puppet high/low and fast/slow to the beat of the music.	**Learning Activity**	**Learning Activity**

Assessment	Assessment	Assessment
Observe the appropriateness of each child's puppet movement.		

References

Aparo, L. (2009). *Influence of sport staking on hand-eye coordination in children aged 7–11.* Unpublished master's thesis, Universita Deglistudi Diroma, Foro, Italy.

Bales, D. (1998). *Building baby's brain: The role of music, educational oasis.* Retrieved from http://www.educationoasis.com/resources/Articles/building_babys_brain.htm.

Bronfenbrenner, U. (1974). Is early intervention effective? *Early Childhood Education Journal, 2*(2), 14–18.

Bronfenbrenner, U. (1979). *The ecology of human development: Experiments by nature and design.* Cambridge, MA: Harvard University Press.

Brown, S. (2008). *Play is more than fun.* TED. Retrieved from http://www.ted.com/talks/stuart_brown_says_play_is_more_than_fun_it_s_vital.html.

Brown, T. (2008). *Tales of creativity and play.* TED. Retrieved from http://www.tec.com/talks/tim_brown_on_creativity_and_play.html.

Campbell, P.S. & Scott-Kassner, C. (1995). *Music in childhood.* New York, NY: Simon & Schuster.

Choksy, L., Abramson, R, Gillespie, A., Woods, D., & York, F. (2001). *Teaching music in the twenty-first century.* Upper Saddle River, NJ: Prentice Hall.

Clark, J.E. (1995). Dynamical system perspective. In R.L. Craink & C.A. Oatis (Eds.) *Gait analysis: Theory and application* (pp. 25–27). St Louis, MO: C.V. Mosby.

Copple, C. & Bredekamp, S. (2009). *Appropriate practice in early childhood programs serving children from birth through age 8* (3rd ed.). Washington DC: National Association for Education of Young Children.

Dewey, J. (1902). *The child and the curriculum.* Chicago, IL: University of Chicago Press.

Gardner, H. (2011). *Frames of mind.* New York, NY: Basic Books.

Ginsburg, K. (2007). Importance of play in promoting healthy child development. *Pediatrics: Journal of the America Academy of Pediatrics, 119*(1), 182–191.

Gordon Institute for Music Learning (2012). *Early childhood.* Retrieved from http://giml.org/mlt/earlychildhood/.

Hannaford, C. (2008). Movement and music: the dance of life. *Perspective: Journal of the Early Childhood Music and Movement Association, 3*(4), 4–8.

Healy, J. (2012). Different learners: why music and movement are brain food for every child. *Perspectives: Journal of the Early Childhood Music & Movement Association, 5*(4), 9–13.

Hedegaard, M. (2007). The development of children's conceptual relation to the world with focus on concept formation in preschool children's activity. In H. Daniels, M. Cole, & J. Wertsch (Eds.). *The Cambridge companion to Vygotsky* (pp. 246–275). New York, NY: Cambridge University Press.

Levitin, D. (2006). *This is your brain on music.* New York, NY: Dutton.

National Association for the Education of Young Children (2009). *Developmentally appropriate practice in early childhood programs serving children from birth through age 8.* Washington, DC: NAEYC.

Parten, M.B. (1932). Social participation among preschool children. *Journal of Abnormal Psychology, 27,* 243–269.

Phillips, J.L. (1969). *The origins of intellect: Piaget's theory.* San Francisco, CA: Freeman & Co.

Sievers, B., Polansky, L., Casey, M., & Wheatley, T. (2012). Music and movement share a dynamic structure that supports universal expression of emotion. *Proceedings of National Academy of Science United States of America,* 110(1), 70–75.

Smilansky, S. (1968) *The effects of sociodramatic play on disadvantaged preschool children.* New York, NY: John Wiley & Sons.

Steele, S. (2013). *Gonna move.* Upper Saddle River, NJ: Pearson Publishing.

Whitwell, G. (2012). Music & sound for the unborn child. *Perspectives: Journal of the Early Childhood Music & Movement Association,* 5(2), 15–18.

Wink, J., & Putney, L. (2002). *A vision of Vygotsky.* Boston, MA: Allyn & Bacon.

Wurm, J. (2005). *Working in the Reggio way: A beginner's guide for American teachers.* St. Paul, MN: Redleaf Press.

chapter 2

Developing Curriculum and Environments for Music and Movement

LEARNING OUTCOMES AND GUIDING PRINCIPLES

Students reading this text will be able to demonstrate Learning Outcomes linked to Guiding Principles based on the National Association for the Education of Young Children's *Developmentally Appropriate Practice in Early Childhood Programs Serving Children from Birth through Age 8* (2009).

Learning Outcomes	Guiding Principles
2.1 Define education and curriculum	Individual Needs Met
2.2 Compare curriculum development models	Individual Needs Met
2.3 Value child decision making and involvement in curriculum	Individual Needs Met
2.4 Discuss curriculum selection	Environment and Curriculum Reciprocated
2.5 Apply curriculum design	Environment and Curriculum Reciprocated
2.6 Analyze curriculum design and the learning environment	Environment and Curriculum Reciprocated
2.7 Apply movement and music and learning	Movement and Music Integrated

Making Connections
What Teachers Do—From a Child's Perspective

Children possess marvelous insight, and we can learn from their perspective. The following example shows that Hwan, Clayton, Liv, Abby, Natalie, and Cassie have both a command of curriculum and an understanding of the teacher's role in learning.

- That's easy. Teachers teach. They teach us math and literacy and science and calendar. (Hwan, 6½ years old)
- Teachers tell you letters and numbers and songs—all the stuff mommies and daddies don't know. (Clayton, 4 years old)
- Teachers wear life jackets and go in the water. (Liv, 4 years old)
- They take care of the children. Mrs. Jaime comes to school on a boat. They help the kids. They get food ready for children. (Abby, 3 years old)
- My teacher teaches me addition and subtraction. She uses silly songs and movement [flaps her arms] to make it fun. (Natalie, 7 years old)
- Teachers go to school to learn how to teach. They teach math, cursive, write and draw on the board. In Eurhythmy we make big movement to make the letters. (Cassie, 9 years old)

2.1 Define Education and Curriculum

Education is seen as a process of preparing children to create an improved society (McLachlan, Fleer, & Edwards, 2010). Decisions as to what activities go into the entire procedure of educating our children, what knowledge and skills should be taught, and what approach or method should be taken to convey the materials to the children are complicated, interwoven, and important questions. It is also important to consider reciprocal interaction between the curriculum design and the learning environment.

The children in "Making Connections: What Teachers Do—From a Child's Perspective" provide us with their views on what teachers do daily in learning programs for young children. It is interesting to realize that these children have covered so many elements of an education program. The children interviewed in "Making Connections" placed a strong

▲ Children engaged in acting out a story.

emphasis on subject areas, pedagogy, and the learning environment when discussing their program of learning or curriculum.

Curriculum Defined

Curriculum is the skeleton of the education experience (McLachlan, Fleer, & Edwards, 2010). As the children in "Making Connections" summarized, curriculum is everything that happens at school. It is the written plan for learning and contains various components, goals, content, pedagogy, and instructional practice (NAEYC, 2003). In addition, cultural elements (ethnicity, racial identity, economic class, family structure, language, and religious and political beliefs) are inherent in how adults and children interact in the learning process (NAEYC, 2003). Two broad curriculum models guide how the weaving can be done.

2.2 *Compare Curriculum Development Models*

The curriculum may be designed around the performance or the competence model (Bernstein,1996). The *performance model* is the most widespread; it emphasizes subject areas and knowledge. Under this model, the goal is to deliver information or knowledge. The key characteristics of this model are use of traditional subject areas and measuring how well the children master the knowledge. The performance model is seen in the majority of schools, where there are separate periods for reading, mathematics, and science, and the material follows a set pattern. Children have little control over the pace and materials. The learning environment design for this model would be desks in rows with a teacher in a command position in front of the desks.

The *competence model* suggests that learners have control over the selection, pace, and sequencing of the curriculum. This model is based on experiences, decision making, and the integration of knowledge and skills into the daily thought processes, and emphasizes involving children in the learning process to optimize learning. Because this model has a more integrated concept of learning and a greater emphasis on child involvement, the learning environment is not centered around rows of desks but rather around interest and activity, exploration and investigation. The children can interact with the broad environment or specific learning areas. Parents and educators must decide what is appropriate for the developmental level of the children.

The following example demonstrates how a third-grade teacher made changes to create a developmentally appropriate classroom.

A third-grade teacher, Ms. Connor, was in a school system that valued the performance model, but she felt that the competence model would be more appropriate for the children she was teaching. Ms. Connor continued to follow the curriculum required by the school system but made some changes to move the classroom more toward a competence model. First, she removed all the desks from the classroom. They were replaced with used stuffed chairs and couches. In addition, she placed low tables around the room and decorated the space with plants and prints by famous artists. Next, she removed all student textbooks; she kept her teacher copies because this was the curriculum she was expected to teach.

From these required texts, she designed individual daily packets for each child. Each child was expected to complete his or her packet each day, but the order of completion was based on individual choice. Therefore, if there were mathematics, science, and literacy learning activities in the packet, the child could choose to do the literacy first, second, or third. All the learning activities revolved around a yearly country theme (e.g., Japan, Italy). As the children worked on their packets, Ms. Connor circulated in the classroom providing assistance to a child or to groups of children.

This example shows that changes made to the curriculum and/or the learning environment can move a classroom toward the competence model. Ms. Connor's children were always high performers on the required state achievement tests, and she was the most requested teacher by parents. The changes she made provided the children with opportunities to be involved in decision making.

M² FUN

Give each child a 2-yard elastic loop. Have the children make various shapes using their arms and legs to stretch the elastic and then name the shape they have formed. They may give it a conventional name, such as "circle" or "triangle," or a nonsense name.

2.3 Value Child Decision Making and Involvement in Curriculum

Decision making and child involvement are important to consider when designing a curriculum. If children are involved in the entire process, they will have a greater interest in what takes place in the learning environment.

The model used by Helm and Katz (2001) places single and integrated concepts (e.g., learning colors in isolation) at one end of the child-initiated and decision-making continuum and teacher-directed inquiry and projects at the other end (see Figure 2.1). There is low child initiation and decision making and high teacher control at the single-concept end of the

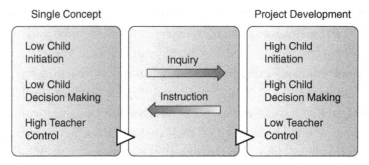

Figure 2.1 Pathway to engagement, decision making, and learning (adapted from Helm and Katz, 2001).

continuum, and high child initiation and decision making and low teacher control at the project or investigation end of the continuum. Curricula should strengthen decision making and inquiry, and the pathway to learning will move in this direction to provide extensive child engagement. At times, the curriculum may flow backward toward single and integrated concepts to provide instruction in a single or integrated concept. The child may be discovering how to measure, for instance, but may need assistance adding single-digit numbers.

The learning process should involve the children and provide opportunities for child-initiated experiences and decision making. If the teacher, in a lecture format, merely tells children about rhythm, the children have little opportunity for making decisions and engagement. However, if the children are given the chance to echo rhythm patterns they hear, they will be engaged in decision making. Some of the echoes may be correct, and some may not. Mistakes are not only acceptable, but also beneficial, because the children are involved in the learning process. If the process is taken a step further and the children are given the opportunity to invent their own rhythms and create their own rhythm instruments, the children's engagement will be higher and more beneficial to their development. Young children from programs that provide opportunities for child-initiated activities show the greatest mastery of the subject areas of reading and mathematics (Marcon, 1992; 1995).

Teachers are involved in the high decision-making and engagement end of the continuum but in a very different manner from that seen in the single-concept end of the continuum. At this end, the teacher becomes a facilitator, guiding the children in the learning process by organizing the learning environment and the materials in the environment. The child's experimentations, investigations, explorations, and play are the sources of knowledge.

Child engagement is a consideration. The high decision-making learning process in movement activities can easily begin by having the children select their own location for the activity. The teacher can guide them initially by telling them that their "self-space" should have the following characteristics:

- Be located away from other children
- Provide opportunities for movement without touching other children
- Enable the child to see the leader at all times, and the leader to see them

Once the children have been told to move to their self-space, they should do so quickly and efficiently. The teacher should then engage the children in a simple activity, such as making a circle or a square with their feet or a scarf, to reinforce the importance of the characteristics. After the basic concepts have been mastered, more difficult ones can be introduced. Child-centered learning has begun.

It is important to provide children with learning activities on the end of the continuum related to teacher-directed inquiry and projects. Children have learned and will learn under both the performance and conceptual models, but educators and families must decide which model will work best for the goals of the learning program and for the children. It is important to capitalize on the proven ways children learn most effectively.

How children learn needs to be understood. The advances over the past several decades in understanding of how the human brain works have been amazing and have helped to shed light on how learning takes place (Soursa, 2010; Willis, 2006). There is a connection between science of the brain and learning. The brain-functioning knowledge base developed through advances in technology and in scientific and medical research has helped to provide an understanding of how children learn.

Most neurons where information is stored are present at birth, but throughout an individual's life there is continued growth in the connecting of cells that enrich communication between neurons. The connecting cells, or dendrites, increase in size and number through learning skills, varied experiences, and information (Willis, 2006). Humans learn by doing. This information can be applied to teaching young children by remembering that they need to be involved in the process, not just the product. Children will derive more information about a process by having sensory and motor learning—for example, by actually baking a cake rather than being told how to bake a cake. (See **video** The Science of Early Childhood Development, Jack P. Shonkoff.)

We know that children learn most effectively when they are engaged actively in interactions rather than being placed in receptive or passive learning activities (Bowman, Donovan, & Burns, 2001). This particular principle of learning for young children was clearly evident in this example of a trip to the beach:

Jesse, a three-year-old boy, was brought to the beach by his parents. While the mother organized the blanket and personal items, the father took Jesse and a bucket and sand shovel to the water. As Jesse and his father drew closer to the water and the waves, Jesse became more and more agitated. The father entered the water, holding the child's hands. Jesse was screaming in fear. The father persisted in his actions and added bouncing the child up and down in the waves. Jesse kept screaming and physically trying to move away from his father and the waves. Neither the father nor the child was enjoying the experience. The boy was afraid of the water and waves, and the father was frustrated with his son's behavior. The father concluded his interaction with Jesse by removing him from the water and placing him on the beach above the water line with the bucket and shovel. He returned to the beach blanket and to the company of the mother.

This would have ended Jesse's swimming lesson at the beach if it had not been for the inward motion of the tide and his own curiosity. As Jesse sat on the sand, the water, due to the wave action, was moving toward the bucket and the shovel. A wave grabbed the shovel and carried it toward the open ocean. Jesse acted quickly and retrieved the shovel from the shallow water. He then intentionally repeated the process over and over, becoming familiar with the action of the waves and the floating characteristics of the shovel. Gradually, Jesse became more and more active in the water, doing the very activities the father tried to encourage in the beginning of the encounter with the ocean. Jesse interacted with his environment and learned about the tides and floating. He became less afraid of the wave action and more confident in his movements.

Researchers, teachers, and parents are always striving to determine how to create an optimal learning experience for children. The more pathways used to introduce and review skills and knowledge, the greater the dendrite growth and connections. We know that learning is accelerated if the situation or material is interesting to the child and if the concept matches the maturational or developmental level of the child (Lee & Lee, 1950). These two factors—developmental level and interests—have been staples of curriculum design for decades .

The concept that children learn by actively interacting with the learning environment (adults, equipment, and materials) has been well documented in the writings of John Dewey, Jean Piaget, and Lev Vygotsky. All three researchers valued play and its role in interactive leaning (Mooney, 2000). Children interact and learn through play, exploration of roles, and their environment, as well as by social interaction with others, not through forced rote learning.

Play is the primary way children prefer to learn. Curriculum choices should provide opportunities for children to play and to assimilate and accommodate information and experiences into their lives. It is important for children to have the opportunity to process information into a form they can understand (*assimilation*) and to adapt current knowledge structures into new experiences (*accommodation*) to reach a comfortable state of equilibrium or stable understanding. The entire process of assimilation and accommodation to reach the desired state of equilibrium is demonstrated in the work of Piaget (1952). He realized, as do many educators, that learning is not the memorization of a body of facts or data, but rather gaining a knowledge base, skills, and dispositions so that the children learn to influence their environment. Children are highly motivated to have control over their environment, and they work hard to achieve this result.

We have all seen the 3-year-old who proudly announces that she can "read." In reality, she has memorized the words of a book and will recite the words to the delight of the adults. Only through the development of additional knowledge and skills in word decoding will she truly be able to read.

Play provides children the opportunity to move beyond their comfort zone into the *zone of proximal development*, where they can begin to construct understanding based on existing knowledge and new concepts (Wink & Putney, 2002). Play is a powerful tool and should be an important component of an early childhood curriculum.

The learning environment should be structured for children to have opportunities to play with a variety of materials and equipment related to movement and music. A music-listening area with music, related books, and instruments provides children with the opportunity to hear and to understand a variety of music, whereas a plastic container and a ball provide children the chance to practice throwing, a fundamental motor pattern. The learning experience can provide more decision-making opportunities by having the children discover objects in the room that make unique resonating sounds that may be used in rhythm activities. Having the children discover various receptacles in the room for the balls can expand the throwing activity. The children are cognitively, socially, and physically involved in the learning process. They are gaining competence or capability in various areas and are in control of their development. Helm and Katz (2001) have praised the concept of the learner being in control of the process.

In recent years, with the strong emphasis on test scores and performance education, play and experimental learning have been moved further and further out of the curriculum. Play is the way children learn and struggle to understand concepts, no matter how difficult they are to comprehend.

Play can help the child understand difficult concepts. In the following example, Martha, a child in an early childhood development program, used role-playing to help her understand an incomprehensible occurrence in her life.

Every day, the program began with the children engaging in choice play. As the children were playing and adjusting to the learning environment, the teacher and the assistant teacher moved around the room, sitting on the floor with each child and engaging him or her in conversation. During this time, each child was encouraged to tell the adult a story; the adult wrote the story down. Later, the authors could do a play about their story. The children selected the actor(s) and props and directed the actor(s) in the play. Four-year-old Martha had written a story about a spider that had climbed into bed with her and scared her. Spiders can be scary to some children, and the teacher recording the story made a mental note to herself but was not overly concerned. It was not until the play began and the teachers saw Martha's level of agitation that they became alarmed. Martha refused to be in the play and selected two other children to play the role of the child and the spider. The "spider" moved into position on the floor next to the "child." Martha became disturbed. She said this was not correct; the spider had to be on top of the child. At this point the alarms went off in the teacher's mind because the child was describing a sexual position. The child was trying, through a "safe" reenactment, to understand the situation that was occurring to her at night in her bed. The other children in the room thought it was a story about an arachnid, but in reality it was about a sexual assault by an adult, the mother's boyfriend, on the child. Appropriate individuals were contacted and the family was helped.

Play assisted everyone to understand the situation, and it should be an important component of curriculum design. Early childhood curriculum cannot be designed without periods of child-directed and adult-assisted play.

The curriculum choices made by educators and families will help the children in the process. Educators and families go about selecting a curriculum appropriate for the children attending the program based on the mission and goals of the program and indicators of effectiveness.

M² FUN

Begin by having the children place an imaginary hat on their heads. Hands are over the head/hat for this activity. Recite the following poem while passing a beanbag called the "cat" back and forth from hand to hand.

There once was a cat

Who jumped over a hat.

He jumped over

And over!

2.4 *Discuss Curriculum Selection*

The mission and goals of the program must be articulated prior to adoption of a curriculum. All stakeholders in the process must have an opportunity to voice their opinions on what is important when adopting or designing a learning program for young children. Based on research, the program should follow the competence model and have a strong foundation in the research of Dewey, Piaget, and Vygotsky. It should also be grounded in Urie Brofenbrenner's (1979) understanding of the important role a family, community, and other ecological systems play in the child's environment.

Once the mission and the goals have been developed, the next criterion to consider is how the prospective curriculum—whether purchased or designed specifically for the program—reflects the range of goals and objectives of the program. The curriculum being selected should provide opportunities to meet a variety of developmental levels and individual differences among children. It is also important to consider the outlook of the licensing state. States now have provided expectations in the form of standards and outcomes for early childhood programs. In addition, the following questions must be considered: Does the curriculum meet the expectations and needs of families and the surrounding community? Does the curriculum have a strong music and movement element? Are the children being exposed to music and movement on a daily basis in a developmentally appropriate manner? The answer must be "yes" to all these concerns.

NAEYC's 2003 Position Statement on Early Childhood Curriculum, Assessment, and Program Evaluation provides additional, more detailed, guidance on the matter of curriculum adoption. According to the statement, the curriculum should have the following characteristics:

- Children are active and engaged.
- Goals are cleared and shared by all.
- The curriculum is evidence based.
- Valued content is learned through investigation; play; and focused, intentional teaching.
- The curriculum builds on prior learning and experiences.

- The curriculum is comprehensive.
- Professional standards validate the curriculum's subject matter.
- The curriculum is likely to benefit children.

(Excerpted from NAEYC, "Early Childhood Curriculum, Assessment, and Program Evaluation," Position Statement [Washington, DC: NAEYC, 2003]. Copyright © 2003 NAEYC. Reprinted with permission. Full text of this position statement is available at www.naeyc.org/files/naeyc/file/positions/CAPEexpand.pdf.)

Optimal learning for children occurs when they are actively engaged in the process; Learning should be developed through play, investigation, and instructional assistance by adults strongly versed in the elements of appropriate practices. The adult realizes that learning quality is based on the child's past experiences, and the learning experience should enhance the whole child.

Curriculum choice should be comprehensive; develop the complete or whole child, physically, cognitively, socially, and emotionally; and have a positive benefit on the child's development. Learning choices for young children should provide learning experiences grounded in sensory learning experienced that enhance physical, language, and social and emotional development, as well as thinking skills. The learning experiences should also be well grounded in current professional standards providing guidance in the development of the whole child (Bowman, Donovan, & Burns, 2001).

Professional standards exist for early childhood education. Arne Duncan's (2010) address to the Early Childhood 2010—Innovation for the Next Generation meeting indicated that all states have early learning standards. Head Start has developed the Head Start Program Performance Standards and Other Regulations (2012). In addition, the Consortium of National Arts Education (2012) and National Association for Music Educators (2012) have adopted standards that support the content areas of dance and music. In the area of movement and physical education, the National Association for Sport and Physical Education (NASPE, 2013), a division of the American Alliance for Health, Physical Education, Recreation, and Dance (AAHPERD), is the leader in designing standards. NASPE sets the standards for appropriate practices in quality physical education and sport.

It is generally agreed that standards (whether state or national) that are developed and reviewed through informed and inclusive process and supported by families and early childhood professionals are an asset (NAEYC, 2003). They help to provide focus on:

- Curriculum content
- Instructional practices
- Guidelines for assessment

When working with standards, it is important to read and understand the standards, learn the terminology related to the standards, and use the standards daily to implement learning activities (Kim & Robinson, 2010). Furthermore, each standard should be viewed critically to determine whether it is developmentally appropriate for the population and teaching situation.

Standards developed by professional organizations such as the National Association for Music Educators and National Association for Sport and Physical Education are content specific to music, movement, and sport. State standards will offer guidance to wider content areas, including the following:

- Arts (music/movement/visual)
- Mathematics/problem solving
- Literacy
- Scientific inquiry
- Social studies/communities
- Health/physical activity

Early childhood programs should follow the standards of the state where the program is practiced but also review national standards. An overview of professional and state standards will serve to ground curriculum, instruction, and assessment. This text will model this practice by providing selected M^2 standards and learning activities for movement and music at the end of each chapter.

Developmentally appropriate practices (DAPs) (NAEYC, 2009) are grounded in research on child development and effective core knowledge for young children. DAP is the framework that all curricula should use because it provides the scale for determining what is best for children. DAP recognizes similarities and differences among children. Therefore, to make sure the needs of all the children are met, a curriculum should provide learning activities designed to be appropriate to the diverse developmental needs among groups of children. If a child has a special need, the learning activity and the environment should be adjusted to meet the wants of each child to provide him or her with the most advantageous educational experience possible. Federal law mandates this through P.L. 94-142 and P.L. 99-457, which govern the services delivered to children with special needs (Bredekamp & Rosegrant, 1992). In addition, position statements published by recognized organizations such as NAEYC (2009) and NASPE (2009) provide guidance in developing quality and developmentally appropriate curricula.

Finally, the selection of the curriculum is not the end—it is the beginning. The curriculum should continue to be evaluated, using the program's goals and standards to ascertain whether quality is maintained (NAEYC, 2003). Assessment of the curriculum should occur regularly whether it has been purchased or developed.

Established Curriculum Choices

Some education programs may decide it is easier to use an established curriculum that has been produced for a broad-interest market. The following curricula have been used and researched and are designed to develop the whole child, cognitively, socioemotionally, and physically. They provide goals and objectives for movement and music. Several choices of established curricula are described here.

High Scope grew out of the work in the 1960s at the Perry Preschool Project in Ypsilanti, Michigan. It is based on the ideas of Dewey and Piaget and the concept of learning by doing (High Scope, 2012). The curriculum has four different age or interest components: infant, toddler, preschool, and elementary. Each component focuses on eight content areas:

approaches to learning, language, literacy, and communication, social and emotional development, physical development and health, creative arts, mathematics, science and technology, social studies. Children learn about the eight components through hands-on experiences in a learning environment that is open and accessible.

Creative Curriculum is a teacher-directed and child initiated program for young children that focuses on the needs of individual learners. The curriculum is aligned with Head Start Child Development and Early Learning Framework (Teaching Strategies, 2013).

The *Bank Street Developmental–Interaction Approach* is named for the Bank Street College in New York City and is strongly influenced by the work of Dewey and of Lucy Sprague Mitchel (Lunenburg, 2011). The goals of this program are to develop the whole child by active learning, and attention is given to movement and music.

The *Waldorf* curriculum places an emphasis on understanding human development and the importance of developing the whole child. This curriculum was developed by Rudolf Steiner in 1919 and places a heavy emphasis on the physical, emotional, and cognitive development of the child. Steiner (1907, as reprinted in Trostli, 1998) identified the three developmental stages shown in Table 2.1.

The teacher presents a focused lesson on one subject area—reading, mathematics, science, or history—in a pictorial and dynamic manner for 2 or more hours, 3 to 5 days each week. Textbooks are not used during this time period; instead, the children record their learning in self-designed main lesson books. The Waldorf program places a strong emphasis on fine

Table 2.1 Developmental Stages of the Waldorf Curriculum (Steiner, 1907, as Reprinted in Trostli, 1998)

Ages	Descriptor Name
Birth to 6 or 7 years old	Imitation
7 to 14 years old	Imagination
14 to 18 years old	Truth, discrimination, judgment, understanding

and gross motor and musical development. Attention is paid to instrument playing and eurhythmics.

The purpose of reviewing these established curricula is to show how each one values a competence model, engaging the child in learning activities appropriate to the developmental level of the child and developing the whole child. Movement and music have an important role in these curricula. Other early childhood curriculum approaches worthy of mention and involving movement and music goals include Project Approach, Reggio Emilia, Montessori, Te Whāriki curriculum, and Kamii-DeVries Constructivist Perspective. Although any of these curricula may meet a given program's philosophy and goals, many programs make the decision to develop their own curricula.

2.5 *Apply Curriculum Design*

A curriculum designed for a large market may not be appropriate for a particular program; it may also be more advantageous to develop the curriculum used for a specific program. This process begins in the same way as the search process for a market curriculum. A mission or a philosophy statement must be developed and a set of goals derived. Mission or philosophy statements and goals are the core items and give direction to the development of the remaining items, curriculum objectives, and learning objectives. Additional consideration must also be given to methods or learning possibilities, how these mesh with state and national standards, and the assessment of both the curriculum and the rate of learning for each child participating in the curriculum activities. Figure 2.2 provides an overview on curriculum development.

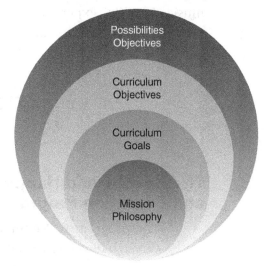

Figure 2.2 Stages of curriculum development.

Once the mission philosophy and the curriculum goals have been established, the process becomes a matter of sifting out the finer points for curriculum objectives and possibility objectives. The sieve becomes finer and finer, providing more detail to the process. Once the progression is completed, providing more and more detail to the learning possibilities, the final circle, it can be reversed, spiraling upward back to the goals and objectives and finally, to the philosophy. The following is an example of curriculum development for a fictional program named Healthy and Happy Early Care and Education Program.

The Healthy and Happy Early Care and Education Program

The Healthy and Happy Early Care and Education program is dedicated to providing a stable and secure learning environment that will enhance the development of the total child with a strong emphasis on movement and music. All skills, experiences, and core knowledge will be presented in a manner appropriate to each child's individual characteristics and family and cultural connections.

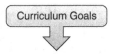

The Healthy and Happy Early Care and Education Program Curriculum Goals

- The program will enhance the development of the whole child through developmentally appropriate learning activities.
- The program will develop the child's fitness level thorough movement and music activities appropriate to each child.
- The program will provide an environment that is safe and secure.

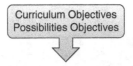

Curriculum Objectives and Possibilities Objectives

❶ The program will provide motor learning activities that will be developmentally appropriate to meet the recommendation of 60 minutes of physical activity for each child.

- Learners will exhibit balance walking on a board on the ground.
- Learners will roll a ball on the ground.

❷ The program will provide developmentally appropriate cognitive activities to stimulate the children's interest in mathematics.

- Learners will use units of measure for measuring objects.
- Learners will track time through the use of a calendar.

❸ The program will provide developmentally appropriate cognitive activities to stimulate the children's interest in literacy.

- Learners will describe pictures using sentences.
- Learner will create a simple story.

❹ The program will offer structured and unstructured opportunities to enhance positive interactions between children and adults.

- Learners will compare their product to others.
- Learners will imitate an adult doing a skill.

❺ The program will provide a learning environment that will grant children the chance to feel secure and safe.

- Learners will play in a toxin-free environment.
- Learners will wash hands prior to eating.

Final Thoughts

This example is a skeleton or frame for a curriculum plan. Additional curriculum objectives and possibilities objectives can be added to the skeleton or frame. All learning activities must refer back to the goals and philosophy. A group of individual learning activities not grounded in goals and a

▲ Physical activity can be incorporated into many of these goals to engage the children and also to help them reach the 60-minute activity goal.

philosophy are not a curriculum. The curriculum is the total package. As the philosophy example of curriculum design shows and the next section will make clear, the learning environment is an important component of the overall curriculum; its design, as well as equipment and materials housed there, will have a huge impact on learning.

2.6 *Analyze Curriculum Design and the Learning Environment*

The learning environment provides an outstanding opportunity to enhance learning. Often teachers do not comprehend how important the environment is in the learning process. Furthermore, they do not understand how to capitalize on the interaction of the children with their environment to enhance learning of knowledge and skills in the physical, cognitive, language, and socioemotional domains.

Learning Environment Characteristics

In the opening section, "Making Connections: What Teachers Do—From a Child's Perspective," Liv placed her teacher in a learning environment outside the normal or traditional classroom. Because learning can and should take place in a variety of environments, it is important to establish criteria for creating and evaluating learning environments for young children.

It is a joy to enter an environment that captures our interest and excites our senses. Why does this happen? Do we feel safe and secure? Does the environment help us make connections to our thoughts and to the thoughts of other individuals? Do the colors excite us? The answer to all of the questions is a resounding "Yes." These items and more, especially safety, are important when designing learning environments for young children. (See **video** Inspiring Spaces for Young Children.)

Safety. The very first consideration in environmental design is ensuring the children's physical and emotional safety. Attention must be paid to the organization of spaces, surfaces, perceptual elements, equipment, and materials to provide optimum safety (Rinaldi, 1998). Children will be spending the majority of their day engaged in learning and life activities in this environment, and every effort must be taken to ensure their safety. Spaces must be defined for a specific activity to ensure adequate room for appropriate movement. If the room is going to be used for ball kicking, for example, space must be provided for a full range of movement of the leg without touching another child or object.

In addition, the space must be designed to provide adequate visual and auditory supervision by adults. For instance, a child care and early learning center had installed a large climbing structure with multiple climbing and sliding tubes. Although the structure was an excellent choice for developing motor skills, it presented a problem because the children could not be observed when they were in the opaque tubes. Out of the view of the teachers, children were engaging in some bullying activities. The teachers made an adjustment by having viewing windows installed in the tubes.

Surfaces should be appropriate for the learning activity. When children are encouraged to run in a space, every effort must be made to ensure that the walls in their path of stoppage are soft. The running surface must be designed to provide traction so slippage is avoided. The air that the children breathe and the materials they touch must be safe and toxin-free, and the space must have adequate lighting In addition, the external noise level must be minimal.

State regulations for child care and education programs will provide guidance in providing a safe environment, such as square footage requirements for indoor and outdoor environments. In addition, the U.S. Consumer Product Safety Commission (2010) provides guidelines for outdoor play learning environments. Teachers and administrators working with children should review and follow the rules, regulations, and/or guidelines for their state.

An additional aspect of safety is security; the learning environment should be a place where a child feels protected, sheltered, and free from stress. Brain research has shown considerable disturbances in the brain's circuits when individuals are in a stressful learning environment (Willis, 2006). Learning must take place in an environment low in stress, where learning activities are relevant and interesting to the children.

Learning Environments That Teach. The learning environment must provide safety and security for the children, but should also be stimulating enough to increase learning and productivity. Rinaldi (1998, p. 119) states that "it is through acting and doing that children are able to understand the path of their learning and the organization of their experience, knowledge, and the meaning of their relationships with others." The children will be motivated to learn by the simple act of engaging in the stimulating and appropriate learning environment.

> When doing consulting work with a group of children (3 to 5 years old) at a school for the blind and the deaf, one of the authors experienced "how the environment teaches." The classroom teacher wanted the children to learn about lines and shapes. Because the children were blind and deaf and therefore unable to be provided with knowledge through the normal auditory and visual clues, and because they were too young to have a command of sign language (and other communication paths, such as tactile signing in the palm of the hand), another learning path through a different one of the child's senses had to be used by the educators to engage the children in the learning process.
>
> The consultant and the teacher designed a learning activity using their sense of touch to assist the children to develop an awareness of lines and shapes. The first activity the children did was to paint a large picture

of their concept of shapes with lines and angles at an easel. This could be considered the pretest. Once this step was completed, the children went outside with buckets of water and large brushes, and were directed to paint surfaces that had distinct edges. They painted decks, fences (picket and mesh), and the sides of a playhouse with windows and a door. It is important to remember that this was all done without the benefit of visual or auditory clues. Once this activity was completed, the children went back to the easel and were directed to paint another large picture. This was the posttest, and the results were absolutely amazing. The pretest of every child was the work one expected to see developmentally; they were what many people would refer to as scribbles. There was not a straight line in any of the pictures. The posttests were entirely different. The paintings were filled with straight lines that did not intersect. Without the benefit of verbal or visual clues from the teacher but with the benefit of a well-designed learning activity and environment, the children were able to grasp the concept of straight lines and spaces.

The environment assists in teaching. Whether the children are engaged in a movement or a musical learning experience, the environment must provide them with space for movement. Children do not learn by sitting still.

The design of the learning environment will set the tone for what will take place and how it will take place. It should have *form* and *fluidity*, where children and adults can do various activities over time. The activities can and should be driven by the children's interests. Therefore, spaces can be changed to reflect the curriculum interests of the children, teachers, and families. Rows of desks or tables do not encourage free movement or exchanges of ideas. Even if the desks can be physically moved and grouped in a separate section of the learning environment, they still require valuable space and hinder movement. Movable partitions, as well as equipment on wheels, may be used to design a fluid environment.

Teachers should review the environment and determine whether the design enhances or hinders curriculum learning in all areas. Movement and music are important in their own right and provide various opportunities for developing skills in language, reasoning, and social skills that will support learning in more academic areas (Bowman et al., 2001). A learning environment that encourages movement and individual and group interactions will strengthen a curriculum revolving around movement and music.

Discussions about learning environments usually divide the environments into indoor and outdoor. Traditionally, the indoor environment is defined as the area where academic material is applied, whereas the outdoor environment is the area that supports movement activities. Although this may have traditionally been true, the characteristics of the learning environment, indoor or outdoor, should be the same. Movement and music activities should be integrated throughout the day, indoors or outdoors. The learning environment should be defined by two broad categories: *what the child will do*, and *how the child will do it.*

What Will the Child Do? How Will the Child Do It? What learning activities the children will be doing and how they will be doing them are important questions. The answers will determine the details of the environmental design. The materials and equipment and their developmental appropriateness will determine what the children will do.

Hedegaard (2007) warns that the selection of equipment and materials should be based on pedagogical issues and not on marketing that could hinder the child's development. A natural outdoor environment with a clubhouse and with opportunities for gardening, bike riding, and water play will encourage movement and social interactions. An indoor environment filled with a wide variety of creative materials, blocks, and boxes will encourage creative thinking and exploration. It is amazing what children can design with a variety of boxes—they create cities, vehicles, and even play structures.

The ratio of pieces of equipment to the number of children will determine how the children will do each activity (taking turns, sharing, waiting). The arrangement of the environment will determine how the children will do the activity and what type of behavior is expected. Finally, the arrangement of the equipment and materials determines the expectations for cleanup after the learning activity is completed.

Table 2.2 lists elements that are part of the learning environment and shows how the elements are categorized into the *What* and *How* columns. The table specifies the components needed for *what* the child will do and the different components for *how* the child will do it. All goals of the program should be reflected in these columns.

Table 2.2 Elements of the Environment: Considering What and How

Element	What the Child Will Do	How the Child Will Do It
Goals of Program	✓	✓
Materials and Equipment	✓	
Health and Safety		✓
Needs of Children		✓
Flow and Pathways		✓
Boundaries		✓
Developmental Level of Equipment	✓	
Adaptation	✓	
Cleanup	✓	

By combining indoor and outdoor activities and looking at the common elements, learning environment design becomes easier to understand, and we are ready to plan how the learning environment will be used.

The *design process* should begin with a review of the program goals. This review reveals any gaps that may exist in philosophy and practice. Are the right types of equipment and materials available to meet the program goals? For example, if a program goal is to have children experience and develop the skill of climbing vertical heights but there is no climbing equipment, some adjustments must be made. In addition, can the materials and equipment be adjusted to meet the diverse developmental needs of the children? Adaptations must always be considered.

Next, the learning environment will have to be assessed for health and safety concerns. As stated before, this is an absolute must. Equipment and materials should be easy to clean. All items should be inspected daily to ensure that there are no loose pieces that can harm children. Remember that children will always find ways to use and experiment with items, including putting them in their mouths.

In addition, the children's developmental needs must be taken into consideration. Is it really necessary, for example, for the children to climb a vertical height? Perhaps laying a ladder on the ground and having the children move their feet—not from rung to rung, but from space to space—

accomplishes the goal. Because the child will be getting the same experience by moving from space to space, lifting one foot and maintaining balance on the other foot, the expensive climbing equipment and the appropriate fall absorption surface would not be needed.

Once these considerations are addressed, we are ready to look more closely at the learning environment. A review of the learning space and the learning activity shows how to design the placement of the equipment and materials. The first consideration must be the pathways around activities and the location of the bathrooms. It would be inadvisable to have children running through striking or kicking areas or through an area where swings are being used. The same consideration should be given to moving from one activity to another. Pathways and the flow of traffic are important.

Physical boundaries must be established. It is a common mistake to not set boundaries. Many times teachers walk into a wide-open space with students and lose control of the children. This can be a safety concern and can also be very frustrating for the teacher and some children. Simple placement of cones or partitions before the children enter the space can prevent frustration and accidents.

The next item to be considered is the equipment and materials used in the lesson. It is important to have a variety of items available to meet all developmental levels of the children. If balls are going to be used for the learning activity, then every effort should be made to provide every child with a ball that is appropriate for his or her developmental level and activity. When selecting equipment, full consideration must be given to the physical capabilities of the children; adaptations may need to be made. There should be a range of balls, from soft and easy-to-grasp ones to balls harder in composition to provide a greater bounce. It is also important to review the equipment to see what adaptations must be made to meet the children's needs and the activity's requirements.

When selecting materials and equipment, make sure to include various colors and textures. Such variety will help to stimulate the children and will increase their productivity.

Finally, considered how cleanup and reorganization will occur in the space. Large containers clearly marked with a pictorial representation of the equipment will expedite the process. An example is a three-sectioned

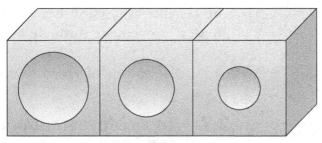

Figure 2.3 Children's ball sorter

container for various size balls, as in Figure 2.3. Children will be required to think about the size of the balls as they sort and place each one in the appropriate section.

Milk crates can also be used for storage of items such as balls, beanbags, and rhythm instruments. Pictures of equipment items, as well as the names of the items, should be placed on the outside of the containers. This will not only expedite cleanup, but also reinforce literacy skills (see Figure 2.4).

Remember that the characteristics listed here are general and may be used when designing a learning environment or any other environment for young children. The choice of equipment to purchase will depend on the program goals as well as on the children's interests. An important goal is developing knowledge, skills, and dispositions in movement and music. Materials and equipment should be simple but usable in a variety of different ways. The listed items in Figure 2.5 have been divided into movement and music categories, but in reality, many of the items on the list, such as balls, beanbags, boom whackers, and scarves, can be used to strengthen movement and music.

Children like stimulation, but they also enjoy consistency. Teachers do not need to provide a wide variety of equipment or materials, just appropriate items for the children's age and developmental level and for the knowledge, skills, and attitudes to which the children will be exposed in the daily curriculum activities. Equipment does not need to be expensive but should be included in the environment.

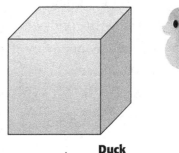

Duck

Figure 2.4 Equipment and material choices.

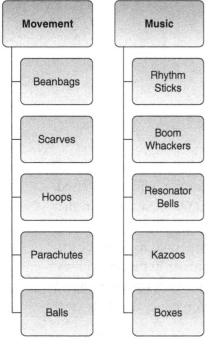

Figure 2.5 Movement and music equipment.

The benefits of physical fitness enhanced by physical movement through play, planned activities, and musical activities are important for the development of a healthy child.

2.7 Apply Movement and Music and Learning

We know that children learn through movement, and what better way to stimulate the body–mind connection than through musical experiences such as dancing, playing an instrument, and singing (Campbell, 1998)? Movement and music should not be separated. Bluestine (2000, p. 50) recommends, "Teach children to move as the music moves—continuously." Music and movement should be integrated into every aspect of the curriculum. The result will be a healthy child.

M² FUN

Give children a beanbag and ask them to move the beanbag to demonstrate the following concepts:

- Over the bridge
- Under the bridge
- Water coming out of a faucet
- Sleep
- Bird
- Around a tree

Emphasize safety in body and beanbag position.

Putting It on Paper

We now have all the pieces necessary to design and build a curriculum that includes all subject areas and, in particular, integrates movement and music. It is also important to remember that the learning environment must be part of any curriculum design.

Remember also that a group of same-age children possesses individual differences based on the children's development, abilities, interests, and culture. Learning activities should be thought of as *possibilities* that provide a variety of methods or procedures to accommodate an assortment of interests and abilities. Not every child will do every step of the activity in exactly the same way, nor should the teacher expect every child to behave the same way. The following example of a lesson plan for a musical learning activity for kindergarten children will help you plan daily and weekly learning activities.

Sample Learning Plan

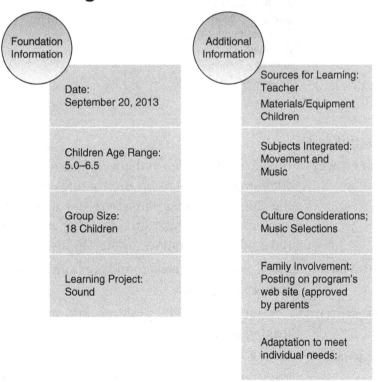

Foundation Information

Date:
September 20, 2013

Children Age Range:
5.0–6.5

Group Size:
18 Children

Learning Project:
Sound

Additional Information

Sources for Learning:
Teacher
Materials/Equipment
Children

Subjects Integrated:
Movement and
Music

Culture Considerations;
Music Selections

Family Involvement:
Posting on program's
web site (approved
by parents

Adaptation to meet
individual needs:

Daily Learning Possibilities

(Learning objectives, goals, and M² standards MUST match all three daily possibilities.)

Curriculum Goal	M² Standard	Learning Objective	Supportive Practices
Child will develop social interactive skills	*M² Music Standard:* Child will demonstrate understanding of the dynamics (high/low, loud/soft) of musical sounds through interruptive movement	Child engages in discussion about making sound	Adult will provide opportunities for input from the children
Child will combine materials in a creative manner		Child combines materials to make a sound	Adult will provide a variety of materials
Child will gain an understanding of the arts	*M² Movement Standard:* Child will construct movement using locomotor skills (walk, hop, skip, gallop) to match the dynamics (high/low, loud/soft) of a musical recording.	Child produces different musical patterns	Adult will model and describe musical patterns
Child will develop gross motor patterns		Child moves to basic musical patterns	Adult will provide opportunities for movement

Possibility 1

Procedure: Discuss sounds: high and low, loud and soft. Stimulate additional discussion on how sounds are made. Give the children various containers and striking materials and have them make sounds, original and imitation. Have the children move to the sounds.

Materials: Metal and plastic buckets and pots and metal, wooden, and plastic spoons.

Assessment: Comments made by children and responses when striking containers.

Summary: Made following completion of possibility as part of the assessment process. Provides guidance for subsequent learning activities.

Possibility 2

Procedure: Discuss sounds: high and low, loud and soft. Stimulate additional discussion on how sounds are made. Give the children various materials and ask them to make sounds with the materials by themselves or in combination with each other. Have the children move to the sounds they have created.

Materials: Paper, cardboard, sandpaper, aluminum foil

Assessment: Comments made by children and creative ways materials are used to make sounds.

Summary: Made following completion of possibility as part of the assessment process. Provides guidance for subsequent learning activities.

Possibility 3

Procedure: Discuss sounds: high and low, loud and soft. Stimulate additional discussion on how sounds are made. Give some of the children a variety of rhythm instruments. Put the children under large boxes and tables and behind barriers and have them make individual sounds and series of sounds. The children not making sounds may move to the sounds made by the children making sounds and offer comments on how the sound changes in the different environments.

Materials: Collection of rhythm instruments, large boxes, and paper and metal barriers

Assessment: Comments made by children and the number of ways the children interact with the containers and partition when making sounds.

Summary: Made following completion of possibility as part of the assessment process. Provides guidance for subsequent learning activities.

The three possibilities, each related to the same goals and objects and standards, will guide learning for different developmental levels and interests. Assessment of each possibility will guide further plans for learning.

Summary

Education is the process of preparing children for a strong future, and the curriculum is the frame or skeleton that helps educators to structure learning. The curriculum is also a way to communicate to all involved parties what is important in the learning process.

When reviewing curriculum choices and design, remember that children learn best by being immersed in the process through play and developmentally appropriate hands-on learning activities. The research work of John Dewey, Jean Piaget, and Lev Vygotsky has provided sound evidence supporting these concepts.

Curriculum selection and design always begin with a clear understanding of the mission or philosophy and the goals of the educational program. The next step is to be sure that there is a connection between the curriculum and the state and national standards and that the curriculum follows the guidelines provided by NAEYC for developmentally appropriate practices (DAP).

Various curriculum programs—including High Scope, Creative Curriculum, Montessori, Bank Street, Constructivist, Waldorf, and Te Whāriki—have gained the respect of educators and families. A program may also choose to build a curriculum to have a better match to the philosophy and goals and objectives. Philosophy, goals, curriculum objectives, and possibility objectives must be developed as part of the design process.

The development of the curriculum must address the learning environment and the basic design characteristics such as safety, assistance in the learning process, and form and fluidity. Finally, consideration must be given to equipment and materials and the format or lesson plans for appropriate learning.

Summary Related to Outcomes

Learning Outcomes	Guiding Principles
2.1 Define education and curriculum	Individual Needs Met
Education prepares children to improve society. The learning activities that are part of the educational process are complicated and interwoven and make up the curriculum.	

Learning Outcomes	Guiding Principles
2.2 Compare curriculum development models	Individual Needs Met
Curriculum is designed around two models, performance and competence. A competence model is effective for movement and music with young children.	
2.3 Value child decision making and involvement in curriculum	Individual Needs Met
Curriculum choices should encourage children to imitate experiences and be decision makers and engaged learners. Play is an excellent way for young children to learn.	
2.4 Discuss curriculum selection	Environment and Curriculum Reciprocated
A curriculum should match the program's philosophy or mission statement. The goals and objectives should be based on the work of Dewey, Piaget, and Vygotsky and develop the whole child. Professional standards help to guide learning. Various curricula have been developed and tested for young children (High Scope, Creative Curriculum, Bank Street Developmental–Interactive Approach, Kamii–DeVries Constructivist Perspective, Waldorf, Montessori, and Te Whāriki).	
2.5 Apply curriculum design	Environment and Curriculum Reciprocated
Programs can decide to develop a curriculum. This curriculum should be based on the program goals and objectives derived from the program's philosophy or mission statement.	
2.6 Analyze curriculum design and the learning environment	Environment and Curriculum Reciprocated
Learning environment is an important part of curriculum design. Safety is the first consideration when designing a learning environment. An appropriately designed environment teaches the children.	
2.7 Apply movement and music and learning	Movement and Music Integrated
Movement and music cannot be separated, especially when working with young children. Daily possibilities provide flexibility in meeting the needs of the children and learning standards.	

Demonstrate Your Knowledge, Skills, and Dispositions

Students will demonstrate knowledge, comprehension, analysis, and evaluation of Learning Outcomes related to Guiding Principles.

Learning Outcomes	Guiding Principles
2.1 Define education and curriculum	Individual Needs Met
• Describe a personal early learning experience. What was important to you? What upset you?	
2.2 Compare curriculum development models	Individual Needs Met
• Was the early learning experience described in 2.1 a performance or competence model? Why do you say that?	
2.3 Value child decision making and involvement in curriculum	Individual Needs Met
• Marcus's mother feels you are having too much playtime in your early learning program. What would your reply be?	
2.4 Discuss curriculum selection	Environment and Curriculum Reciprocated
• Review early childhood standards for your state. Pick two movement standards and two music standards. What did you like about the standards you selected?	
2.5 Apply curriculum design	Environment and Curriculum Reciprocated
• You have been hired to begin an early child care and education program. Describe what curriculum choices you would make.	
2.6 Analyze curriculum design and the learning environment	Environment and Curriculum Reciprocated
• Pick three pieces of equipment you would buy for the program and describe why you made these selections.	
2.7 Apply movement and music and learning	Movement and Music Integrated
• Marcus's mother wants to know why you are spending time every day doing movement and music activities instead of doing reading and math activities. What would your response be?	

Planning for Engaging

The following learning activities provide three possibilities or ways to develop a standard taken from the **M² Movement Standard**:

M² Movement Standard: The child will be creative and invent a movement pattern to represent or match musical notation or style.

Possibility One	Possibility Two	Possibility Three
Children will be shown a large musical notation. Children will then use their bodies alone or with others to represent the notation.	Children will be exposed to a variety of music (marches, waltzes, rock, jazz, orchestral). Children will move their bodies to the music patterns.	Children will move to a variety of music (marches, waltzes, rock, jazz, orchestral) as different animals (elephant, eagle, snake, lion).
Assessment Observation of letters formed by the children. Variety used to represent the letters.	**Assessment** Observation of the variety of patterns used by the children and how the patterns matched the music.	**Assessment** Observation of how children matched the music tempo. Observation on creativity used to represent the animals.

Now You Try It

Complete the following standard-based learning activity designed to meet various interests and developmental levels by designing two possibilities/ learning activities to develop a movement or music standard taken from the **M² Movement Standard**.

Standard:		
M² Movement Standard: The child will use movement and vocal expressions to demonstrate characters in a story.		
Possibility One	**Possibility Two**	**Possibility Three**
Design a "story can" by decorating a coffee can with a plastic lid. In the can put in small plastic animals and people, and a few nondescript objects. Each child will select an item from the can and, using voice and body movements, will act out a story about the object.		

Assessment	Assessment	Assessment
Did the child use both movement and voice when creating a story about the object?		

References

Bernstein, B. (1996). *Pedagogy, symbolic control and identity: Theory, research and critique* (2nd ed.). London, UK: Taylor and Francis.

Bluestine, E. (2000). *The ways children learn music: An introduction and practical guide to music learning theory.* Chicago, IL: GIA Publications, Inc.

Bowman, B., Donovan, M. S., & Burns, M. S. (Eds.). (2001). *Eager to learn: Educating our preschoolers.* Washington, DC: National Academy Press.

Bredekamp, S. & Rosegrant, T. (Eds.) (1992). *Reaching potentials: Appropriate curriculum and assessment for young children.* Washington, DC: National Association for the Education of Young Children.

Bronfenbrenner, U. (1979). *The ecology of human development: Experiments by nature and design.* Cambridge, MA: Harvard University Press.

Campbell, P. (1998). *Songs in their heads: Music and its meaning in children's lives.* New York, NY: Oxford University Press.

Dodge, D. T. (2004). Early childhood curriculum models: Why, what, and how programs use them. *Child Care Information Exchange,* January/February.

Duncan, Arne (2010). Working together for early learning. Paper presented at the Early Childhood 2010—Innovation for the Next Generation meeting. Retrieved February 21, 2013, from http://www.ed.gov/news/speeches/working-together-early-learning-secretary-arne-duncans-remarks-early-childhood-2010-in.

Hedegaard, M. (2007). The development of children's conceptual relation to the world, with focus on concept formation in preschool children's activity. In H. Daniels, M. Cole, & J. Wertsch (Eds.). *The Cambridge companion to Vygotsky.* New York, NY: Cambridge University Press.

Helm, J., & Katz, L. (2001). *Young investigators: The project approach in the early years.* New York: NY: Teachers College Press.

High Scope. (2012). Curriculum. Retrieved February 7, 2012 from http://www.highscope.org/Content.asp?ContentId=1.

Kim, J., & Robinson, H. M. (2010). Four steps for becoming familiar with early music standards. *Young Children,* March, 42–47.

Lee, J. M., & Lee, D. M. (1950). *The child and his curriculum.* New York, NY: Appleton Century Crofts, Inc.

Lunenburg, F. C. (2011). Curriculum models for preschool education: theories and approaches in the early years. *Schooling, 2*(1), 1–6.

Marcon, R. A. (1992). Different effects of three preschool models on inner-city 4-year-olds. *Early Childhood Research Quarterly, 74*(5), 19–20.

Marcon, R. A. (1995). Fourth-grade slump: The cause and cure. *Principal, 74*(5), 19–20.

McLachlan, C., Fleer, M., & Edwards, S. (2010). Early childhood curriculum and planning, assessment, and implementation. Cambridge, UK: Cambridge University Press.

Mooney, C. G. (2000). *An introduction to doing Montessori, Erickson, Piaget, and Vygotsky.* St. Paul, MN: Redleaf Press.

National Association for the Education of Young Children (NAEYC) (2003). *Early childhood curriculum, assessment, and program evaluation: Building an effective, accountable system in programs for children birth through age 8.* Washington, DC: NAEYC.

National Association for the Education of Young Children (NAEYC) (2009). *Developmentally appropriate practice in early childhood programs serving children from birth through age 8.* Washington, DC: NAEYC.

National Association for Sport and Physical Education (2009). Appropriate practices in movement programs for children ages 3–5: A position statement from the National Association for Sport and Physical Education. Reston, VA: AAHPERD.

Piaget, J. (1952). *The origins of intelligence in children.* New York, NY: International Universities Press.

Rinaldi, C. (1998). The space of childhood. In G. Ceppi, G. & M. Zini, (Eds.). *Children, spaces, relations: Metaproject for an environment for young children.* Reggio Children's Publishing, Italy: Grafiche Maffei.

Soursa, D. (Ed.) (2010). *Mind, brain, and education: Neuroscience implications for the Classroom.* Bloomington, IN: Solution Tree Press.

Teaching Strategies (2013). The creative curriculum for preschool: What preschool leaders say. Retrieved from https://www.teachingstrategies.com/page/adwords-learn-Leaders-page-cc-latest-edition-4-2013.cfm?gclid=CMyN3trej7oCFU-Z4AodaREAwQ.

Te Whāriki: Early Childhood Curriculum (1996). See http://www.educate.ece.govt.nz/~/media/Educate/Files/Reference%20Downloads/whariki.pdf. Material corrected.

Trostli, R. (1998). *Rhythms of learning: Selected lectures by Rudolf Steiner* (pp. 11–43). Hudson, NY: Anthroposophic Press.

Willis, J. (2006). *Research-based strategies to ignite student learning: Insights from a neurologist and classroom teacher.* Alexandria, VA: Association for Supervision and Curriculum.

Wink, J., & Putney, L. (2002). *A vision of Vygotsky.* Boston, MA: Allyn & Bacon.

chapter 3

Music Provides the Rhythm for Movement and Healthy Lifestyle

LEARNING OUTCOMES AND GUIDING PRINCIPLES

Students reading this text will be able to demonstrate Learning Outcomes linked to Guiding Principles based on the *National Association for the Education of Young Children's Developmentally Appropriate Practice in Early Childhood Programs Serving Children from Birth through Age 8.*

Learning Outcomes	Guiding Principles
3.1 Describe the importance of music	Movement and Music Integrated
3.2 Define music	Movement and Music Integrated
3.3 Discuss musical experiences for young children	Environment and Curriculum Reciprocated
3.4 Recognize music standards	Standards and Assessment Provide Guidance
3.5 Identify notable musical teaching methods	Movement and Music Integrated
3.6 Describe how to teach music	Movement and Music Integrated
3.7 Identify musical suggestions	Environment and Curriculum Reciprocated

3.1 *Describe the Importance of Music*

Music is a form of communication, but this is certainly too simple a definition. It is also a way to share feelings and experiences. It has the ability to soothe, arouse interest, stimulate thought, and regulate social behavior (Trehub, 2003). Music's ability to transform behavior and thought makes it a powerful tool, which has been used for centuries and in every culture. Music should be an important part of the lives of young children because early interaction with music positively affects the quality of children's lives (MENC, 1991). In addition, early interaction creates a strong foundation for future music learning (MENC, 1991).

Studies of brain development have demonstrated the effect stress can have on the young child's maturing central nervous system, the brain and spinal cord, and the entire body—encompassing the peripheral nerves, muscles, glands, and related hormones (Flohr, 2010). In "Making Connections: The Power of Music," Madeline was under stress. She was away from her mother and father, and she was tired. The stress Madeline was experiencing was reduced by her mother's singing the lullaby and her grandmother's physical rubbing of her back. Music and movement are good partners when attempting to comfort a child (Edwards, 2011). Early

▲ Three-year-old boy showing his excitement as he sings and plays the drums for his family.

music and movement experiences have a therapeutic benefit in that they can be an antidote to stress and can be beneficial to the brain's developing structure (Healy, 2010). Parents and caregivers know that a stressed infant or young child can be soothed by a melodic vocalization.

Research shows that in addition to reducing stress, music has the benefit of supporting skills in mathematics and creativity (Jensen, 2001). Music should be in the lives of every child because it is important to children's social, emotional, physical, and cognitive development.

3.2 *Define Music*

Music has importance to different cultures and peoples. Our lives are filled with various sounds that make us feel joy, sadness, annoyance, or contentment. These sounds are the raw material used to make music.

Table 3.1 Characteristics of Sound

Sound Characteristic	Description	Example
Pitch	High or low (number of vibrations)	Violin makes a high sound; double bass makes a low sound
Timbre	Quality of sound/ pitch	Piano and guitar sound different even when producing the same pitch or loudness
Dynamics	Soft or loud	Whispering or yelling
Duration	Beat and rhythm	Clapping hands to a steady drumbeat or a song

The four characteristics of sound listed in Table 3.1 are the foundation of music.

Pitch

Sounds occur when the source of the sound moves the surrounding air molecules, creating vibration (Winner, 1982). Vibrations repeating quickly will produce a high pitch. The greater the gap between the vibrations, the lower the pitch. The concept of pitch is easy for children to hear and comprehend. Teachers can have the children lower or raise their bodies to demonstrate a high or low pitch as they listen to the corresponding sound. Another way to encourage children to explore pitch and their own vocal range is to have them follow the teacher's hand with their own voices as the teacher imitates a roller coaster (Stacey Steele, personal interview, October 7, 2012).

Timbre

The quality of a pitch is referred to as *timbre*. Timbre tells the listener what sounds are different from one another even when they have the same pitch and loudness. Helping children to note the differences between the qualities of the sound is important. For instance, Sergei Prokofiev composed *Peter and the Wolf* to cultivate musical tastes in young children. Characters in this story about a boy and a wolf are denoted by the use of musical instruments, including strings, oboe, clarinet, French horns, bassoon, timpani, and bass drum. Children who are guided as they listen to this composition develop the concept of timbre and intensity or dynamics.

Teachers can assist the children in recognizing timbre by asking them to raise their hands when they hear the French horn, the oboe, or any of the other featured instruments. By asking the children a question such as "Which instrument is louder, the bass drum or the clarinet?" dynamics can be emphasized as well.

Dynamics

Dynamics, the loudness or the softness of a sound or musical piece, is also an easy concept for children to grasp. Children will enjoy making loud sounds and soft sounds. The *Surprise Symphony* (Symphony No. 94) by Franz Joseph Haydn was intentionally written to have soft sections followed by loud sections to "surprise" the listeners. To further develop the concept of dynamics, give a set of rhythm sticks to each child and have them play the sticks with the following dynamics. They will enjoy learning the Italian words as well:

- Very soft (pianissimo, *pp*)
- Soft (piano, *p*)
- Moderately soft (mezzo piano, *mp*)
- Moderately loud (mezzo forte, *mf*)
- Loud (forte, *f*)
- Very loud (fortissimo, *ff*)

Duration

The *beat* indicates the steady pulse of music. It can be compared to the beat of the heart. Children can feel the beat by walking in time to the music.

Rhythm is the way the words to a song move. Sometimes the rhythm of a song moves steadily, using sounds or notes the same length, as in "Twinkle, Twinkle, Little Star." Or the rhythm may be very irregular or uneven, as in "The Itsy Bitsy [Eency Weency] Spider." Songs that move steadily could be used for natural body movements such as walking or, if the music moves quickly, running, whereas pieces that move with an uneven rhythm inspire galloping or skipping. Including movement with music will helps children develop a greater sense of rhythm and beat. They will discover that music is fun!

You may also help children move to a preset beat, such as a recording of John Philip Sousa's *Washington Post March* or *Stars and Stripes Forever*, or to Johann Strauss's *Blue Danube* waltz. Encourage free expressive movements by waving scarves to the contagious rhythm of a Strauss waltz.

The previously discussed elements of pitch, timbre, dynamics, and duration produce organized sounds or music. Harvard psychologist Howard Gardner (2011) felt that music intelligence is as important as logical–mathematical intelligence, linguistic intelligence, spatial intelligence, bodily–kinesthetic intelligence, interpersonal intelligence, and intrapersonal intelligence. Music is not a frill (Levinowitz, 2012); children must be provided with experiences in music to enhance their overall learning.

M² FUN

Using the characteristics of sound, tell a story or sing a song using your voice to demonstrate pitch, timbre, dynamics, and duration. A good story to use would be that of Rapunzel or Snow White.

3.3 *Discuss Musical Experiences for Young Children*

Musical experiences for young children are vital to the education of every child, and therefore should be available and developmentally appropriate for every child. The Music Educators National Conference (MENC) of the National Association for Music Education (NAfME) in 1991 adopted a set of beliefs to guide early childhood teachers in the design and execution of a quality music curriculum for young children. The belief framework involves a clear understanding of the following:

- Importance of each child's unique and diverse musical potential
- Significance of the musical learning environment
- Development of critical thinking skills through music
- Importance of an effective musical model

These points should be understood and used to guide music curriculum development and learning experiences.

Children's Musical Potential

Children are musical beings from the first rhythmic beat of the heart in the uterus. Research shows that maturing infants interact and learn from their environment. Prenatally, a six-month-old fetus moves in rhythm to the mother's speech. The sounds the developing infant hears are muffled because of the surrounding tissue and fluid. Only low to medium frequencies, 40 to 4000 Hz (number of times sounds go up or down in a second), corresponding to the notes on a piano and a human melodic voice, are heard by the developing fetus (Blythe, 2004).

The sense of hearing is fully developed before birth (Whitwell, 2012), and infants are born ready to interact with the elements of music, rhythm, pitch, and melody (Edwards, 2011). After birth, infants remember lullabies sung during pregnancy (Arabin, 1992; Polverini-Rey, 1992). Infants as young as 2 months old are able to recognize the ups and downs of a melody and are able to distinguish between a familiar melody and a novel one (Edwards, 2011). Children's music potential is substantiated, and they are ready to experience musical skills through quality experiences in a learning environment designed to maximize learning.

Musical Learning Environments and Culture

Each child is unique and is encapsulated in a diverse cultural background. These individual differences will affect how each child reacts to the musical learning environment. The environment should be rich in opportunities for all children to interact with various equipment and materials at their own paces and interest levels. The equipment and materials available in the musical environment should reflect the unique background of each child represented in the group.

Music has been referred to as the universal language, but the music children absorb and learn initially is specific to their culture. Generally, children in the United States develop while listening and learning Western music. In contrast, children in other parts of the world may not be familiar with Western music. The difference is the scales—arrangement of pitches—used in different parts of the world (see **video**).

▲ Making music using pots and spoons in the kitchen is always fun.

Music is made up of different pitches. Western music is divided into repeating octaves, with each octave consisting of 12 notes. If you look at the black and white keys on a piano or a keyboard and played them consecutively from C to the next C, you would be playing the Western music scale or the chromatic scale (Winner, 1982). The majority of cultures in the world, however, do not use the 12-note chromatic scale. Non-Western countries and peoples, such as China and India, use scales that vary in the number of notes in the scale. Indian music uses the diatonic scale consisting of seven (C-D-E-F-G-A-B) of the 12 notes in the Western scale. Chinese music uses a pentatonic (five-note) scale (C-D-E-G-A). The pentatonic scale is the most widely used scale in the world. A YouTube video featuring Bobby McFerrin demonstrates the pentatonic scale (Pentatonic Scale). The instruments used to play the music vary according to the country and the musical scale used by the country or region (see Table 3.2) (see **video** Power of Pentatonic Scale–Demonstration by Bobby McFerrin).

Table 3.2 Country/Regional Musical Scales

Country or Region	Musical Scale Number	Musical Instruments
China	Five notes (pentatonic)	• Stringed instruments (plucked, bowed, struck) • Bamboo woodwinds • Metal gongs • Hide drums
India	Seven notes (diatonic)	• Chordophones (string) • Aerophones (wind) • Membranophones (drums)
Arab North Africa Arabian Peninsula	Twenty-four notes	Varies according to region. Includes extensive variations of string, wind, and percussion instruments. Arabic ensemble can include: • Oud • Nay • Ganum • Kaman
Latin American	Five notes (pentatonic)	• Maracas • Whistles • Panpipes • Trumpets • Guitars
Native American	Five notes (pentatonic)	Varies according to geographic region. Can include: • Drums • Flutes • Shakers

The listing in Table 3.2 provides an overview of the diversity and similarity of scales and musical instruments used throughout the world (Musical Instruments from Around the World). We should be careful not to present a single picture of a culture, such as assuming that all Mexican children wear sombreros or German children wear lederhosen. Children should be exposed to a many cultures and the complexities of the culture. In the 21st century, children live in a global society and should be made aware of different cultures by families and teachers. There should be a blending of cultural experiences and an appreciation for the similarities, as well as differences, among cultures (see **video** Musical Instruments from Around the World).

African-American children, for example, should be able to listen to and to have experiences with movement tunes and instruments reflective of the African-American culture—and other children should share these experiences as well. Similar equipment and materials should be provided for many forms of diversity and cultures.

Chin Ho and his family have just arrived from China. His kindergarten teacher, Ms. Marvin, is very aware that Chin Ho's learning environment should reinforce his previous cultural environment and should also expose his classmates to the music of the Chinese culture. One way she is doing this is to play *Rabbit Days and Dumplings* by Elena Moon Park, a collection of mostly traditional songs from, Korea, Japan, China, Tibet, and Taiwan.

The learning environment should have an area designated for musical play. Remember, children learn best through play and exploration. The area should contain the following:

- Recordings of quality children's songs, classical music, and folk tunes from various cultures (see music suggestions at the end of this chapter).
- Tape or CD player
- Percussion instruments (sticks, rattles, shakers, tom-toms, cymbals)
- Melodic instruments (bells, xylophones, tone bars)
- Boom whackers (individual plastic tubes tuned to specific notes)
- Sundry noisemakers (oatmeal containers, coffee cans and paper tubes filled with beads or sand/corn meal, blocks of wood, sandpaper, and metal bowls)

The musical experiences children have should be of high quality and not trite in nature. This means that the musical environment should develop quality music experiences through personal interactions. Through the use of high-quality materials and equipment, children begin to build discriminating skills and attitudes. They develop critical thinking skills related to music.

Mrs. Collier, Anm Ang's violin teacher, does not want her student to listen to some of the commercial recordings designed for children. She feels the recordings are not of high quality and will not provide good musical experiences for Anm Ang.

Development of Critical Thinking Skills

Young children are capable of developing critical thinking skills through music (National Association for Music Education, 2012). It is important to review Bloom's Taxonomy of Learning Domains when discussing the topic of critical thinking skills. Benjamin Bloom was an educational psychologist who, in 1956, led a group of fellow educational psychologists in the development of a classification system for intellectual behaviors. Bloom's Taxonomy was revised in the 1990s to reflect relevance to the 21st century (Overbaugh & Schutz, 2012). The revised Bloom's Taxonomy (RBT) provides the same basic structure or levels as the 1956 version (see Figure 3.1). The differences are the changing of the names of the levels from nouns to verbs and reversing the top two levels.

When developing a music curriculum and associated critical thinking skills, it is important to employ the RBT levels. Nursery rhymes are used by parents, caregivers, and teachers to entertain and stimulate young children. Many musical elements, such as rhythm or beat, are incorporated into even the simplest nursery rhymes. In *remembering*, the first level of RBT, traditional rhymes will begin to build the child's musical memory repertoire. To develop the next level, *understanding*, the curriculum leader can have the children draw a picture about a nursery

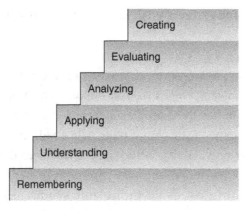

Figure 3.1 Critical thinking skills related to Bloom's Taxonomy.

rhyme or a simple song. The child's playing or singing a tune provides experience at the *applying* level. The educator can play different patterns with rhythm sticks, enabling the children to develop skills to recognize patterns, thereby engaging the *analyzing* level. Two recordings of the same music can be played to the children, who can then discuss which version they like best. This activity develops the *evaluating* level. Finally, the children can compose a simple song to experience the *creating* level. An effective music educator can select appropriate learning experiences to enhance all levels of RBT.

Effective Musical Model

Music education for young children applies developmental learning experiences in singing, moving, listening, creating, and playing instruments (NAfME, 2012). These experiences can be introduced by an adult or a child and/or stimulated by the environment surrounding the child.

It is important that the individuals involved in music education are loving, respectful, enthusiastic, and encouraging toward young children. In addition, it is helpful for the individuals to value music in the lives of children. We have all seen adults and children wanting to share a favorite song or movement with each other. They are effective musical models.

> Ms. Sanchez was a first-year teacher who enjoyed music, and who had a vast quantity of camp songs from her days as a camper and a counselor. Each day in her third-grade classroom, the children began with the day singing some of the camp songs. The children and Ms. Sanchez enjoyed this opening activity. Although Ms. Sanchez did not have any formal musical experience, she was confident in her realization that there are many ways to provide musical interactions to affect children's musical growth. Everyone had a wonderful time enjoying the musical experience. Later, when the trained music teacher taught a song to add to Ms. Sanchez's morning repertoire, the children were excited even though it did not quite sound the same as Ms. Sanchez's version.

Ms. Sanchez was an effective role model because she realized she could affect the musical interest of the children even though she was not professionally trained. In addition, she had engaged the children in a fun and playful manner that stimulated their interest in a varied musical repertory. She created an appropriate musical learning environment.

The environment can be an effective role model, too. If the environment provides many opportunities for children to listen and to engage in musical activities, it can become an operative musical model. Simply having classical music playing in the background while the children are engaged in play or other activities is an important way to use music in the environment.

Many parents and educators of young children may be apprehensive about engaging children in musical experiences. Although it is important for children to be exposed to activities developed by musical educators, this is not always possible. Whether or not a program does have a musical educator who frequents the classroom, however, it is important for the children to be constantly exposed to music on day-by-day or hour-by-hour bases. Music should be the rhythm of the classroom. Musical standards help both the trained musical educator and the enthusiastic teacher provide a quality music curriculum.

3.4 *Recognize Music Standards*

The Music Education National Conference (NAfME, 2012) has adopted national standards for music. The standards are undergoing revision (2013–2014) by NAfME; here, we present the 2012 standards. The current national standards are presented in a musically appropriate manner in a video (see **video**).

The music standards can be adapted to be developmentally appropriate for younger and older children. All children sing to some degree. They sing spontaneously. It often seems as if it may be a means to calm or reassure themselves. Madeline, in "Making Connections" earlier in this chapter, loves to sing and sings often in the day. It is understandable that she could be calmed by the melodic nature of the voice. Teachers and parents can encourage singing simply by singing to the children throughout the day.

Instead of telling the children it is time clean up, for instance, the adult can sing:

> This is the way we pick up blocks, pick up blocks so early in the morning/afternoon.
>
> This is the way we pick up books, pick up books so early in the morning/afternoon.

This simple improvisation of the song, "This Is the Way We Wash Our Clothes," can encourage improvisation.

Improvisation of a song can encourage composition and note reading when appropriate to the interests and abilities of the children. Simply having a child sing high and low notes while moving his or her hand up and down can signal the beginnings of composition. The actual notation and reading of music can be introduced as children gain understanding of musical concepts.

Listening to music should be nurtured prenatally and throughout the lifestyle of the child. Children should be exposed to a variety of musical styles. The concept of evaluating music can also begin young by simply asking, "Do you like this music?" Later adults can ask, "Why do you like it [or not]?" Peter, for example, drives his two daughters to school each day. During the drive, they have developed the habit of picking their favorite song for the week. Peter records the song and plays it to the girls throughout the week.

Children from a young age can enjoy simple instruments, even if the instrument is a pot lid or a cereal box. Gradually, children can be exposed to other instruments such as rhythm instruments, and, finally, they can progress to string and wind instruments.

Music is strongly related to the other arts—dance, visual art, and drama. This connection should be encouraged by using music in all the art areas and in other academic areas. For example, playing musical recordings such as historical and/or patriotic songs can help to increase the understanding of abstract historical facts.

Standards provide reminders of what we should be teaching, but the way the material is presented can vary to match the developmental levels and interests of the children. How the standards are introduced and taught can also vary. There are several notable methods to help the educator. The methods of Jaques-Dalcroze, Kodály, Orff, and Suzuki are covered next.

3.5   *Identify Notable Musical Teaching Methods*

The educational methods of Jaques-Dalcroze, Kodály, Orff, and Suzuki are possible ways to meet the Music Educator National Conference (MENC) Standards (Choksy, Abramson, Gillespie, Woods, & York, 2001). Teachers who have a clear concept of musical goals and the philosophical understanding of each of the methods will have an advantage when selecting the method matched to their own abilities and teaching approach (Choksy, et al., 2001).

Émile Jaques-Dalcroze

Émile Jaques-Dalcroze (1865–1950) was a Swiss composer and teacher known for developing *eurhythmics*, an approach to music education involving the entire body. Jaques-Dalcroze understood that music is a combination of rhythm and sound and thus recognized the important role rhythm plays in learning music (Jaques-Dalcroze, 1921). He noticed that the children in his classes had a weak understanding of musical rhythm—patterns formed

Table 3.3 Jaques-Dalcroze Movement Vocabulary

Movements in Place	Movements in Space
Clapping	Walking
Swinging	Running
Turning	Crawling
Conducting	Leaping
Bending	Sliding
Swaying	Galloping
Speaking	Skipping
Singing	

from joining sounds and silences. However, he felt that children possessed a sense of musical rhythm in their bodies when they moved by breathing, walking, running, and swinging their arms, and this movement could be used to teach musical rhythm. By using natural bodily movement to represent musical values or beats, Jaques-Dalcroze felt he could reinforce the study of musical rhythm.

Although rhythm is a component of dance, what Jaques-Dalcroze defined as eurhythmics is not dance. Dance is movement used to describe the feelings and concepts of the dancer or choreographer, whereas Jaques-Dalcroze used movements to express the elements of musical rhythm (Choksy, et al., 2001). The movement vocabulary used by Jaques-Dalcroze is recognized by young children and is categorized into *movements in place* and *movements in space* (see Table 3.3) (Choksy, et al., 2001).

It is clear that Jaques-Dalcroze valued the importance of movement in learning music. His theory has also been absorbed into the various methodologies of Zoltán Kodály and Carl Orff (Choksy, et al., 2001).

Zoltán Kodály

Zoltán Kodály (1882–1967) was a Hungarian composer who developed the Kodály method, in which he combined separate pedagogy techniques from various sources in Italy, England, and France, as well as the work of

Jaques-Dalcroze (Choksy, et al., 2001). The philosophy behind the Kodály method is simple:

- Singing is the most effective way to teach music to all children.
- Folk songs familiar to the children's culture should be the means for musical instruction.
- Quality music, especially folk songs, should be used to develop critical learners who value music.
- Music should be taught at a young age.

To develop this philosophy, Kodály emphasized a highly sequential and developmentally appropriate approach using the following tools:

- Solfège (system of syllables: do, re, mi, fa, sol, la, ti, do)
- Hand signs (hand placed in different positions between the waist and the top of the head to denote do, re, mi, fa, sol, la, ti, do)
- Rhythm duration syllables (ways to voice rhythm)

The Kodály method is a highly active approach to teaching and learning music, with the ultimate goal of developing the musical abilities inherent in all children (see **video** Miss Mei Music Class).

Carl Orff

Carl Orff (1893–1982), a German composer who is most well known for composing *Carmina Burana*, developed the Orff-Schulwerk methodology. This process is based on exploration through movement, thereby providing participating children with musical experiences. There is a strong emphasis on the use of singing, chanting, dancing, drama (improvisation), and percussion instruments (xylophones, glockenspiel, tambourines, gongs, and others) (Choksy, et al., 2001).

Shinichi Suzuki

Dr. Shinichi Suzuki (1898–1998) was a Japanese violinist who developed a method for children, as young as 2 to 3 years of age, to learn to play the violin.

A major feature of the method is for children to listen to classical recordings they will be playing to develop a musical ear. Although the method was developed for the violin, it has been expanded for the piano, flute, and guitar.

Interestingly, all four men—Jaques-Dalcroze, Kodály, Orff, and Suzuki—developed the music pedagogy associated with their names in the 20th century, but their methods reinforce the nine NAfME standards developed for the 21st century, which emphasize that musical pedagogy for young children should emphasize singing, playing of instruments, improvising and composing, reading and notation of music, listening, and evaluating music.

3.6 *Describe How to Teach Music*

The nine NAfME standards provide guidance to help educators (teachers and parents) develop an appropriate music curriculum. Music should be incorporated throughout the child's day, not just at a specific time period during the day and/or week. Ms. Sanchez, in the earlier example, recognized this important fact and used her knowledge of camp songs to enhance the classroom's musical environment. She also recognized the value of having an area of the classroom devoted to music, where the children could learn about music through exploration of materials and equipment. Both the classroom singing and the music center strengthened the once-a-week visit of the music specialist to the class.

Singing

Using the voice to sing is the most natural way to introduce music to the early childhood learning environment. The voice is a child's first instrument—one each child has been using since birth. Crying, cooing, and babbling are all human vocalizations that make a natural foundation for singing. A good beginning is to use simple nursery rhymes in daily activities. Many musical elements are present in the simplest rhyme, and the rhymes are the foundation for a repertoire of language and music skills (Burrell, 2011). Chants are also helpful.

As you incorporate singing into your class, remember that it is easier for children to learn words to a chant or song that is short and repetitive (Fallin, Horton, Bennett, & Taylor, 2010). Leonard Bernstein, the famous

Figure 3.2 Child's chant.

composer and conductor, argued for the concept of children's universal chant (Bernstein, 1976). This chant is simple and familiar to everyone: "nya, nya, nya, nya." (Figure 3.2).

The tune "Ring Around the Rosy" uses the chant pattern of pitches (Fallin, et al., 2010). Simple chants and echo songs are a good way to begin the learning process. The chants can be made up by the teacher and should be appropriate for the time of the day and the age of the children. A simple melodic chant, "How are you today?" as each child enters the learning environment, is a good beginning. Upon completion of the chanted question, the teacher can smile and wait for the child to reply in a melodic chant, such as "I am fine," or "I have a cold."

Kodály recognized the importance of folk songs in the musical learning process. Certainly, many folk tunes and rhymes are familiar to most educators and can be used in the music curriculum. Some examples are:

- "A-Tisket, A-Tasket"
- "Are You Sleeping" (Frère Jacques)
- "Baa, Baa, Black Sheep"
- "Bingo"
- "Farmer in the Dell"
- "Hickory Dickory Dock"
- "Hot Cross Buns"
- "Lavender's Blue"
- "London Bridge"
- "Looby Loo"
- "Mary Had a Little Lamb"
- "Mulberry Bush"
- "Pat-a-Cake"
- "Pop Goes the Weasel"
- "Ring Around the Rosy"
- "Row, Row, Row Your Boat"
- "Twinkle, Twinkle Little Star"

All these songs are on the royalty-free list and may be used without restrictions by the educator.

Songs selected for young children should be sung in the voice range of the children, with limited pitches, and should be accompanied by movements and actions (Melville-Clark, 2006). Appropriate pitches for K–2 children are from the middle C to the octave (series of notes forming a scale). Songs that are not in the child's natural vocal range will not be comfortable for the children to sing. Songs such as "Twinkle, Twinkle Little Star" and "Ring Around the Rosy" are examples of songs that fit easily into the appropriate range (Fallin, et al., 2010). Children enjoy learning songs with motions. The motions can be with the hands (fine motor) or the body (gross motor).

The following familiar songs can be used with hand/finger movements or total body movements:

- "Head, Shoulders, Knees, and Toes"
- "If You're Happy and You Know It"
- "Do Your Ears Hang Low?"
- "The Itsy Bitsy Spider"
- "The Wheels on the Bus"
- "The King of France" (see Figure 3.3)
- "Hickory, Dickory Dock" (see Figure 3.4)

Parents and teachers can easily design movements to go with most songs suitable for children by first listening to the song and noting action

The King of France [Touch finger on hands to make crown]
He had ten thousand men
He marched them up the hill [March in place]
And marched them down again

And when you're up you're up [Rise on toes]
And when you're down you're down [Lower body]
And when you're only halfway up [Rise part way]
You're neither up nor down [Up and down]

Figure 3.3 "The King of France," with motions.

Hickory, dickory dock [Wave hand back and forth]

The mouse ran up the clock [Move fingers in upward motion]

The clock struck one [Hold up one finger]

The mouse ran down [Move fingers in downward motion]

Hickory, dickory dock [Wave hand back and forth]

Figure 3.4 "Hickory, Dickory Dock," with motions.

verbs and repeating nouns. The next step is to decide what motion to use for the nouns and verbs. The children will be eager to help with this selection process, or you may tell them what motions you have chosen. Sing the song through yourself with the new movements until you feel comfortable. The song is now ready to introduce to the children. The physical movements help the children to learn and to remember the words of the song.

Teach a Song

Once a song has been selected—using the criteria of appropriate voice range for children, limited pitches, and with or without motions—it is now time to teach the song to the children. Begin by humming or singing the song or playing a recording of the song, and then teach the entire song (Melville-Clark, 2006). Songs can also be broken down into phrases and taught in sections, as Stacey Steele explains in this **video**.

As the song is sung over and over, the children will begin to remember the combination of pitches, rhythm, and melody. Melody is the combination of one pitch after another. The contour of the melody will be noted by the rise and fall of the pitches and later by the intervals between the pitches. A new tune is stored in the child's memory in a rising and falling pattern ($+ + - + - +$) (Winner, 1982).

Daniel, 3 years old, loves music. He developed his love of music listening to music with his mom. He can sing the music of the Beatles, Bob Dylan, Van Morrison, Adele, and others. Daniel accompanies his singing while strumming a guitar or banging drums.

Children remember melodic contour. To help them memorize a new melody, the contour can be drawn on a piece of paper for the children to visualize, or a sandpaper line can be made for tactile reinforcement. Songs can also be taught one or two lines at a time until the entire piece is learned. Listening to the melody repeatedly will help children learn the song. For example, the song "Gonna M^2" in "Making Connections" (Chapter 1) can be taught line by line or as a whole because of its strong repetitive qualities.

Listening

Listening to music is valuable not only to learn a new song, but also to develop an understanding and enjoyment of music. *Hearing* is the ability to receive sensory information, whereas *listening* requires participation by the listener (Jensen, 2001). Listening requires concentration on the part of the individual. Teachers can develop listening skills in children by using the following activities (Popuce, 2012):

- Listening to a variety of sounds
- Listening to the contour
- Developing a musical vocabulary
- Developing concentration skills
- Relating a piece of music to personal experience

Children can listen to a variety of sounds and identify the sounds (bells, animals, thunder, cans and bottles, rattles). Having the children listen to a musical selection while noting the contour of the intervals by raising or lowering their hands may further develop listening skills. Providing children with a musical vocabulary will assist children in developing their listening skills. The use and understanding of such words as *rhythm*, *pitch*, *timbre*, and *melody* are beneficial. All people need assistance in learning to concentrate. Playing a musical selection that is enjoyable to children, while keeping the concentration time period short, can help children attend to the musical selection and avoid distractions. Providing the children with something to listen for, such as the bass drum, or an activity, such as drawing while listening, may increase concentration. Finally, have the children discuss the musical selection and have them relate the selection to their own experiences. Ask questions such as "Have you ever heard this song before?" and "What does the music make you want to do?"

Encouraging an open discussion about music and the instruments used in the selection will enhance listening skills, and it will assist children to become familiar with the sounds of musical instruments. Playing an instrument will also be a wonderful experience for children.

Playing Instruments

Suzuki realized how important it is for all children to learn to play an instrument. He concentrated first on a string instrument, the violin. Violins vary in sizes to match the size of the child—one-quarter or one-half the size of a full-size violin; thus, the instruments will be sized appropriately for a young child's fingers and arm length. Although this may be advantageous, many families or schools cannot afford to provide a violin for each child, and trained Suzuki teachers are not always nearby or available to provide instruction.

Percussion instruments are an economical way to introduce musical instruments to the classroom. Rhythm sticks and a drum for the teacher are an excellent way to introduce musical instruments. Parents and teachers can expand the number and variety of instruments as time, money, and interest increase. Teachers can form a rhythm band by giving each child an instrument and playing a tune. It is good to emphasize the beat, sounds, and rests while the band members are playing.

Henry is 4 years old and a member of a music class. His instrument for the day's lesson is the triangle. As the music and the teacher's instructions emphasize the rhythm, Henry strikes the triangle on the beat. His classmates are doing the same on various other percussion instruments. The sound is glorious.

An excellent and appropriate musical tool is a boom whacker or boomophone. These are hollow plastic tubes in bright colors graduated in length and tuned to a scale. They are a marvelous tool for improvisation and composition. Children can strike each tube to obtain an individual pitch.

Six-year-old Naaz received a set of boom whackers from her grandmother for her birthday. Her mother showed her how each tube, when struck, produced a sound or pitch. The entire set provided a musical scale. The next step was to see how the pitches could be combined to make a tune by striking various tubes in succession. After some instruction, Naaz was left alone by her mother to explore the boom whackers while her mother cooked dinner. When Naaz's mother returned to check on Naaz's activities, she was treated to a creative sight. Naaz had taken the cylinders and stood them perpendicular to the floor and next to each other in a graduated order, longest to smallest, to make a wall. In front of the wall was her toy red piano. Naaz had made an organ that showed she grasped the concept of pitches and demonstrated her awareness of the musical instrument, the organ. Naaz's exposure to a simple instrument was a beneficial learning experience that developed both her auditory skills and her fine motor skills.

There are a variety of advantages to learning to play an instrument (see **video**):

- Strengthen auditory skills
- Increase attention skills
- Increase memory skills
- Strengthen fine motor skills
- Develop awareness musical concepts

The benefits of playing an instrument are vast and serve to develop the child's cognitive and motor skills (see **video** Children, Free Play and 60 Homemade Musical Instruments). Developing an understanding of the structure involved in musical concepts is the final step in how to teach music.

Exposing children to the structure of music and teaching the musical concepts involved may be difficult for many parents and teachers. The best scenario is that the adult working with children has some background in music, or that there is a music professional on the teaching staff to advise the teachers. Individuals working with children when music is part of the curriculum should certainly be familiar with these structural elements and music notation.

We have already learned about the elements of sound: pitch, timbre, and dynamics. The foundation for the next step has been built.

Structural Musical Elements

The structural elements of music are similar to the elements of sound that we have already discussed (pitch, timbre, dynamics, and duration). But now we will be talking about the musical elements of melody and harmony. When a song is written down or notated, the composer of the song uses the notes of a scale to determine what the song will sound like. Worldwide, there are many scale systems, some that sound very different from those we are used to hearing and using. The music of our American culture that sounds familiar to our ear is based primarily on the music of Western Europe. The scale we use most often for musical composition is called *diatonic,* and it has eight pitches. Eastern cultures often use the *pentatonic* scale, which has five pitches.

Notes (♩) are placed on a staff, which consists of five lines and four spaces, to show the pitches used in a musical piece. The higher up the scale, the higher the pitch. Notes are given letter names (E-F-G-A-B-C-D-E-F). The letters E-G-B-D-F are located on the lines of the staff, from bottom to top, and the letters F-A-C-E are located on the spaces of the staff, also from bottom to top (see Figure 3.5). Vertical lines on the staff mark measures; they provide organization to the music.

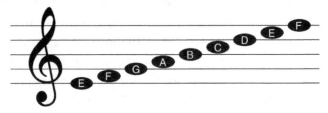

Figure 3.5 Staff with space and line notes.

Table 3.4 Clef Information

Clef	Clef Symbol	Note	Description
Treble		G	The second line of the staff, which passes through the curl of the G clef symbol is called G.
Bass		F	The fourth line of the staff, which passes through the two dots of the F clef, is called F.

The musical staff is read from left to right and supplies the performer with all the information about how the selection should be played or sung. The first thing you see on the left side of the staff is the *clef* symbol, which establishes what the pitches of the musical score are called. Once that clef is in place, all the other notes can be arranged on the staff. The most common clefs are the treble (G) and bass (F) clefs (see Table 3.4).

The treble clef is used for higher-pitched notes and the bass clef is used for the lower-pitched notes. The two clefs divide the piano keyboard in half, with the "middle C" as the middle of the keyboard (see Figure 3.6).

The numbers next to the clef indicate the time signature, such as ¾. It shows how many beats there are in a measure. The top number tells how many beats there are in a measure and the bottom number tells the kind of note that gets one beat; thus, in a ¾ measure, there are three beats to a measure, and a quarter note gets one beat (see Figure 3.7).

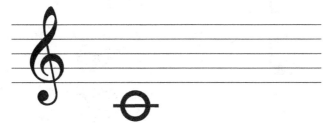

Figure 3.6 Middle C.

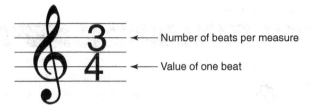

Figure 3.7 Time signature.

This raises the question: What is a quarter note? Notes are grouped according to whole, half, quarter, and eighth (see Table 3.5). The type of note determines the duration of the beat. To reinforce the beat, have the children "put the beat in your feet" and walk while listening to music or singing (Stacey Steele, personal interview, October 7, 2012).

Children Singing

When pitches or notes are strung one after another with an even or uneven rhythm, the result is a *melody*. This is what we all hum when we hear a familiar tune. When two or more pitches are played or sung simultaneously, the result is *harmony*. A barbershop quartet is a good example of harmony. The four singers are using four melodies in different pitches at the same time. The easiest way to create harmony with young children is

Table 3.5 Note Value in 4/4 Time Signature

Note	Figure	Duration in 4/4 Time Signature
Whole	𝅝	Four beats
Half	𝅗𝅥	Two beats
Quarter	𝅘𝅥	One beat
Eighth	𝅘𝅥𝅮	One-half beat

to have them sing in a round, such as "Row, Row, Row Your Boat." Teach the song first. Sing it multiple times until the children can sing it independently. Then divide the children into two groups. The first group begins and the second group starts after the first group gets halfway through the song.

> ## M² FUN
>
> Give each child an empty can and a stick. Demonstrate that by tapping the can, sounds can be made. The children will make a short sound on the outside of the can and long sounds on the inside of the can. Children can then design a composition using notation of their design, such as @_____ @@_____ @@@_____.

Whereas there are many varieties of music—classical, opera, folk, jazz, rock, rap, blues, and music from other cultures—the elements are the same. Once children have a basic knowledge of pitch, rhythm, timbre, melody, and harmony, they are on the way to understanding and enjoying music. The elements can be adapted to meet the developmental level of the children. Young children should be exposed to rhythm, pitch, and melody. Timbre and harmony are more sophisticated and can be added later. It is most important that children develop the appropriate knowledge and skills to appreciate music and to integrate the joy of music into their lives. Children love to sing; wise teachers will make sure they have an opportunity to use music often in the daily curriculum.

Integrate Music Into the Curriculum

Music can—and should—be thoroughly integrated into any curriculum area. It should not be a once-a-week activity; instead, it should be available to enhance all subject areas. Music may be the reason for mathematical and science excellence in Japan, Hungary, and the Netherlands, where music instruction is required (Jensen, 2001). Furthermore, musical curriculum activities can enhance cognitive and emotional development, and

Table 3.6 Integrating Music Into the Curriculum

Subject Area	Learning Activity
Movement	Play Handel's *Water Music*. Have the children move like animals (frog, fish) to the music.
Literacy	Read a story with a variety of characters. Have the children select a percussion instrument (sticks, drum, shakers) to represent the character. Read the story again and have the children use their instrument when the character's name is mentioned.
Mathematics	Give each child a felt shape (circle, square, triangle). Sing the "Hokey Pokey" song but change the words *hand*, *arm*, and *foot* to *circle*, *square*, and *triangle*.
Science	Have children move at different beats (slow, fast) to match the music. Measure neck pulses after the fast music and after the slow music. Compare the pulses.
Creativity	Using boom whackers, have the children compose a tune. The teacher can place stickers on a staff to indicate the tune.

may help to remediate or prevent potential learning problems (Healy, 2010). Finally, research demonstrates the benefits of music in strengthening verbal learning (Jensen, 2001). Start to think how music can be integrated into the curriculum (see Table 3.6).

3.7 Identify Musical Suggestions

Teachers, caregivers, and parents who have a musical background are fortunate—but not all of us have had musical training. This, however, is not a reason to restrict musical experiences for children. It is important for the total development of children to make an effort to ensure that music is part of the curriculum offerings to every child. Each rhyme repeated, song sung, and instrument played builds confidence in the child. Fortunately, many recordings are available to help build confidence while ensuring a positive learning experience for the children. The Internet site "Best Children's Music" by Fred Koch (1999) (see Table 3.7)

Table 3.7 Examples of Music That Children Love

Category	Album	Musician
Infant and Toddler		
	I Will Hold Your Tiny Hand	Steve Rashid
	Lullabies with Mandolins	Simon Mayer & Hilary James
	On a Starry Night	Various artists
	Say Hello to the Morning	Kathy Reid-Naiman
	40 Winks	Jessica Harper
	Smart Sleep with Classics	Heidi Brende
	Rock the Baby	Mr. Al
	The Mozart Effect: Music for Babies Volume 1 & 2	Various artists
Early Childhood		
	Did You Feed My Cow?	Fred Koch Presents the Songs of Ella Jenkins
	CELLAbration! A Tribute to Ella Jenkins	Various artists
	Meltdown!	Justin Roberts
	Jim Gill Sings Moving Rhymes for Modern Times	Jim Gill
	Nora's Room	Jessica Harper
	Reading Rainbow's Greatest Hits	Various artists
	Kids in Motion	Greg & Steve
	Great Big World	Joe McDermott
	Jo Jo the Scarecrow	Joel Frankel
	Fun & Games	Greg & Steve
	I've Got Imagination	Rachel Summer
	Ralph's World	Ralph Covert

at http://bestchildrensmusic.com/, for example, offers some excellent suggestions.

The following are some other excellent music sources:

- Amazon: Source for Chinese, classical, German folk, jazz, Korean, rock, hip-hop, opera music, or any other genre of interest www. amazon.com/)
- Children's Public Radio (www.kidspublicradio.org/)
- Raffi (raffi.com/)
- YouTube (www.youtube.com/)
- Pete Seeger (www.peteseegermusic.com/)
- Hap Palmer (www.happalmer.com/)
- Ella Jenkins (www.ellajenkins.com/)
- iTunes Store Top 10 Children's Albums

Now, go find some music and enjoy. The children will enjoy, too!

Summary

Music is very important in the lives of all people, especially children. The elements of sound—pitch, timbre, dynamics, and duration—provide the basis for understanding music. The national music standards developed by the National Association for Music Education can be used to develop an appropriate music curriculum. To teach children music, begin with rhymes, chants, and simple songs. It is also important to assist children in developing listening skills and playing simple percussion instruments.

Summary Related to Outcomes

Learning Outcomes	Guiding Principles
3.1 Describe the importance of music	Movement and Music Integrated
Music is an important form of communication used throughout the world. It also strengthens mathematics and creativity while reducing stress.	

Learning Outcomes	Guiding Principles
3.2 Define music	Movement and Music Integrated
The characteristics of music are pitch, timbre, dynamics, and duration.	
3.3 Discuss musical experiences for young children	Environment and Curriculum Reciprocated
The National Association for Music Education (NAfME, 1991) has adopted beliefs to guide music curriculum for young children. Culture considerations should be used when planning musical environments and learning experiences.	
3.4 Recognize music standards	Standards and Assessment Provide Guidance
The National Association for Music Education has designed music standards for K–2.	
3.5 Identify notable musical teaching methods	Movement and Music Integrated
The educational methods of Jaques-Dalcroze, Kodály, Orff, and Suzuki are possible ways to meet the Music Educator National Conference (MENC) standards.	
3.6 Describe how to teach music	Movement and Music Integrated
Teaching of music should begin with chants and rhythms, followed by singing. Other important techniques are listening, playing instruments, understanding of musical notation, and integrating music into daily curriculum choices.	
3.7 Identify musical suggestions	Movement and Music Integrated
It is beneficial to be aware of various commercial recordings available to assist the integration of music into daily curriculum choices.	

Demonstrate Your Knowledge, Skills, and Dispositions

Students will demonstrate knowledge, comprehension, analysis, and evaluation of Learning Outcomes related to Guiding Principles.

Learning Outcomes	Guiding Principles
3.1 Describe the importance of music	Movement and Music Integrated

- A child in your classroom is showing aggression toward another child. How would you use music to help the child cope with her feelings?

Learning Outcomes	Guiding Principles
3.2 Define music	Movement and Music Integrated
• Pick a sound characteristic (pitch, timbre, dynamics, duration). How would you teach this characteristic to a group of 5-year-olds?	
3.3 Discuss musical experiences for young children	Environment and Curriculum Reciprocated
• Develop a music pocket or corner in your classroom. Pick three things you would put in the pocket or corner, and tell why you picked the item and how you would use it.	
3.4 Recognize music standards	Assessment and Standards Provide Guidance
• Six-year olds Salina and Raja want to perform a song for the class. Pick a song to sing and an instrument(s) for the children to use. What standards would you be meeting?	
3.6 Identify notable musical teaching methods	Movement and Music Integrated
• Pick a song. Using hand signs, teach the song using solfège. Critique your lesson.	
3.7 Identify musical suggestions	Movement and Music Integrated
• Go to the suggested Internet sites in the Musical Suggestions section. Listen to four songs at different sites. Describe movements you would do with each song.	

Planning for Engaging

The following activities provide three possibilities or ways to develop M^2 Movement Standards.

M^2 Music Standard: The child will be exposed to a variety of music rhythms.		
Possibility One	**Possibility Two**	**Possibility Three**
Each child will be given a coffee can and a rhythm stick. The children will be encouraged to make sounds with the instruments. The teacher will play a percussion recording by John Cage or Daniel Adam as an accompaniment.	Play one or two Ella Jenkins songs: • "I Can Sing High Notes, I Can Sing Low Notes" • "Kuluba, Beat the Drums" Discuss pitch and rhythm. Have children clap loud sounds and soft sounds to a beat.	Echo Game: Give each child a set of rhythm sticks. The teacher plays a rhythm on the sticks. The children will repeat the pattern. Have the children take turns being the echo leader.

Assessment	Assessment	Assessment
Observe how consistent the children are in making rhythm patterns.	Listen to how the children clap. Determine whether they have grasped high/low.	Observe whether the children can repeat a pattern.

Now You Try It

Complete the following standard-based learning activity designed to meet various interests and developmental levels. Design two learning possibilities or learning activities to develop M^2 Movement Standards.

M^2 Music Standard: The child will determine the mood created through music.		
Possibility One	**Possibility Two**	**Possibility Three**
Have the children draw three circles on paper. Have them make faces: (1) Happy (2) Sad (3) Neutral Play four different types of music. Have children point to the face/circle that best describes how they feel about the musical selection.		
Assessment	**Assessment**	**Assessment**
Degree of participation from each child. Note whether they are varying their selection or just picking the same face/circle.		

References

Arabin, B. (1992). Music during pregnancy. *Obstetrics & Gynecology*, 20(5), 425–430.

Bernstein, L. (1976). *The unanswered question: six talks at Harvard*. Cambridge, MA: Harvard University Press.

Blythe, S.G. (2004). *The well-balanced child: movement and early learning*. Gloucester, UK: Hawthorn Press.

Burrell, M. (2011). The benefit of music sessions for very young children with their parent or carers through the eyes of a music therapist. In J. Edwards (Ed.), *Music therapy and parent-infant bonding* (pp. 93–114). New York, NY: Oxford University Press.

Choksy, L., Abramson, R.M., Gillespie, A.E., Woods, D., & York, F. (2001). *Teaching music in the twenty-first century*. Upper Saddle River, NJ: Prentice Hall.

Edwards, J. (Ed.) (2011). *Music therapy and parent-infant bonding*. New York, NY: Oxford University Press.

Fallin, J., Horton, S., Bennett, S., & Taylor, D. (2010). Infusing music in early childhood learning. *Perspectives*, 5(4), 14–17.

Flohr, J. W. (2010). Best practices for young children's music education: Guidance from brain research. *General Music Today*, 23, 2.

Gardner, H. (2011). *Frames of mind*. New York, NY: Basic Books.

Healy, J. (2010). Different learners: Why music and movement are brain food for every child. *Journal of the Early Childhood Music & Movement Association*, 5, 4.

Jaques-Dalcroze, E. (1921). *Rhythm, music, and education*. New York, NY: G.R. Putnam's Sons.

Jensen, E. (2001). *Arts with the brain in mind*. Alexandria, VA: ASCD.

Koch, F. (1999). Best children's music. Retrieved from http://bestchildrensmusic.com/.

Levinowitz, L.M. (2012). Importance of music. Retrieved from http://www.musictogether.com/importanceofmusic.

Melville-Clark, P. (2006). Music, moving, learning in early childhood: a manual of songs, lesson plans and basic theory for teachers, students, and parents. *Music and Movement Education in Australia*. Darling Heights, Queensland, Australia: Electronic and Database Publishing Inc..

National Association for Music Education (NAfME). (1991). Early childhood (position statement). Retrieved from http://musiced.nafme.org/about/position-statements/early-childhood-education/.

National Association for Music Education. (2012). National Standards for Music Education. Retrieved from http://musiced.nafme.org/resources/national-standards-for-music-education/.

National Standards of Music Education (2006). http://www.youtube.com/watch?v=kliX7dnroEY.

Overbaugh, R.C. & Schutz, L. (2012). Bloom's taxonomy. Retrieved from http://ww2.odu.edu/educ/roverbau/Bloom/blooms_taxonomy.htm.

Polverini-Rey, R.A. (1992). Intrauterine musical leaning: the soothing effect on newborns of a lullaby learned prenatally. *Dissertation Abstracts*, 9233740.

Popuce, M. (2012). How to listen to music: a vintage guide to the 7 essential skills. Retrieved from http://www.brainpickings.org/index.php/2012/04/12/elliott-schwartz-music-ways-of-listening/.

Steele, S., (2013). *Gonna move*. Upper Saddle River, NJ: Pearson Publishing.

Trehub, S. (2003). The developmental origins of musicality. *Nature Neuroscience*, 6, 669–673.

Whitwell, G. (2012). Perspectives. *Journal of the Early Childhood Music & Movement Association* 5(2), 15–18.

Winner, E. (1982). *Invented worlds: The psychology of the arts*. Cambridge, MA: Harvard University Press.

chapter 4

Matching the Individual, Task, and Environment to Enhance Learning

LEARNING OUTCOMES AND GUIDING PRINCIPLES

Students reading this text will be able to demonstrate Learning Outcomes linked to Guiding Principles based on the *National Association for the Education of Young Children's Developmentally Appropriate Practice in Early Childhood Programs Serving Children from Birth through Age 8.*

Learning Outcomes	Guiding Principles
4.1 Match the task and the environment to the individual child	Individual Needs Met
4.2 Explain Newell's model of constraints	Individual Needs Met
4.3 Differentiate among individual, task, and environmental factors that increase and decrease task difficulty	Individual Needs Met
4.4 Match the individual, task, and environmental constraints to select culturally relevant activities for a developmentally appropriate movement lesson	Environment and Curriculum Reciprocated

Making Connections
Developmentally Appropriate Physical Activity

Watching the children in his class practice kicking, a fundamental motor pattern and sports skill, Mr. Lopick was pleased that all the children were actively involved. Each child had a ball to kick into his or her own trash can. Every time they were successful in reaching the target, they took a step back to increase the difficulty of the task. Everyone was laughing, having fun, and being successful at his or her own level of skill. However, what Mr. Lopick saw in his class was different from what he observed in Ms. Smith's class.

Ms. Smith believed, contrary to Mr. Lopick's approach, that the children would learn fundamental motor patterns and sport skills by playing a game of kickball. At the start of the game, Ms. Smith told the children where to stand and what positions they were going to play. Half the children were spread out in the outfield and the other half were clumped around home plate. Ms. Smith had one of the strongest athletes "pitching" the ball. Even though the 5-year-old was good at rolling, getting the ball across the plate was difficult for her. When the pitcher was able to get the ball across the plate, it was rare that the kicker could make contact with the ball. Sometimes the kicker would kick before the ball arrived; sometimes he would fall on top of the ball. On the rare instances that the pitcher got the ball across the plate and the kicker did make contact with the ball, the kicker did not appear to know what to do. Ms. Smith would yell at him to run to first base, for instance, but he would take off to third base. The outfielders, if they were paying attention, would watch the ball fly by them and then start chasing the ball. As they got close, they would bend down to get the ball, but instead of picking the ball up, their foot would hit the ball and cause it to shoot away. Eventually they would retrieve the ball and run to home plate. Tired of standing in the outfield and bored watching one child kick at a time, one child, Eliza, decided to practice her skipping.

Most of the children in Ms. Smith's class did not have the previous experience or prerequisite skills to play kickball. Ms. Smith did not understand that she needed to do the following:

- Understand the growth (structural) and maturational (functional) levels of the children to see whether they had the strength, coordination, and motivation to perform the skills
- Determine the task requirements (constraints)
- Evaluate the environmental conditions (constraints) in which the children would play

The children needed to learn how to roll, throw, catch, and kick prior to attempting to put the skills together to play an organized sport.

4.1 Match the Task and the Environment to the Individual Child

How many organized team sport games, such as T-ball, softball, and soccer, have you watched during which the children are playing with their caps, making a horn with grass between their thumbs, doing cartwheels, or entertaining themselves watching butterflies? Mr. Lopick realized the importance of young children acquiring motor skills and knew that until children learn the movement skills required to play a game, they cannot be successful at the game. Success was built into Mr. Lopick's lesson. The children in his class were actively engaged in motor skill development, not standing around and watching others practice the skills.

▲ Child with a tennis racquet that is too large. The child has to support her arm with her body.

The early childhood years are an opportune time to acquire both gross and fine motor skills. *Gross motor skills* are movements that require large muscle movement, and include skills such as walking, running, throwing, and kicking. *Fine motor skills* require the use of small muscle groups and require precision; examples are coloring, grasping, and releasing. It is easier for children to develop gross and fine motor skills when they are young, rather than when they are older, because of their developing brain pathways. For optimum learning to occur, a progression of activities should be designed for each child. To plan a developmentally appropriate lesson, teachers need to analyze the individual characteristics of the child, the prerequisite skills he or she has, and the complexity of the task (*task constraints*) to be learned. Matching the child's level of performance to a developmental progression of the skill and structuring the environment to match the child's level of performance (*environmental constraints*) assist the teacher in guaranteeing success during the learning process.

The purpose of this chapter is to develop the knowledge to evaluate the individual characteristics of the child, understand the components of the task, and evaluate the environment in which the child performs the task. This information is used to create a developmental sequence appropriate to the age and developmental level of the child, while attending to the hierarchical steps to perform the task. A task analysis is used to develop the lesson that assists the child in being successful. For example, a skip is a combination of a step and a hop on one foot. If Arli cannot hop or jump on one foot, he is not ready to skip. The child's developmental level is discussed first, followed by evaluation of the task and the environment.

4.2 Explain Newell's Model of Constraints

To help understand the development of motor skills or tasks, we have chosen Newell's Model of Constraints (1986) to understand the interactions of the child, the task, and the environment. The basis of Newell's model is an understanding of *constraints*, which are characteristics of the child that either assist or restrict the child's movement. A toddler learning to walk is constrained, or limited in his movement, by the size of his head and the length of his legs. The only possible walking movement a toddler can perform because of these constraints is short and flat-footed steps. Gradually, these constraints are changed as a result of physical growth or increased exploration of the environment and experience. Prior to changes in the child due to growth, an adult can modify the constraint by adjusting the movement via the assistance of a hand or providing a child-size walker.

Maddie had a riding giraffe on wheels, with a high back. She could sit on the giraffe, or she could hold onto the back of the giraffe for support while walking. Later, when Maddie was 5 years old and learning to ice skate, she was given a walker on wheels to hold onto while learning to move from short steps to long skating glides. Constraints can be modified by changing the effect the constraints have on the child and the movement.

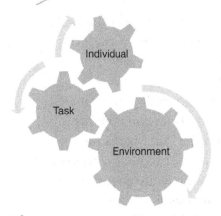

Figure 4.1 Newell's model of constraints.

The child will always have constraints, but the effect the constraint has on the child can be modified by growth and development, experience, or adaptation of the task or the environment by an adult. Obviously, there is little an adult can do to modify a child's growth and development, but an adult can positively adapt the task and modify the environment so the child can accomplish the skill.

Constraints can be modified to assist movement. A toddler can walk first while holding onto a parent's hand. With practice and development, the toddler becomes able to walk without support. In another example of a movement constraint, if a child is asked to jump as high as she can, at first she typically lifts one foot off the ground while keeping the other placed on the ground. However, if she sees her mom's cooking pots or a bunch of balloons hanging from a ceiling, she is motivated to move both feet off the ground to reach the pots to hear the clanging, or to see the balloons swaying in space.

We will now examine the three types of constraints we have introduced—*individual*, *task*, and *environment*—as described by Newell and shown in Figure 4.1.

Individual Constraints

The individual has both structural and functional constraints that affect performance. *Structural constraints* change slowly over time and include physical growth and maturation. A child's body proportions change slowly with age. At birth, the head forms 25 percent of the body, but when the child reaches adulthood, the head is only one-eighth of the body's height. Similarly, between the first year and adolescence, the child's legs grow proportionately more than the trunk. Around age 11 years, children typically run faster than they do when they are younger. One factor in this change is increased leg length.

In addition to structural constraints, the individual also experiences *functional constraints*. These are related to behavioral change and tend to change more quickly. For example, Alexander loves to swim in the heated swimming pool at home but refuses to go into the pool at his child development center because the water is cold. John will spend hours with his aunt, who pitches balls for him to hit, but will spend only two minutes reading. Theresa will play outdoors when the weather is warm, but will not go outside when it is cold. In the remainder of this section, we review key concepts of structural change, including biological maturation, and functional change, including cognitive and affective maturation.

Structural constraints include physical changes. Biological makeup begins with heredity and plays a continuing role in the development of the child. The interaction of the hereditary blueprint and the environment in which the child lives sets the stage for development of the child. Neural development, physical growth, and physiological factors are structural constraints that are important in assisting the child's development of successful movement skills.

Neural changes are important to consider when developing movements in children. A link has been established among movement, experience, and neurological development. Experiences appear to strengthen the neural connections within the brain such that if connections are not made or are weak, they are pruned. If the connections are made and used, these pathways are strengthened and become parts of the brain (Greenough & Black, 1992). If the pathways are not used, they fade. Thus, what we use, we keep, and what we do not use, we lose!

Researchers are discovering the importance of early stimulation. Children lacking in stimulating environments have brains that are 20 to 30 percent smaller than normal. The years of development prior to age 5 years are extremely important; a child has the ability to overcome some devastating problems during this time. Children below the age of 3 years who have lost a complete hemisphere of the brain have matured into highly functioning adults. During this time of development, the brain is very plastic and new connections are made. Experience is critical in the wiring of the child's brain (Greenough & Black, 1992). Children must have a variety of hands-on experiences to develop strong pathways; the time to develop these pathways begins in early childhood and continues throughout early school years (until around 10 years of age). If the developing child undergoes physical or mental stress, problems in the wiring process may arise. As the child matures, the ability to rebound from serious problems declines.

The research of Ramey and Ramey (1994) provides an example of experience affecting development of the child. They conducted a series of studies on children between the ages of 4 months and 8 years who lived in disadvantaged environments and found that intensive early education using blocks, beads, and games had positive long-term effects on IQ and academic achievement. An important finding was that the earlier the children enrolled in the programs, the longer the results lasted. Children enrolled after the age of 5 years demonstrated few benefits.

With the rapid expansion of neural connections through use and pruning due to disuse, there appear to be windows of opportunity for brain development—times in development when it is easiest for an individual to develop a skill, even though the skill can still be developed later. The main circuits required for responses such as breathing, regulation of heartbeat, and reflexes are already set and windows of opportunity do not exist; however, the environment shapes and refines the connections for conscious control. The variety of sensory experiences progressively refines these connections, making environmental stimulation extremely important to development.

Gabbard (2008) summarized research on brain development, suggesting windows of opportunity for various functions. These windows occur while the child is growing physically, frequently during the rapid growth spurts for specific systems. Gross motor development has a sensitive period from prenatally to about age 5 years, whereas fine motor development takes place shortly after birth until approximately 9 years of age. Visual development demonstrates a window of opportunity from birth to about 4 years, whereas that for second language learning extends from 1 year to about 10 years of age. The math/logic window of opportunity ranges from 1 year to about 4 years.

The window of opportunity for music is from about 3 to 10 years of age. From brain and early childhood research, Fox concludes that active engagement in music changes the brain structure. A music curriculum

"should involve active and expressive modes of music making . . . singing, moving, and playing sound-making objects, including instruments. Listening activities should be designed to actively engage the children, through attending to sounds and the changes in sounds as they occur" (Fox, 2000, p. 25).

Although windows of opportunity are ideal or optimal times for development and learning, teachers should always expect that children can learn outside these periods of opportunity as well.

Windows of opportunity change from childhood to adolescents (see **video** Critical Periods of Brain Development). The adolescent window of opportunity focuses more on experimenting, thinking for oneself, and taking risks.

Physical growth includes proportional changes in body structure and rate of growth, which are important to understanding structural constraints of the child. Proportional changes include the changes in relationship of the size of the body segments. The child's rate of growth determines how quickly he or she reaches physical maturity.

Physical growth includes changes in height and weight. The child grows very rapidly during the first year of life. During this time, in many cases, children increase their birth height by nearly 50 percent (from 20 inches for boys and 19.75 inches for girls to 30 and 29.25 inches, respectively) and triple their weight, to 22.5 pounds for boys and 21 pounds for girls. The second year of life shows continued growth but at a slower rate, with children growing an average of 4.75 inches. Until the adolescent growth spurt, children's height and weight increase at a slow and steady pace, although some children will experience a small growth spurt in middle childhood.

Throughout growth, both absolute and relative sizes of the body parts change. As mentioned earlier, a newborn's head accounts for 25 percent of the body size in relation to body length, whereas the legs account for about three-eighths of the stature. On the other hand, the head is one-eighth and the legs half of the total height for an adult. Think how difficult it would be to maintain a balanced position if your head was twice the size it is now!

Not only are there proportional differences in relation to total height, but there are also width differences. The width of a newborn's head is similar to that of the shoulders and hips, whereas the width of an adult's head is only one-third the width of the shoulders. During infancy and early childhood, the legs grow faster than the trunk—thus the leggy look of early adolescent children. The trunk grows at a faster rate than the legs throughout adolescence, thus reducing the proportional length of the legs. Another example is changes in arm length with increasing age. Think of an infant with a hand raised—the hand barely reaches the top of the head. For the

▲ How far does the child's hands go above his head? How far do yours? Can he swim the same way as you do? What constrains the child's action?

adolescent and adult, though, the elbow is above the head. A younger child is not physically ready to swim using a mature pattern due to the length of his or her arms; this child is unable to generate the required force.

The *rate* of growth differs for all children. Children can be categorized as early, average, or late maturing. Early-maturing children—those who reach adult height typically two years earlier than their peers—tend to be bigger and stronger than their late-maturing counterparts throughout childhood. The size advantage can predispose a child to early success in movement merely due to a size advantage. Late-maturing children, on the other hand—those who reach adult height typically two years after their peers—might not experience success in movement outcomes (to see the effects of size differences in children, watch the **video** Teaching Ball Skills and Fitness).

Who appears to be a late-maturing child, and who seems to be an early-maturing child? What is the reason their skills are different from those of the others? A late-maturing child might be skilled (demonstrating a mature pattern), but owing to size mismatching, may not perform well when he or she is playing with early-maturing children. Shanti, for example, won a swimming meet, not because she had a mature swimming pattern but because she was bigger and stronger than the other children in her age group. Thus, emphasizing skill development, not outcome, is critically important for young children.

Physiological factors are related to movement performance constraints. Two factors—aerobic endurance and anaerobic endurance—are discussed here. The ability of the child to sustain moderate to intense physical activity over time is *aerobic endurance,* whereas *anaerobic endurance* is the ability to produce short bursts of muscular force. Both aerobic and anaerobic endurance increase with physical growth.

The aerobic endurance of children, when viewed relative to their body size, is comparable to that of an adult; however, because the adult is bigger, the child cannot last as long as an adult at a given activity. This means that although children should not be restricted from participating in aerobic activities that require moderate to intense physical activity, distance and time must be scaled to their individual body size and endurance capabilities. Because of this fact and an understanding of body proportion differences, youth sport organizations have modified the size of the fields, game time, and, in many cases, equipment.

Relative to body size, the anaerobic performance of children is not similar to that of adults. Muscular strength increases with age because of growing muscle mass and improvements in skill performance. Strength and power increase with the aging process and directly influence the ability of the child to perform many movements successfully. For example, without the level of strength needed to lift the body weight, a 4-year-old child's attempts to jump up are not successful. Pairing children to compete against each other can predispose the smaller child to failure. The larger child will win merely because he or she is stronger than the smaller child, not because of superior skill.

In summary, a child's state of biological maturation may require an alteration of activities. When playing catch with a child, the educator needs to use a soft, light, and large ball while standing fairly close. When pitching a ball for a child to hit, the child moves closer to the pitcher to be able to track the ball, whereas the pitcher moves away in order to avoid being hit! The change in biological maturation is directly related to task constraints and is discussed in a later section.

Functional constraints include cognitive, affective, and motivational constraints and are reviewed in this section. Recall that functional constraints can change more quickly than biological constraints. Cognitive maturation relates to thinking and learning, whereas affective maturation focuses on the child's social and emotional development. Motivation is related to persistence at the task.

Cognitive maturation is explained using Piaget's stages of cognitive development to provide a foundation. Children who are less than 2 years of age are in Piaget's *sensorimotor* level of cognitive development. During this phase, movement is critical to thinking, and the child basically learns through movement by interacting with the environment. The second stage of development, *preoperational thought*, is from 2 to approximately 8 years of age. During this stage, the child begins to use symbols to represent objects in the environment and verbal communication emerges. The *concrete operational* stage generally spans ages 7 through 11 years. Problem-solving skills are enhanced and children start to use memory strategies (cuing, selective attention, and rehearsal) to improve learning and retention. The final stage of cognitive development is *formal operations*, which begins at approximately 11 or 12 years of age. Abstract thought is the major emphasis during this stage.

Knowledge development and play go hand in hand. Piaget believed that play assisted the child in the construction of knowledge. He outlined three major types of knowledge: physical knowledge, logical–mathematical knowledge, and social knowledge.

As Kristin plays with a set of keys, she is developing *physical knowledge—* knowledge about the physical properties of the objects she manipulates. *Logical–mathematical knowledge* provides the child with a comprehension of relationships among objects, people, and ideas. In her classroom of 5-year-olds, for instance, Ms. Gail noticed that the children had difficulty keeping their hands off other people and kept running into objects. She decided to help the children understand how to move around the room while being alert to other children and objects. Several lessons on self-space (the space around the individual) increased children's awareness of how they can change their body shape from big to small, wide to narrow, and high to low.

Lessons on general space (where they are in relationship to other children and objects) assist the children in moving safely around the room. Practice changing the size of self and general space also assists the child in developing the third type of knowledge, *social knowledge*. Moving in general space, the children move without bumping into other children and thereby avoid behavioral problems.

Children are constantly adding information to their knowledge base and/or changing the format of existing knowledge through assimilation and accommodation. The child constructs knowledge through play and the interactive process of assimilation and accommodation. During *assimilation*, the child uses knowledge and skills without adaptation. *Accommodation* involves changing current ways or patterns of thinking to take new information into account.

> In T-ball, Joel practices hitting a ball off the tee. The ball is always at the same place in space, so each time Joel hits the ball he is assimilating the information into replicating the same pattern or schema. During an actual game, however, Joel, who could hit the ball off the tee 100 percent of the time during practice, strikes out. The coach and his parents blame the performance on the stress of the game. That is not the case, however—Joel needed to practice accommodation to change his hitting pattern to adapt the pattern to account for the various positions in space that the ball may occupy. Instead of continually practicing hitting the ball in the same position, he needs to practice striking the ball in different positions in space.

Affective development focuses on the social and emotional development of the child. For movement programs, we need to be concerned with the development of self-concept and a positive attitude toward physical activity. The terms *self-esteem* and *self-concept* have been used interchangeably. In a review of 84 studies, Gruber (1985) concluded that involvement in directed play or physical education enhanced self-esteem. Around 8 years of age, children begin to verbalize their feelings of self-worth and make judgments about their self-esteem. By age 12, they are able to differentiate academic and athletic competence, peer social acceptance, physical appearance, and their own conduct. Applying this to teaching young children, it is important that the child has more success experiences than failures to enhance self-concept. Teachers can assist the child in experiencing success by developing a task analysis and a skill progression.

> Anod's parents enrolled her in swimming classes when she was 4 years old. The teacher did not have an understanding of developmentally appropriate learning, so she taught swimming using a teacher-centered approach. Even though it was evident that Anod had a fear of the water and did not like to get her face wet, she was dunked in the water on the first day and was forced to work repetitively on kicking. As a result, Anod struggled through the lessons and cried hard enough that her parents removed her from the program.

Subsequently, Anod was put in a developmentally appropriate program, in which she first played and splashed in the water to get her acclimated, then worked on "blowing out birthday candles," followed by blowing bubbles and playing "Ring Around the Rosy," but instead of falling down, she put her face in the water. At each point, Anod was successful by building on previous successes.

Motivational constraints are relevant to engaging the child in the activity. Even if the individual constraints are positive (good balance) and the child has the physical capabilities to perform the task, motivation can be lacking. We typically think that children have short attention spans—and, for many activities, this is true. When you ask a child to take out the trash, you have to continually remind her to do so. However, when playing ball with your 5-year-old nephew, who stops first? We are sure it is you! What is the reason a child persists at one task and not the other? Playing ball is fun for a child, whereas taking the trash out is not. A different child engages in reading for fun but has to be pushed to participate in physical activity. Why is he not motivated to participate in physical education? One reason might be the way the lesson was taught—the activity was not fun and he did not feel successful.

A feeling of competence is important for motivation; it is important that the child develop a feeling of self-confidence in the activity. Children need to be successful and thus feel competent. It does not take too many experiences of failure for a child to discontinue participation in an activity. It is always disappointing to hear a child say, "I can't." We want children to feel secure and confident, but it is also important for each child to develop a strong sense of self. A child's knowledge of what he or she can do very well and what skills may need to be improved is important.

Task Constraints

Task constraints are related to the requirements of the movements and skills outside the body. Goals, rules, and equipment are all considered task constraints. Separate from the individual, task constraints are specific to the movement. For example, the task constraints in the "Chicken Dance" require children to first open and close their four fingers against the thumb (forming a beak) four times, followed by tucking their hands under their armpits to form wings four times, and finally with hands on their waist, twist four times. They clap the next four beats. After these moves, they link elbows with a partner and skip in a circle until the music returns to the beginning. All this is performed to the beat of the music. The task can become easier with slower music and harder with faster music.

As the child grows and matures, it is necessary to match equipment (a task constraint) to the child. Asking young children to learn on adult-size equipment or adult-size fields puts them at a disadvantage. We tested the success of children using child-size golf clubs (Wood, Gallagher & Martino, 1990). When JL used a child-size golf club at age 8, he demonstrated a skilled swing pattern. When he used either a woman's club or a cut-down man's club, however, his skill deteriorated. An example of how a task constraint can cause an adult to use a less mature pattern is an adult walking up steps that have a high riser and short width. The adult uses a mark-time pattern (the same foot leading) instead of the usual alternate stepping pattern when the step riser matches the adult's leg length. Similarly, the child who is given an adult tennis racquet does not have the strength to hold the racquet in one hand (see **video** Kennedy Swinging Tennis Racquet).

Environmental Constraints

Weather conditions, temperature, culture, and surrounding environment are examples of environmental constraints. These constraints are global and not directly related to task constraints. Haywood and Getchell (2009) categorize environmental constraints into physical and sociocultural constraints. *Physical constraints* are directly related to the physical environment—a toddler, for example, will have no difficulty walking on level ground, but an uneven surface can present difficulties.

Sociocultural constraints also play a role in constraining a child's movement. Critical here is *cultural congruence* (Bredekamp & Copple, 2009). Cultural differences relate to a specific group of individuals. The educator needs to understand the value of cultural rules of the home to facilitate development and learning and design learning activities that are congruent with children's cultures. Teachers can cause conflict in children if they do not understand the cultural environment of the child. For example, the Kinder Kinetics Program, a gym and swim program for children between 3 and 12 years of age, serves children from various countries. Several children from Muslim countries attend, and their culture must be valued. The girls have worn swimsuits that cover their bodies. They wear long pants, long shirts, and swimming caps. Expectations for children that are consistent with the home are important. This is also a learning experience for the children from a more mainstream American culture to understand and value different cultures.

> Kirk was raised in a family that liked to play soccer, cross-country ski, and swim. The family participated in these activities together. Kirk had been in the water since infancy and had been on many ski outings with his mother, father, and sister. However, the area where the family lived placed a great deal of emphasis on the sports of football and baseball. Kirk was not aware of this "sports culture" conflict until he started kindergarten. During his first gym class, the class played baseball. Needless to say, Kirk did not do well. The gym teacher called Kirk's mother and told her that Kirk was delayed in his motor skills and needed to take a remedial gym class. Clearly, the family culture and the regional culture were in conflict. Kirk was not delayed—he just did not have the experiences in football and baseball that the other children had.

Teachers of young children must remember that cultural differences do exist and must be sensitive to this aspect of development and learning when assessing, planning, and implementing movement activities.

4.3 Differentiate Among Individual, Task, and Environmental Factors That Increase and Decrease Task Difficulty

The way a growing child moves in a changing environment can be explained through the interaction of the individual (structural and functional), task, and environmental constraints. A toddler who is acquiring the skill of climbing steps has a structural constraint not evident in older children. The size of the toddler's legs in relation to the riser height and step width forces the child to use a mark-step pattern, continually stepping up with the same foot. If toddlers climb steps (task constraint) that are proportional to their leg length, with shorter risers and shorter step width, they walk up the steps using an alternate stepping pattern. If it is raining (environmental constraint), however, even with appropriately sized steps, their pattern would revert to the mark step. A functional individual constraint that can motivate the child to stand up is by placing a favorite toy on a low table. A potential

> **M² FUN** **Ball Rolling with Infants**
>
> To help the infant who can sit begin, you can explore pushing and receiving a large, light, brightly colored ball. Sit facing the child with legs spread. Push the ball to the young child and have the young child push the ball back to you.

task constraint related to a structural physical constraint is if the child still displays the plantar grasp reflex (see **video** Palmar—palm of the hand grasp reflex/reaction 1). If she still curls her toes under when touched on the bottom of the foot, standing would be difficult. A task modification for a 3-year-old learning to catch would include using a large, light, brightly colored ball. Children at this age are attracted to the bright color, a light ball will not hurt them, and the large size makes it easier for them to catch with two hands. An environmental modification to assist standing and walking is a smooth surface. The smooth surface provides a base on which to walk where the individual does not have to worry about obstacles. If the surface becomes uneven, unstable, or covered in ice, the walking pattern changes to adapt to the changing conditions by using wide, short, steps.

Our goal in using Newell's model is to understand the growing and maturing child and the task requirements and environmental conditions, so we can assist the child in developing skilled movement. If we can help the child to be successful, we are developing a strong functional constraint called *motivation* that will keep the child engaged in physical activity. Through the interaction of individual, task, and environmental constraints, we can understand task complexity, analyze the task, and develop a progression of movement experiences that builds successful performance.

4.4 *Match the Individual, Task, and Environmental Constraints to Select Culturally Relevant Activities for a Developmentally Appropriate Movement Lesson*

This section expands on the task constraints and develops the knowledge to analyze or break down a skill to teach the child using developmentally appropriate guidelines. To do so, we first discuss two types of sequences, intertask and intratask. Next, we create a general developmental intertask sequence followed by providing specific examples of intratask sequences. Finally, we examine how to create your own task analysis for the skills you want to teach.

To help the teacher in planning a lesson in which all children are successful, it is important to understand the two types of sequences covered in this chapter—intratask and intertask.

Intratask sequences are changes that occur within a specific skill; they are the qualitative changes in a skill from the first attempt through the attainment of skilled behavior. When children first start to run, their arms are held high and close to the body to control the action, and their steps are short, almost moving more vertically than horizontally. The teacher can hear the children running because they contact the ground with flat feet, sounding like a herd of elephants. As the skill of running is developed, the arms gradually move down and swing in opposition to the legs, the stride length increases, the base of support decreases, and a heel–toe roll appears. The next section provides an overview of the timing of skill development throughout childhood (intertask sequence) followed by increases in skill performance (intratask sequence).

An *intertask developmental sequence* is a general progression of skill attainment in which the new skill is based on movements acquired from previously learned skills in the sequence. As the child progresses through the intertask sequence, complexity of the movement increases (see **video**). An example of an intertask sequence for an infant is the development of walking. Children will initially push up to balancing on their hands and knees. As they develop this skill, they start to rock back and forth. As they then develop the strength and then balance to lift one hand, crawling and creeping appear as they lose and regain balance and start to move forward. After they learn to creep, they start to pull to a stand. Holding onto an object to develop the required balance and endurance, they eventually let go of the support, stand for a few moments, then fall. These experiences eventually allow the toddler to stand unsupported and subsequently walk without support.

A general intertask sequence used for developing dance, sport, and fitness skills is based on Seefeldt's (1980) model with the inclusion of movement and fitness concepts (see Figure 4.2). The first level of the sequence includes *reflexes* and *reactions*. Reflexes are involuntary, subcortically con-

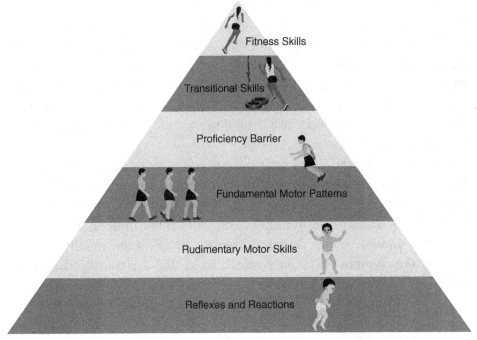

Figure 4.2 General intertask sequence of motor skill development.

trolled movements and are elicited by a particular sensory stimulus, such as light, sound, touch, or pressure. Developing during the first year of life, postural reactions are automatic and assist the infant in maintaining the body in an upright posture. Reflexes and reactions allow the infant to gain information about the immediate environment and learn more about the relationship between the body and outside world. They are important for survival (e.g., sucking, rooting), perception (e.g., depth perception, object constancy), and maintaining posture (e.g., tonic neck, head righting).

Rudimentary movement involves *stability movements*, such as gaining control of the head, neck, and trunk muscles; the manipulative tasks of reaching, grasping, and releasing; and the *locomotor movements*, such as creeping, crawling, and walking. Many of the motor milestones (sitting, crawling, creeping, and standing) are developed during this phase of development and can occur only after the infant has gained control of a series of body parts. The averages of attainment of the motor milestones are well documented (Bayley, 1935; Shirley, 1963) and are fundamental to skilled performance.

Rudimentary movements are the beginning combinations that excite parents and increase their anticipation concerning their child's impending motor milestones, but, more important, these combinations provide the infant with the ability to practice emerging motor skills. We see this in practice when infants on all fours rock back and forth in rhythm to their cooing. Another example is seen when an infant who has just gained the ability to ungrasp an object will drop a toy (or maybe food or utensils) to the ground repeatedly.

Previous general developmental pyramids have been based on the development of motor skills. A component that has been missing from the pyramids but critical to learning motor skills is the development of *movement concepts*. To learn motor skills, the child must understand the concepts that underlie motor skill performance. The learner initially needs to develop a movement vocabulary before being able to understand, analyze, and modify motor skills. Movement concepts should be developed in early childhood. Concepts are typically divided into the following areas:

- Body awareness—what the body can do
- Space awareness—where the body moves
- Movement qualities—how the body moves
- Relationships—to whom and to what the body relates

As children gain strength and develop postural control and balance, they start to acquire *fundamental motor patterns*, classified as locomotor (walking, running, chasing, fleeing, sliding, galloping, hopping, skipping, and dodging), nonlocomotor (turning, twisting, rolling, balancing, transferring weight, jumping and landing, bending, stretching, pushing, pulling, and curling), and manipulative (catching, throwing, striking, kicking, punting, dribbling, and volleying). Typically, children develop these skills during the preschool and early elementary school years. The level of performance is directly related to experience.

Seefeldt and Haubenstricker (1982) have documented age-related attainment of the various levels of fundamental motor patterns. Boys and girls display an immature overhand throw for force around the age of 3 years and acquire a more efficient pattern around 5 years of age for boys and

8.5 years of age for girls. Mature catching develops before 7.5 years of age for girls and after 7.5 years for boys. These age-related guides should be used to determine the ages at which most children are likely to have demonstrated the mature skill pattern and are ready to begin to adjust the skill for more advanced sport-specific movement. More important, these guides emphasize the importance of teaching the fundamental motor skills. Remember, from a developmental perspective, if an 8-year-old child displays an immature running pattern—his foot lands flat—he is not wrong; that is simply the level he has achieved.

M² FUN   Understanding Self-Space

Prior to this lesson, we cover *boundaries*, the space in which we move. For 15 children, we spread 15 large hoops within the boundaries, one hoop for each child. The children move from hoop to hoop with the task constraint that only one child can be in a hoop at any time. After they learn to move among the hoops with relative ease and spacing, we increase task complexity by increasing speed of movement or by requiring different locomotor skills. Finally, all hoops are removed— making the task more abstract and more difficult.

After reading the last paragraph you might have noticed gender differences in movement. The question is, "Are these differences between boys and girls genetic or are they due to practice?" The basic answer is— practice! French and Thomas (1985) analyzed 64 previous studies on gender differences in motor skills. They found that gender differences were related to age for balance, catching, dash, grip strength, long jump (jump for distance), shuttle run (run between two lines), sit-ups, tapping speed, and the vertical jump (jump for height). Boys were typically somewhat ahead of girls, but the gender differences were minimal until the adolescent growth spurt, at which point males gain a distinct size advantage. French and Thomas (1985) attributed these gender differences to environmental constraints such as encouragement, practice, and parental and peer expectations. However, for throwing, they found that the boys were very different from the girls. There was minimal overlap in the throwing outcome scores, and the average boy's distance throw was greater than the 99th percentile for girls. The question remains as to why gender differences in throwing performance are much greater than those for other tasks. Are they due to mechanical differences in throwing form, or are they due to early encouragement? Needless to say, we must have equally high expectations in all areas of movement for both boys and girls.

Fundamental motor patterns are the building blocks that allow the child to successfully develop more complex movements. It is essential that early movement experience begin with exposure and instruction in fundamental skill development of fundamental motor patterns and apply movement concepts to learning fundamental motor patterns.

Between fundamental motor pattern and transitional skill development, a *proficiency barrier* commonly exists. If the child has not learned prerequisite fundamental skills, combinations of fundamental motor patterns will not occur. For example, a child who has not learned both efficient running and long jump patterns will not be able to combine the two patterns to form a running long jump.

Commonly occurring during the late elementary and middle school years, the *transitional period* includes what traditionally was viewed as lead-up games that begin to combine the fundamental motor patterns into gamelike situations. It is important to recognize that lead-up games are structured to permit success without the level of skill or complexity of the environment that are required in the adult versions of the games. Once children have learned to throw and catch, they can play a game of "three-player keep-away." The purpose of this game is to practice the skills of throwing and catching under changing conditions. The throws are no longer easy to catch, and the catcher must move to catch the ball. Adding to the complexity and fun is the person in the middle trying to grab the ball from the others.

The final level of skill progression is *dance, sport-specific skills, and fitness,* the specialization of sport skills, dance, and the maintenance of fitness. Early learning and sport achievement do not automatically lead to successful performance. Clark (1967) demonstrated a low correlation for prediction of future success based on sport performance. Only 25 percent of the boys deemed outstanding athletes in elementary and junior high school were considered outstanding during their senior high school years. Because physical size and coordination advantages may disappear, childhood athletes and their parents should understand that continued practice and skill development are essential for continued success.

Additionally, parents should understand that less success, as measured by winning and losing, does not indicate lack of effort. Caution must be taken that prepubertal children not overspecialize in any one sport activity to the exclusion of other sports, because of changes in physical structure. Early specialization is aimed at developing an elite athlete, but the research does not support the need for early specialization to obtain the elite levels of performance. Moesch, Elbe, Hauge, and Wilkman (2011) found that elite athletes actually specialize in sport later than near-elite athletes. The elite athletes also participate in their first national and international competitions later than their near-elite peers. By late adolescence, the individual has the physical, cognitive, social emotional, and motor skills required to enter high levels of specialized training in one sport.

The general intertask sequence of motor skills should be used to develop a general progression. The teacher must understand that preschool children are moving among reflexes and reactions, rudimentary movement, movement concepts, and fundamental motor patters. It is important to understand the quality of movement by reviewing intratask sequences, which are covered next, followed by skill progression and task analyses.

Intratask sequences focus on quality of movement changes that occur within a given task until the task is mastered. The components of the skill are analyzed to determine levels of progression. An example of development of the skill of walking is found in this **video**, "Baby on the Move."

This sequence describes the change from an immature motor skill to an advanced pattern. When Suelyn first attempted to throw a ball, she merely flexed and extended her arm at the elbow (see Figure 4.3). Sometimes it was even hard for her to let go of the ball; at other times, she let go too soon and the ball would fall to the side. As she gained experience, though, Suelyn began to add some trunk motion by bending backward and forward at the waist. With continued practice, Suelyn added trunk rotation—her shoulders and hips would turn sideways—and she added a unilateral step (step with same foot as the throwing hand). The next level included stepping with the foot opposite the throwing hand and hip rotation forward, followed by the shoulders, upper arm, and forearm.

Developmental skill analyses exist for basic motor skills, including running, sliding, hopping, skipping, leaping, throwing, striking, sidearm

Level 1:
Arm
motion

Level 2:
Adds
trunk

Level 3:
Unilateral
step

Level 4:
Contralateral
step

Figure 4.3 Intratask sequence for throwing.

striking, overarm striking, catching, kicking , and punting (for more extensive information of intratask sequences of the fundamental motor patterns, see Pangrazi & Beighle, 2013; and Thomas, Lee, & Thomas, 2008).

Skill Progression

The difficulty of learning tasks is directly related to the nature of the movement and the conditions in the environment. Skills may be classified according to whether the performer's interaction with the environment is consistent and whether the body is stable or requires transport. Skill classification can generally be simplified and thought of as a continuum from a stationary (the child throws the ball to a stationary target) to a moving environment (the child has to move to catch the ball) and no variability to variability of the skill. This classification is commonly called a continuum of closed to open skills, respectively.

The environmental requirements of a skill vary (see Figure 4.4). A forward roll, for example, differs from batting a pitched ball in two ways. First, the environment is stable for the forward roll; the child tries to complete the task the same way each time. Body stability (balance) is required without modifying the skill to meet environmental demands. Skills of this type are termed *closed skills* and are generally considered to require a consistent pattern of response on each movement attempt. In addition to repeating the skill and having time to decide what to do, the individual is able to choose when to initiate the movement; the skill is self-paced.

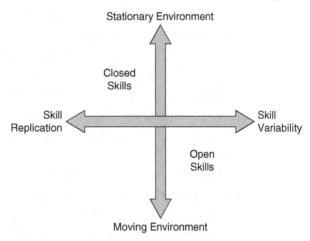

Figure 4.4 Level of motion of the environment and required adaptability of the skill.

Batting a baseball differs from the forward roll in that the child must match movements to the demands of a changing environment. When batting a pitched ball, the child is not free to arbitrarily choose how, when, and where to swing. The swing of the bat must occur neither too high nor too low, too early or too late. This type of skill, termed *open skill*, requires the child to develop an understanding of how to modify the swing to accommodate the changing environment. The child must adjust the level of the swing to the level of the ball. In addition, the skill is externally paced. The child must time the movement to the flight of the ball. The swing can be neither too soon nor too late.

For skill learning, the nature of the performance environment dictates the successful patterns that are developed by the child during practice. Successful performance of a closed skill requires development of highly consistent movement patterns (Higgins & Spaeth, 1972). Effective performance in open skills requires the child to adapt the movement to each specific situation. Most movement skills are considered to be open skills.

Relating to task complexity, performing in a moving environment is typically more difficult than in a stationary environment. A child must attend to the important aspects of the environment (e.g., flight of the ball, speed) and quickly choose the appropriate skill to use (e.g., whether to swing or not). Developmentally, it has been thought that the child should learn a skill in a fixed environment prior to practicing the skill in a moving environment. For example, young children initially play T-ball (closed environment), move to having coaches pitch (a highly predictable environment), and finally play ball with a peer pitching (open environment).

However, practicing an open skill in a closed environment for too long may cause the child to have difficulty performing the skill in a changing environment. For instance, when teaching sidearm striking with a bat, success at hitting must be weighed against striking different pitches. Consequently, the progression from T-ball to coach pitching to peer pitching is appropriate as long as the child is able to progress to the next level after early success is achieved. Moving to the next level can be embedded in practice.

Each skill a child undertakes has a *progression*—a series of skills that increase in complexity. An example of a skill progression for a young child is crawling, creeping, walking, and running, followed by jumping. If a child can successfully run, he or she has the prerequisite strength and balance for jumping. Associated with skill progression, *task complexity* is important in modifying the skill. Factors that can be varied to increase task complexity in a skill such as catching include ball size, speed, color, and trajectory, in addition to distance thrown, type of throw, and where thrown (Roberton, 1984). These factors can be progressively modified to help the child's skills improve. The novice, for instance, would catch a large, light ball thrown at chest height. As the child becomes more successful, the teacher can decrease the size of the ball and throw the ball so that the child has to reach to catch the ball. Continuing to increase complexity, the ball can be thrown from different angles and at different speeds. Finally, the child must move to catch a small, forcefully thrown ball. A developmental sequence for jumping is shown in Figure 4.5.

Task Analysis

A task analysis is important when determining what skills to practice in each day's lesson. A combination of intratask and intertask sequences aids the teacher in determining the learning hierarchy. First, the teacher reviews the general intertask sequence presented earlier in this chapter. What general skills are the children able to perform? Are they new walkers, or are they already racing from room to room? Do the infants still exhibit reflexes and reactions that prohibit the development of locomotion?

Once a general developmental level (e.g., rudimentary movement, fundamental motor patterns) is determined, the specific concepts and skills

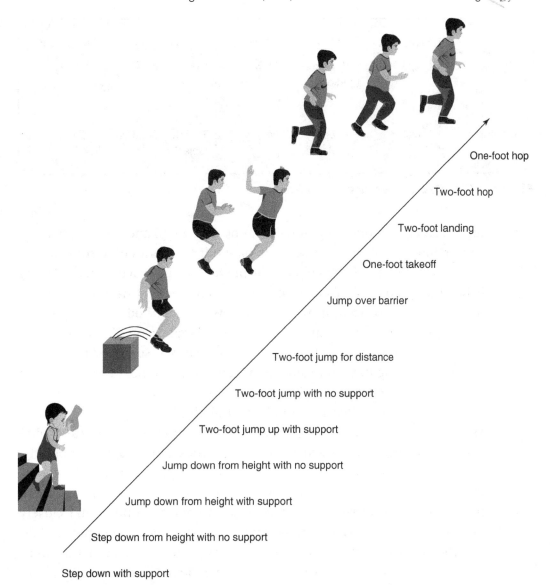

One-foot hop

Two-foot hop

Two-foot landing

One-foot takeoff

Jump over barrier

Two-foot jump for distance

Two-foot jump with no support

Two-foot jump up with support

Jump down from height with no support

Jump down from height with support

Step down from height with no support

Step down with support

Figure 4.5 A developmental sequence for jumping.

are chosen. One of the first movement concepts developed with 3-year-olds in the Kinder Kinetics Program is space awareness, or moving in space. We have refined a task analysis to develop the concept of where the child can move (see Figure 4.6). Young children typically congregate together; they move close to other children. When they are close to other children,

	Size	Concrete	Speed	Relationships	Movement
Simple	Large	Self-Space Marked	Slow	None	Stationary
Complex	Small	Self Space Not Marked	Fast	To Other Children/ Objects	Moving

Figure 4.6 Task analysis for general space.

the probability of bumping into one another is high, and the likelihood of getting into trouble is increased. We plan our first series of lessons to help children understand the concept of movement in space (thus avoiding behavioral problems). To accomplish this goal, we first have the children understand the concept of self-space: How do their bodies change shape and require more or less space? If there is a large group of children, how can they move without touching (using a small self-space)? After several lessons exploring how to change their self-space, we next concentrate on developing an understanding of general space.

For motor skill learning to occur, the child must receive adequate amounts of practice. Therefore, games of exclusion (e.g., musical chairs) and games with limited participation (e.g., Duck, Duck, Goose) should be avoided. The teacher's role is to ensure that the practice of a skill is monitored so that efficient movement patterns develop. In addition, practice of the individual skill should be performed under conditions that closely match situations in which the skill will be performed. The required skills and the practice environment must be adjusted to meet the changing individual constraints (both structural and functional constraints). Both task and environmental constraints should be altered to challenge the child to increase skill performance but not force failure.

Putting It on Paper

To create a task analysis, the various factors that affect the skill must be considered. The first-grade M^2 Movement Standard used to develop the following task analysis is M^2 Movement Standard: Movement Concept

Development: Understand the concept of stability and apply to safe movement in space. The objectives of this series of lessons based on these standards are:

- Understand stable and unstable movement
- Demonstrate how to maintain balance when stationary and moving

To begin the lesson, the concepts of base of *support, center of gravity,* and *line of gravity* are discussed (see Figure 4.7). The child will understand that the most stable position is a wide base, with a low center of gravity and the line of gravity that is within the base of support. Lying on the ground is the most stable position and one cannot be pushed over. An unstable position is a narrow base of support with a high center of gravity. It is very easy to push over someone who has his hands above his head while balancing on his toes. Due to the unstable position, the line of gravity is wavering inside and outside the base of support. Once children understand the factors affecting stationary balance, they can apply them to moving (dynamic) balance. Surface and speed are some of the factors that affect the difficulty of moving balance.

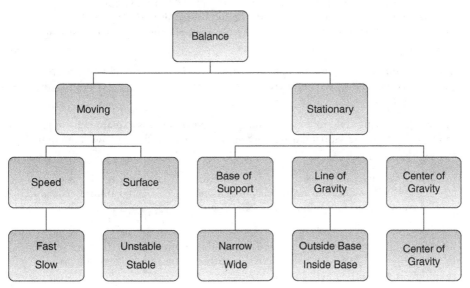

Figure 4.7 Developmental sequence for balance.

Summary

Movement is important for individuals of all ages. The purpose of this chapter was to develop the knowledge, skills, and dispositions needed to create developmentally appropriate movement lessons that scaffold children's development of motor skills. The following points are important in planning developmentally appropriate movement lessons for children.

Summary Related to Outcomes

Learning Outcomes	Guiding Principles
4.1 Match the task and the environment to the individual child	Individual Needs Met
Learning both gross and fine motor skills is important during the childhood years. To assist children in learning the skills, the task and the environment need to be matched to the child's structural and functional levels.	
4.2 Explain Newell's model of constraints	Individual Needs Met
Newell's model of constraints provides the foundation for understanding the individual child. The changes in the child include both structural constraints and functional constraints. Knowing how the structural constraints—the size of the child—change are important for selecting the appropriately sized equipment and determining criteria for activities. Functional constraints are related to motivation and change quickly. Matching task constraints to the child's prerequisite skills provides guidance in developing the lesson. Changing the environmental constraints allows simple increasing/decreasing of task difficulty.	
4.3 Differentiate among individual, task, and environmental factors that increase and decrease task difficulty	Individual Needs Met
The way a growing child moves in a changing environment is explained through the interaction of the individual (structural and functional), task, and environmental constraints.	
4.4 Match the individual, task, and environmental constraints to select culturally relevant activities for a developmentally appropriate movement lesson	Environment and Curriculum Reciprocated
Selection of the culturally relevant activities is important. The activities are selected based on the size of the child, the child's cognitive maturational level, the task requirements, and the environment.	

Demonstrate Your Knowledge, Skills, and Dispositions

Students will demonstrate knowledge, comprehension, analysis, and evaluation of Learning Outcomes related to Guiding Principles.

Learning Outcomes	Guiding Principles
4.1 Match the task and the environment to the individual child	Individual Needs Met
• Recall a physical activity class when you were a first grader, describe the lesson, and reflect on whether the task and environment were matched to you.	
4.2 Explain Newell's model of constraints	Individual Needs Met
• Choose an age group and a physical activity standard to plan a movement lesson. • Determine the individual constraints (structural and functional) of the age group you selected earlier.	
4.3 Differentiate among individual, task, and environmental factors that increase and decrease task difficulty	Individual Needs Met
• Using the preceding standard, determine a concept/skill to be taught and develop a task analysis for the concept/skill to be developed. Match the individual constraints to the task analysis to develop a developmental sequence.	
4.4 Match the individual, task, and environmental constraints to select culturally relevant activities for a developmentally appropriate movement lesson	Environment and Curriculum Reciprocated
• Develop a lesson for the concept/skill selected previously. Select activities for a developmentally appropriate movement lesson. Include at least three different culturally relevant activities that provide experience to develop the concept/skill.	

Planning for Engaging

The following learning activities provide three possibilities or ways to develop a standard taken from the M^2 Movement Standard.

The child will be able to:
• Differentiate the factors that promote health-related fitness from the factors that do not promote health-related fitness.
• Know that health-related fitness is required to function effectively, which allows the individual to feel good and perform the desired activities.

Possibility One	Possibility Two	Possibility Three

• Discuss what it means to be physically fit.
• Name activities that are beneficial to health.
• Name activities that are detrimental to health.
• Define:
  • Red light—stop—rest/refuel
  • Green light—go
  • Yellow light—slow down
• What happens to your breathing for red light, green light, and yellow light?
	• Learn to take heart rate.
	• Sitting down, place two fingers lightly on the side of the neck; run around for 1 minute, place two fingers on the side of the neck; discuss the difference.
	• Explore activities that make the heart beat faster/slower.
		• Children explore what happens to the heart rate when they move faster/slower; use more/less muscle; and so on.

Assessment Each child records activities that are beneficial to health.	**Assessment** Children record their heart rate for each of the activities they practice.	**Assessment** Each child identifies what makes the heart beat faster: moving faster/slower, using more/less muscle, and so on.

Now You Try It

Complete the following standard-based learning activity designed to meet various interests and developmental levels by designing two possibilities/earning activities to develop a movement or music standard taken from the M^2 Movement Standards.

M^2 Movement Standard: The child will be able to:
- Differentiate the factors that promote health-related fitness from the factors that do not promote health-related fitness.
- Know that health-related fitness is required to function effectively, which allows the individual to feel good and perform the desired activities.

Possibility One	Possibility Two	Possibility Three
Children sit in self-space and think about their breathing.		

Children walk around the room and think about their breathing. Children run around the room and think about their breathing. Class discussion on what happened to their breathing when they moved faster.		
Assessment Quick observation, teacher calls out "breathe heavier," "breathe less," and observes the children speeding up or slowing down.	**Assessment**	**Assessment**

References

Bayley, N. (1935). The development of motor abilities during the first three years. *Monographs of the Society for Research in Child Development*, 1(1), 26.

Bredekamp, S. & Copple, S. (2009). National Association for the Education of Young Children. *Developmentally appropriate practice in early childhood programs* (N.A.E.Y.C. Series #234). Washington, DC: National Association for the Education of Young Children.

Clark, H. (1967). Characteristics of the young athlete: A longitudinal look. In *AMA Proceedings of the Eighth Annual Conference on the Medical Aspects of Sport—1966*. Chicago, IL: American Medical Association, 49–57.

Fox, D. (2000). Music and the baby's brain early experiences: Do young children benefit from early childhood music instruction? Here is a research-based answer. *Music Educators Journal*, 87, 23–50.

French, K.E., & Thomas, J.R. (1985). Gender differences across age in motor performance: A meta-analysis. *Psychological Bulletin, 98*, 260–282.

Gabbard, C. (2008). *Lifelong motor development* (5th Ed.). San Francisco, CA: Benjamin Cummings.

Greenough, W.T., & Black, J.E. (1992). Induction of brain structure by experience: Substrates for cognitive development. In M. Gunnar & C. Nelson (Eds.), *Minnesota Symposia on Child Psychology*, Vol. 24, *Developmental Behavioral Neuroscience* (pp. 155–200).

Gruber, J. (1985). Physical activity and self-esteem development in children: A meta-analysis. *The Academy Papers, 19*, 30–48.

Haywood, K.M., & Getchell, N. (2009). *Life span motor development* (5th Ed.). Champaign, IL: Human Kinetics Publishers.

Higgins, J.R., & Spaeth, R.K. (1972). The relationship between consistency of movement and environmental conditions. *Quest, 17*, 61–69.

Moesch, K., Elbe, A., Hauge, J., & Wilkman J. (2011). Late specialization: The key to success in centimeters, grams, or seconds (cgs) sports. *Scandinavian Journal of Medicine, Science and Sports, 21*, e282–e290. doi: 10.1111lj.1600-0838.2010.01280x.

Newell, K. M. (1986). Constraints on the development of coordination. In M.G. Wade & H.T.A. Whiting (Eds.). *Motor development in children: Aspects of coordination and control* (pp. 341–361). Amsterdam: Martinus Nijhoff Publishers.

Pangrazi, P., & Beighle, A. (2013). *Dynamic physical education for elementary school children.* New York, NY: Pearson.

Ramey, C., & Ramey, S. (1994). Which children benefit the most from early intervention? *Pediatrics, 94*, 1064-1066.

Roberton, M.A. (1984). Changing motor patterns during childhood. In J.R. Thomas (Ed.). *Motor development during childhood and adolescence* (pp. 48–90). Minneapolis, MN: Burgess.

Seefeldt, V. (1980). Developmental motor patterns: Implications for elementary school physical education. In C. Nadeau, W. Holliwell, K. Newell, & G. Roberts (Eds.). *Psychology of motor behavior and sport.* Champaign, IL: Human Kinetics Publishers.

Seefeldt, V. & Haubenstricker, J. (1982). Patterns, phases, or stages: An analytical model for the study of developmental movement. In J.A.S. Kelos and J.E. Clark (Eds.). *The development of movement control and coordination* (pp. 309-318). New York: John Wiley & Sons.

Shirley, M. M. (1963). The motor sequence. In D. Wayne (Ed.), *Readings in child psychology.* Englewood Cliffs, NJ: Prentice-Hall.

Thomas, K., Lee, A., & Thomas, J. (2008). *Physical education methods for elementary teachers.* Champaign, IL: Human Kinetics Publishers.

Wood, C., Gallagher, J., & Martino, R. (1990). Large equipment and small children: Implications for club fitting based upon age and standing height for junior golfers. In A. Cochran (Ed.), *Proceedings of the First World Scientific Congress of Golf* (pp. 88–93). London: E. & F.N. Spon.

chapter 5

Movement Content During the Early Childhood Years

LEARNING OUTCOMES AND GUIDING PRINCIPLES

Students reading this text will be able to demonstrate Learning Outcomes linked to Guiding Principles based on the *National Association for the Education of Young Children's Developmentally Appropriate Practice in Early Childhood Programs Serving Children from Birth through Age 8.*

Learning Outcomes	Guiding Principles
5.1 Understand the relationship of movement and music	Environment and Curriculum Reciprocated
5.2 Know the content of developmentally appropriate movement	Environment and Curriculum Reciprocated
5.3 Create lessons to enhance understanding of movement concepts	Environment and Curriculum Reciprocated
5.4 Create lessons to enhance development of fine motor skills	Environment and Curriculum Reciprocated
5.5 Understand the role culture plays in planning movement and musical activities	Family and Community Involved
5.6 Enhance family and community involvement in movement and music	Family and Community Involved

A Dalcroze eurhythmics class for 3- and 4-year-olds has just begun. The children are standing and ready to move while their teacher is seated at the piano. The music starts and the children begin to move following the instructions of the teacher. Their movements are based on Dalcroze's philosophy of using rhythmic movement to gain understanding of musical aspects such as timing, tone, and phrasing. The teacher and the children are all smiling. The children are enjoying moving to the music, and it is gratifying for the teacher to support movement through music and music through movement.

The first activity is moving to a pleasant dance tune. Part of the dance is done on tiptoe. As the music progresses to a faster time, the pace of the children increases. Surprisingly, the pianist then slows the timing, and the children must decrease their speed. Later, the children form groups of four and pass a tennis ball to each other, timing the grasping release to the rhythm of the music. Clapping with a partner also enforces beat and the phrasing of the music. The fun continues when each child is given a small hoop. They spin the hoop and when the hoop falls, the children move to where their hoop has landed.

Musical scales are emphasized as the pianist plays notes up and down the musical scale, while the children raise and lower their bodies. They discover that this takes balance and strength, and comment to each other their enjoyment of this ascending and descending movement. Finally, the children move about the room using arm and leg movements to act out a story about a princess who goes to a mountain to visit her aunt. What fun everyone had!

5.1 Understand the Relationship of Movement and Music

Watching the children move in the "Making Connections" eurthymics class provides convincing evidence of the relationship between movement and music. Musical concepts are strengthened through body movements. The baby automatically moves her body to music; the child taps his foot in time to music or swings his head back and forth. Movement and music share emotions and tell stories. Happy music is upbeat and fast; sad is slow and low. Music tells a story as we take an imaginary trip with a princess, to the zoo, or to a forest searching for a bear, or as we march as pretend soldiers. Music can also be used to calm movement and help the child sleep.

Emotion is a component of both music and movement, which is represented by a combination of features that are the same both within and across cultures (Sievers, Polansky, Casey, & Wheatley, 2013). Using a computer program for adults to create their own melodies or bouncing ball animations, Sievers et al. (2013) found that regardless of culture, the components of the music and movement were the same. An adult in Cambodia creates the same structure of emotion (anger, happy, peaceful, sad) for both movement and music as an adult from the United States.

Music and movement are connected through multisensory information. We hear the rhythm in the music and feel the beat. Moving with music involves the following:

▲ Girls engaging in creative movement.

- Proprioception (perception of body position)
- Vestibular perception (perception of movement and balance),
- Visual system
- Auditory system

An example of the use of multisensory information was demonstrated when infants who were presented with music without rhythm but were bounced on a specific beat preferred to listen to a rhythm similar to the bounced training condition (Phillips-Silver & Trainor, 2005).

Because music and movement share components, music can be used to guide movement. The young child who runs flat-footed can be guided by music that has a light, smooth flow. Children learning to skip can perform a more fluid motion if they skip to music with a low-high beat (step-hop, step-hop, step-hop, and so on).

Movement and music are linked in the development of movement concepts, the language of motor skill development and learning. The initial goal of this chapter is to understand the development of movement concepts during the early learning years; these concepts are then used for motor skill learning. A child needs to understand the concepts of "fast" and "slow" before being able to speed up or slow down the movement. We use this information to develop creative movement lessons, followed by understanding the importance of culture and family in early childhood learning.

5.2 Know the Content of Developmentally Appropriate Movement

The National Association of Sport and Physical Education (NASPE), an association of the American Alliance for Health, Physical Education, Recreation and Dance (AAHPERD), has developed national standards for physical education for children (National Association for Sport and Physical Education, 2004a). The standards (see Table 5.1) are general and define a *physically educated person*. Skill benchmarks are developed for grades K–2, 3–5, 6–8, and 9–12. Here, we are concerned with pre-K to third-grade development.

A committee within NASPE, the Council for Physical Education for Children, has provided a variety of documents on developmentally appropriate practice for children. Some of the position statements they have been instrumental in developing include the following:

- *Looking at Physical Education from a Developmental Perspective: A Guide to Teaching* (NASPE, 1995)
- *Recess for Elementary School Students* (NASPE, 2006)
- *Physical Activity for Children: A Statement of Guidelines for Children 5–12* (NASPE, 2004b)

Table 5.1 National Standards for Physical Education for Children (NASPE, 2004)

Standard 1:	Demonstrates competency in motor skills and movement patterns needed to perform a variety of physical activities
Standard 2:	Demonstrates understanding of movement concepts, principles, strategies, and tactics as they apply to the learning and performance of physical activities
Standard 3:	Participates regularly in physical activity
Standard 4:	Achieves and maintains a health-enhancing level of physical fitness
Standard 5:	Exhibits responsible personal and social behavior that respects self and others in physical activity settings
Standard 6:	Values physical activity for health, enjoyment, challenge, self-expression, and/or social interaction

Reprinted with permission from the American Alliance for Health, Physical Education, Recreation and Dance, www.AAHPERD.org.

- *Active Start: A Statement of Physical Activity Guidelines for Children from Birth to Age 5* (NASPE, 2009)
- *Appropriate Practices in Movement Programs for Children Ages 3–5* (NASPE, n.d.)

The International Council for Health, Physical Education, Recreation, Sport, and Dance (ICHPER·SD, n.d.) has also developed international standards that parallel those of AAHPERD and include benchmarks for grades 3, 6, 9, and 12. Although these guidelines start at grade 3, the guidelines include developmental suggestions for younger children that lead up to the third-grade standard. These global standards need to occur regardless of nationality, with each nation customizing the curricula to culturally related standards. Culturally neutral content is based on providing all children with physical education content that they are capable of learning regardless of where they live. The right-to-learn premises address the rights to physical education that must be part of schooling.

These organizations stress the importance of children moving. Whether in sport, physical education classes, at school, or at home, the child needs to be active. The child must be actively engaged in the activity

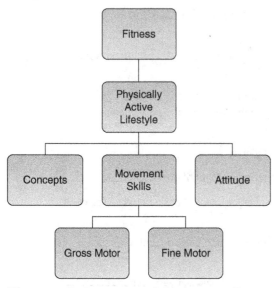

Figure 5.1 Content of developmentally appropriate physical education.

and should be moving for 95 percent of the activity period. Instruction is important—but the child should not be sitting and listening, but moving as teachers provide instructions, cue words, and feedback.

Developmentally appropriate physical education includes development of concepts, movement skills, and a positive attitude applied to dance, games, and sports that lead to a physically active lifestyle (see Figure 5.1). *Concepts* provide the foundation for understanding movement and *motor skills* (gross and fine) provide the children with the skills to move.

Motor skills develop in a cephalocaudal (head to foot), proximal–distal (body core to fingers), and gross to fine motor direction. Gross motor skills encompass large muscle movements, which lead to physical fitness (Wrotniak, Epstein, Dorn, Jones, & Kondilis, 2006). Fine motor skills—small muscle movements, such as buttoning, tying a shoe, and writing—are developed in early childhood.

Attitude fosters the motivation that is important for maintaining physical activity across the lifespan. This chapter covers the development of movement concepts and fine motor development and discusses how culture and family involvement influence learning of concepts and fine motor skills.

5.3 Create Lessons to Enhance Understanding of Movement Concepts

The major emphasis of movement programs for young children is the development of concepts. The teaching of movement concepts began in the 1800s with the work of François Delsarte (Abels & Bridges, 2010), who emphasized expression of thought and emotion and connected this to mind, body, and spirit. He emphasized the idea of time, space, and motion, suggesting that movement toward and away from the body was the basis of all movement. He included nine "laws" of motion: altitude, force, motion, sequence, direction, form, velocity, reaction, and extension.

Moving into the 1930s, Liselott Diem focused on building movement skills and balance. She encouraged physical education teachers to ask the children questions, such as "Who can do this?" and "How can this be done differently?" (Abels & Bridges, 2010, p. 4). Her focus was on body awareness, force, time, and space.

Rudolf von Laban is considered the father of modern movement education (Abels & Bridges, 2010). His major emphasis was on effort for both expressive (creative movement) and functional movement (movement skills). Laban identified the factors of weight, space, time, and flow. Movement concepts include both movement and fitness content. Linking movement concepts and fundamental motor skills, Laban and Ullmann (1963) described movement focusing on body awareness, space awareness, movement qualities, and relationships (see Figure 5.2), concepts

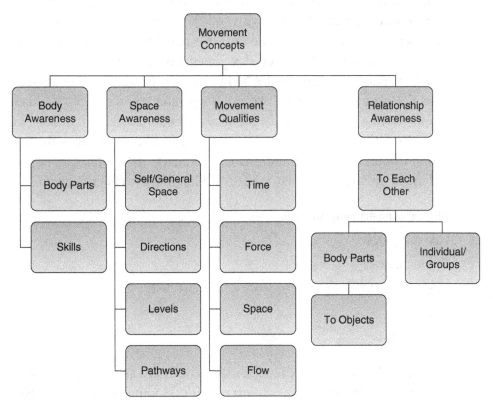

Figure 5.2 Movement concepts.

used by modern movement theorists. Fitness concepts are the health- and skill-related components of physical fitness. We next cover movement concepts, followed by fitness concepts.

Movement Concepts

Body awareness, space awareness, movement quality, and relationship awareness are included in movement concepts (see Figure 5.2). Development of this knowledge provides the foundation for all skill development.

Body Awareness. Identification of body parts followed by an understanding of the skills the body can perform (*what the body does*) is part of developing an awareness of the body. In learning the parts of the body, the child is first able to identify the body parts. If the parent says, "eyes," the child points to the eyes (recognition) (see Body Parts **video**). Subsequently, the parent points to the eyes, and the child names the body part (recall). The child's ability to name body parts is due mainly to practice. For instance, every time Cyrus's mother said, "chin" (recognition), and he pointed to his chin, his mother rewarded Cyrus with smiles and excitement. A more difficult concept for Cyrus was to name the body part (recall) when his mother pointed to her chin; this, however, developed with practice.

Good songs to sing to emphasize body parts are "Head, Shoulders, Knees, and Toes," "Hokey Pokey," and "If You're Happy and You Know It." A made-up chant, "Move Around My Body, Squirrel," is an interactive chant done by making a fist with the left hand and inserting the first finger between the first finger and thumb of the left-hand fist. The "squirrel" then moves to various parts of the body, such as a knee, while the adult and the children chant,

> Move around my body, squirrel,
>
> Hop to my knees,
>
> Pop to my head,
>
> Stop at my feet,
>
> Flop,
>
> Chop to my toe.

Learning the names of the skills that the body can perform is also included in body awareness. The children are developing knowledge of *what* their bodies can do and *when* they should perform a given skill. For example, children learn the concept of a jump, and when they should use the jump. They can jump off a chair, jump up to hit the pots and pans, or jump across a brook—but they should not jump down the steps, for safety reasons.

Knowing what skills they can perform also relies on the quality of the skill performance. An inexperienced basketball player, during a free throw, would choose to throw the ball using a two-handed underhand throw (granny shot) rather than using a one-handed overhand throw. We are more likely to make the shot this way because we do not have the prerequisite strength nor the skill to get the ball to the basket. It is important to remember that children who perform a skill this way are not wrong; they are working at their individual developmental level, and the teacher needs to determine the next developmental level.

M² FUN Body Awareness

The children create their own "bodies" by lying on a large sheet of brown paper. Someone traces their bodies and then cuts out the figures. The body shape can then be cut to create a puzzle for the child/children to assemble.

Connecting moving in general space and body awareness, the children get a partner and move in general space while they are touching specific body parts (e.g., hands, elbow, back).

Play "Simon Says" with a beanbag. The teacher or child calls out a body part and the child puts the beanbag on the body part. When all children have the beanbag on the correct body part, the next body part is called. No one is eliminated.

Space Awareness. Self and general space, directions, levels, pathways, planes, and extensions are part of space awareness. This defines *where the body moves*. The child needs to understand self-space (personal space) and general space (area within the boundaries). Infants and toddlers begin to understand the concept of space awareness by crawling under tables of different sizes. For some tables, they do not need to alter their size, but to go under other tables they need to move on a low level. An example of a developmental task anal-

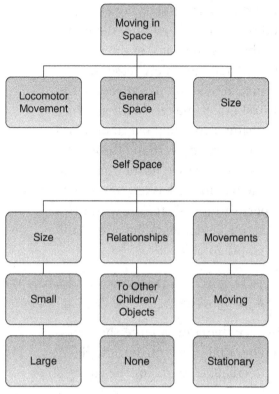

Figure 5.3 Developmental sequence for general space.

ysis/sequence for developing the concept of self-space and general space is given in Figure 5.3. The children should explore self-space and understand how self-space changes and what can be done in self-space.

During a lesson on space awareness, children first explore self-space to determine how it changes shape. Self-space can be tall, when the child is standing, or it can be small, when the child is crouched down. A good song to sing is "I Am Tall, I Am Small":

I am tall, very tall [stretch upward],

I am small [crouch down to the ground].

I am tall, I am small, now I am—? [child decides, through body position, whether to be tall or small].

Children understand general space when they are able to move without bumping into one another and spread throughout the entire space instead of huddling together or moving as a group in a circle.

Other key concepts to develop during early childhood include directions, levels, and pathways. Directions include forward, backward, up, down, sideways, and, eventually, right and left. Children understand directions when they are able to change directions within two steps when asked and change direction without hesitation. They do not understand directions if they have to stop and think before they change, or follow others as they change directions.

Levels relate to high, middle, and low. We crawl at a low level but jump into a high level. Children need to travel and freeze at different levels, move while different body parts are at different levels, and rise and sink to create different levels. They understand levels if they are able to freeze in space at the level indicated without hesitation. If they have to stop and think, they do not understand levels.

An extension of space awareness after the general concept is learned is to develop the concept of *pathways*. Pathways are straight, curved, and zigzag (created by combining straight paths). Initially, the children can move a ribbon stick (or even just a long ribbon or strip of crepe paper) in the three pathways while standing. A straight pathway can be a vertical, horizontal, or diagonal path. The children can create a zigzag path by making a Z, W, or an M. For circles, they move the ribbon in a circle above their heads, or swing it around in front, or create the letter O or the number 0. The children can increase complexity by moving and creating a path. Children should explore and design pathways and play "follow the leader" through pathways. They understand pathways if, when required to change pathways, they create the path, change without hesitation, and their speed does not change.

Shapes are made of a combination of pathways. This understanding of shapes will lead to identification of letters and other cultural symbols.

Once a child has a grasp of directions, levels, and pathways, integration of the concepts is important. For example, it is important for children to know they are moving backward at a high level in a curved path. The teacher asks the children with their tricycles or scooters (real or pretend) to drive on the road (lines on the floor). As the children drive, they need to be aware of the space in which other children are moving. Sometimes, when a child parks a car or truck and returns later, he or she needs to move backward to move out of out of the parking space. To accomplish this, the children need to know they are moving backward at a high level.

M² FUN   Space Awareness—Follow the Path Map

Children work in groups of two or three; there are a leader and followers, and each child gets to participate in both roles. Each child creates a combination of straight, curved, and zigzag paths. One child becomes the leader and leads the other children through the path. At the end of the path, the other children draw a map of the path. The followers then compare the path to that drawn by the leader. Each child has a turn to do each task.

Movement Qualities. The components of time, force, space, and flow are concepts that relate to the quality of movement and describe *how the body moves.*

Time refers to the speed of movement and can change from slow to fast. A turtle creeps slowly, whereas a rabbit moves quickly (see Figure 5.4). The children should explore different speeds in self-space, move at different speeds, and travel and freeze at different speeds. Children understand time and changes in speed when they can change speed from fast to

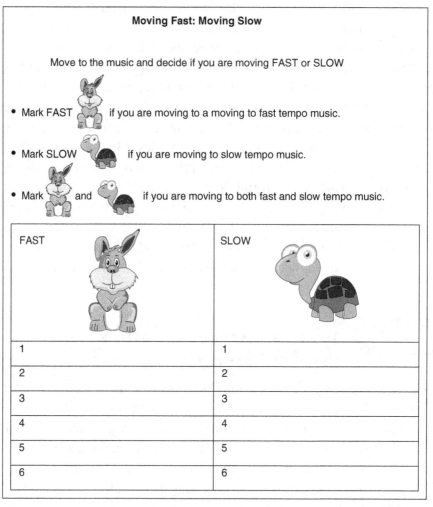

Figure 5.4 Task sheet for children to indicate whether they were moving fast or slow.

slow on command, without hesitation, and the difference between speeds is evident.

Force is the amount of energy used to complete the movement. We impart force to a throw, but absorb force when catching. Children should explore various levels of force, travel, and change qualities of force. Children understand the concept of force when they use strong force and the involved muscles show tension. The tension is different for light, moderate, and strong. They demonstrate changes in force without hesitation or stopping to think.

The space used in the movement ranges from direct to indirect. We follow a direct pathway, or we use an indirect route. A direct movement would have little flexibility and a rigid, straight path. An indirect movement is more flexible, and the path can meander. Rivers follow an indirect path.

Flow, a more advanced concept, ranges from bound to free. The mover has complete control of a bound movement and can stop the movement instantly. These are constrained and cautious movements. Walking while balancing a beanbag on the head is an example of bound flow. A free movement is continuous and cannot be stopped once initiated. A child running down a hill is an example of free flow. Children understand flow if they can change from bound to free flow and bodies are tense for bound flow but relaxed for free flow. The child's range of motion narrows for bound flow and expands for free flow.

M² FUN   Movement Qualities—Time

Move like the animals: The teacher calls out the name of an animal and the children move like that animal. The teacher questions the children as to whether the animal moves fast or slow. Children then take turns naming animals. To make the activity more difficult, the teacher or children call out fast, slow, faster, or slower, and the children select the animal. Another revision would be to have a child name an imaginary animal and demonstrate how the animal would move. The group would follow the lead child.

Relationships.   The relationships of body parts to one another and of the individual to other individuals, groups, or objects is the focus of movement relationships (*with whom and what the body moves*). Relationship awareness covers such concepts as *over, under, around,* and *through*. The child can stand *beside* a friend, jump *over* the obstacle on the floor, and go *under* the bridge, *around* the mulberry bush, or *through* the door. Singing the songs "London Bridge Is Falling Down," "Ring Around the Rosy," and "Mulberry Bush" can help provide practice relationship awareness.

Obstacle courses are always fun for children to develop movement relations. You can use cones with a dowel to create something to crawl *under* or step *over*. A trash can can be moved *around*; a line on the floor can be walked *over*.

Relationship awareness also includes leading and following, in front of and behind, meeting and parting, near and far, mirroring, and so on, in relation not only to objects but also to people. Awareness of where others and objects are in relationship to the individual is very important in all physical activities and sports. For safety, children need to know where they are in relation to other children moving.

In addition to movement concepts used to develop mastery, children also need to understand concepts related to physical activity and development of health-related fitness. Health-related fitness concepts are covered next.

M² FUN   Movement Relationships—Mimic

Identify a leader and a follower. The leader moves through general space, performing different movements, and the follower mimics the leader. Scarves can used to vary the movement.

Fitness Concepts

Fitness can be either skill related or health related. Skill-associated fitness is important for improved skill performance, whereas health-linked fitness is critical for health (see Table 5.2). Appropriate nutrition also plays a role in health-related fitness. If children do not consume foods that provide needed nutrients, they will be unable to obtain and maintain a healthy and fit lifestyle.

Table 5.2 Fitness Concepts

Skill Related	Health Related
Speed	Cardiovascular
Reaction time	Strength
Agility	Flexibility
Balance	Muscular endurance
Coordination	Body composition
Power	

Not only do children need to understand the components of health-related fitness, but they also need to understand the factors that influence fitness. Fitness concepts cover the knowledge related to how to develop and maintain physical fitness (see Figure 5.5) and include an understanding

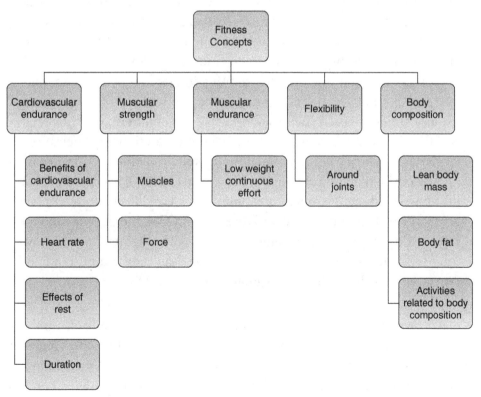

Figure 5.5 Fitness concepts.

of the benefits of physical activity. It is important to understand health-related fitness concepts even at a young age, but it is not necessary to focus on developing fitness just yet. The goal is for children to learn the concepts, develop the skills, and love to move. Children learn to take their heart rate and learn the relationship between heart rate and level of physical activity. On her developmental level, Gwen, a 3-year-old child, can put the "heart-o-meter" (toothpick in a small piece of clay) on her wrist and see that it does not move when she is quiet. However, when Gwen finishes running, she places the heart-o-meter on her wrist and it moves rapidly back and forth.

M² FUN   Fitness Concepts

Ask the children how they feel: Are they breathing heavily, are they sweating, can they feel their muscles? Take the children on a "mountain climb." To reach the mountain, they have to hike through thick grass (high knees); then they see a stream and have to jump from rock to rock to rock (three times) to reach the other side of the river. To climb the mountain, they have to do "mountain climbers" (hands and feet on ground in push-up position, bring in one foot at a time to middle, and alternate feet). When they get to the top, they have to jump up four times to reach the peak. Now ask the children how they feel: Are they breathing heavily, are they sweating, can they feel their muscles? What did they do that made them sweat and breathe heavily?

By pushing objects of different weights, a child will begin to develop an understanding of strength and endurance. Provide children with an array of box sizes and ask them to make a train. Ask them: What do you have to do with a heavier weight compared with a lighter weight? How long can you push a heavy object, and how long can you push a light object? (See **video** What Is Imagination Playground.)

An awareness of how strength differs from endurance is also important. Children can understand the concept of flexibility and range of motion—how far they can bend without stretching beyond their range of comfort. They can certainly see what happens when a rubber band is stretched too far. Finally, they can understand body composition, knowing that a body is composed of lean body mass and fat. Children can begin to realize that too much fat can be harmful to a healthy lifestyle.

Movement and fitness concepts provide the child with the language to improve skill performance. Next we provide ideas on how to develop movement concepts.

Teaching Movement Concepts

Teaching children movement concepts typically use movement education, in which the teacher is considered a facilitator. The teacher provides the children with a series of questions that require them to solve a movement problem. This helps the child explore and understand his or her body, what it can do, where it can move, how it moves, and with what or whom. This type of teaching style encourages creativity and the ability to adapt and modify movements. The child is asked to explore, analyze, and apply knowledge to find solutions to a problem. Children are questioned and explore a variety of ways to solve a problem. How the body can move? In what levels? Would a one-handed or two-handed catch work best?

M² FUN   Balance

Ask the children to assume three positions requiring balance:

Straddle-balance: While standing, children will move their feet apart gradually until they reach the widest straddle possible without losing their balance.

V-sit: Children are asked to sit and raise their feet into the air, as straight as possible, while positioned on their seat. Arms should be positioned out to the side.

Airplane: Children are asked to stand on one foot and bend forward while lifting the non–weight-bearing leg and lifting arms to the side.

Which action is most difficult for balance?

Movement education uses a teaching style that is similar to two elements of Mosston's spectrum of teaching styles (Mosston & Ashworth, 2002):

- Guided discovery
- Inclusion

The *guided discovery* style poses a series of questions that assist the learner in discovering the specific concept. The teacher provides a variety of levels of difficulty for the child to select a task that provides him or her with a challenge, but that is able to be accomplished. For example, one child can move quickly in general space without touching anyone, whereas another has to move more slowly to be successful. The *inclusion* style allows for adaptation for children of all ability levels, including children with disabilities.

Over the past several decades, as a result of the increasing obesity epidemic, there has been a major emphasis on teaching fitness. We do not feel that early childhood educators need to be concerned with "increasing fitness levels"; we are more concerned with children developing skill, feeling competent, loving to move, and therefore moving for a lifetime

5.4 Create Lessons to Enhance Development of Fine Motor Skills

During the early childhood years, children are also developing fine motor skills. Small muscles of the body are coordinated to perform fine motor skills such as grasping, drawing, writing, buttoning, and piano playing. It is important for infants, toddlers, and children to be provided with appropriate materials to explore and to develop fine motor skills.

Development of Fine Motor Skills

Fine motor development is frequently thought of as eye–hand coordination. However, fine motor movements also include control of precise movements throughout the body. For example, fine motor control includes not only picking up a small object, but also controlling the muscles in the foot while dribbling a soccer ball and then precisely kicking the ball to a specific point in the goal to score.

We see evidence of the beginning of the development of fine motor skills in the newborn with the grasping reflex. These skills are important in most activities in school, as well as required for everyday tasks such as eating and dressing. The remainder of this section reviews reaching and grasping, bimanual control, and eye–hand coordination.

To develop fine motor skills of the hands, stability of the trunk, development of the shoulder girdle, head control, and visual tracking need to be present (Brook, Wagenfeld, & Thompson, n.d.).

Reaching and Grasping. A newborn demonstrates the beginning of eye–hand coordination through reaching and grasping. Changing with age and experience, the infant initially shows crude shoulder and elbow movements, followed by the movements of the hand becoming finer, followed by use of the fingertips. With practice come increased speed and efficiency.

Grasping is initiated with the palmar grasp reflex, which is present prenatally at approximately four months. If an object is placed in the newborn's hand, the infant's hand closes tightly around the object. Around 3 months of age, the child attempts to reach for an object that draws his or her attention. The beginning of an intentional grasp begins with the infant squeezing the object using the four fingers against the palm (primitive squeeze, power grip). The thumb is eventually used in opposition, but the object remains in contact with the palm (squeeze grasp). Between 7 and 9 months of age, Sheliah intentionally dropped objects on the floor. Not only did she have fun as her dad picked up the objects, but she was also practicing releasing the object. Between 9 and 12 months of age, infants use the thumb and index finger to grasp small objects. As the grasp becomes more precise, the infant explores the object by moving, rotating, and shaking. Throughout the first year, the power grip transforms into a precision grip by about 1 year of age, by which time the infant is able to pick up small objects using the thumb and finger or fingers in a pincer grasp (see **video** Developing Milestones).

The grasp used depends on the size and shape of the object (Lee, Liu, & Newell, 2006). Because babies frequently place objects in their mouths, it is critical during this time that objects with small parts be removed from the area. Independent sitting also frees the babies' hands to perform a variety of manipulations. Through this exploration of objects, infants begin to determine the objects' size, shape, weight, hardness, and texture.

The learning environment for infants and toddlers should provide a variety of materials to stimulate the development of grasping. Common kitchen items and different sized balls of yarn or string are easily obtainable and provide wonderful experiences for the infant or toddler.

Coordinated manipulation of objects with the fingers moving independently does not occur until around age 4. This is when a child starts to learn to button a shirt. To manipulate an object with skill, the fingers must be capable of moving independently of one another. For example, if the thumb and fingers work as a unit, it is impossible to rotate an object held in the fingertips. The hand also requires sensory information to manipulate an object, along with appropriate grip strength. An excellent tool to reinforce this developmental sequence is a block crayon. These one-inch by two-inch rectangles can be used on the side for broad markings or on the corner/edge to make finer markings. For ideas on activities to develop fine motor skills, view "Fine Motor Development Ideas for Preschool Children" (see **video**).

With age, there is a decrease in the amount of time it takes for the fingers to move independently (e.g., each finger touches the thumb with minimal movement of the other fingers). There is not much change between 5 and 7 years, but there is greater control by 11 years of age.

Applying this to coloring and later to printing and writing, the grip changes with development. The first grip is a fisted grip, in which the

M² FUN   Finger Play

Select a slow song with a strong beat. Name the fingers, thumb, pointer, middle, ring, pinky. To start, have the children tap all the fingers on the table eight times. Next, starting with the thumb, they tap each finger eight times in order. In the next round, they will tap four times, followed by two, and then one. As they are able to independently move their fingers, the beat can speed up.

▲ Finger play is a fun way to work on independent use of the fingers.

thumb is at the top and the pinky finger closer to the paper (arm and hand are moved as a unit). The movement initiates with the shoulder to move the marker across the paper. With continued use and practice, the infant uses a palmar grasp, in which the palm faces down and the elbow is out to the side. The next type of grip is an immature five-finger pencil grasp. Five fingers hold the pencil and the wrist is usually off the table, with the initiation of movement changing from the shoulder to the wrist, an example of proximal to distal development. By around 5 to 6 years of age, a three-finger pencil grip is used. Eventually, wrist movements change to finger muscle control to draw and write letters. The dynamic tripod, the most efficient way to grip a pencil, develops by 7 years of age. In this grasp, the pencil is positioned between between the thumb and index finger and the pencil rests on the middle finger. With age and practice, the child's posture becomes more upright and the trunk and hand more stable. Additionally, the positioning of the hand is more in line with the forearm (see **video** Improving Fine Motor with Occupational Therapy: Meet Sylvie).

Reaching does not appear to be a continuous change. Infants develop reaching skills by doing (Thelen, et al., 1993). Within the first few months of life, the infant's arm movements change from random, reflexive actions to the successful reaching for objects. This change in action appears to be due to "learning by doing" (Thelen, et al., 1993). Infants appear to adjust the tension in their arms and to move the hand close to the object. As they repeat this action, their actions become more efficient and consistent. Older children and adults have a controlled smooth motion when reaching for an object. The movement is initiated by the arm moving forward as the hand opens to the size of the object.

Vision is important in the development of reaching and grasping. Infants frequently knock at an object before actually grasping, whereas older children and adults configure the size of the hand prior to contact with the object. Infants reach and then grasp, whereas older children and adults open the hand as they are reaching toward the object. The use of vision changes between 5 and 10 years of age to optimize anticipation of the grasp and accuracy. Six- and 7-year-olds depend more on vision to configure their hand for the grasp (Kuhtz-Buschbeck et al., 1998), whereas 9- to 10-year-olds slowed down more than adults at the end of the reach (Pryde, Roy, & Campbell,1998) to successfully anticipate the closure of the hand around the object.

Eye–Hand Coordination.   The development of eye–hand coordination is critical to the ability to interact with the environment. The visual and tactile systems work together to provide us with information about objects in our environment. The information we receive from each system is similar, but not identical. The central nervous system receives, processes, and translates visual and tactile information into motor behavior. For eye–hand coordination to work, the eye muscles must direct the eye to what the hand is about to touch. Skills we use on a daily basis depend on basic eye–hand coordination skills. Patterns of muscular coordination are necessary to complete everyday skills such as dressing, writing, and even self-feeding. These activities contain three important motor operations: looking, reaching, and grasping. Puzzles, shape sorters, coloring, modeling clay, finger knitting, and throwing and catching help to develop eye–hand coordination.

Bimanual Control.   Reaching and grasping, as discussed previously, are for unilateral movements (movement of one side of the body); this section is focused on bilateral movements (use of two sides of the body), as most activities require coordination of both hands. There are two types of coordinated bimanual movements. One type involves active participation of both hands with similar or symmetrical movement. Some examples of this type of movement include clapping, playing patty-cake, finger knitting, knitting, and, eventually, juggling. The other type of movement involves the two hands using asymmetrical movements. One hand is used to manipulate while the other hand holds or stabilizes an object. Examples of this kind of movement include putting a block in a puzzle, buttoning, and using scissors. Alfonso, for instance, had learned to cut with his child-appropriate scissors. He practiced this bimanual motor activity over and over, creating a large pile of confetti. His caregiver had to make sure he had a large selection of scrap paper available for his work and that important papers were out of his reach!

Use of the two arms together appears around 2 months of age, with the infant extending and raising the arms. The infant clasps the hands at the midline of the body. By about 5.5 months, the infant can reach for an object with both hands; however, at this time, one hand usually grasps the object. Around 8 months the infant starts to independently use the two arms and will hold one object in each hand. Around this age, many infants will insist that they have a cracker in each hand! After around 12 months, infants can pull objects apart and insert one object into another. Between 8 and 18 months, children use a variety of bimanual actions, ranging from holding a toy with both hands and switching an object from one hand to the other, to more complex symmetrical actions, such as holding a jar and turning the lid to explore and manipulate toys (Greaves, Imms, Krumlinde-Sundholm, Dodd, & Eliasson, 2012). By the end of the second year, children start to perform complementary activities, such as threading large beads on a string or stick (Haywood & Getchell, 2009).

The size, configuration, and complexity of toys may interfere with the child completing the task if he or she has not previously watched and experienced some of the possibilities. Showing the child how the toy works can assist in the use of the toy (Greaves et al., 2012). When the size of the object is matched to the scale of the child, the pattern and quality of the movement parallel the pattern and quality of an adult. Thus, task constraints play a major role in grip pattern.

Some children have trouble with coordinated use of the hands. Children with developmental delays have very brief visual monitoring of their hands, inaccurate reaching, and immature hand grasp. Children born blind do not use their hands to explore objects; they simply bring them to their mouths. Creating objects with different textures, shapes, and weights can provide novel information and perhaps help engage the child in exploration with the hands.

Some children have difficulty with bilateral hand use. This difficulty usually stems from a combination of motor and cognitive delays. Children with cognitive delays are unable to attend to two things at once. They have difficulty using one hand to stabilize and the other to perform a different task. Activities that encourage bilateral hand use include pushing large objects with both hands, holding a cup while pouring rice and then a liquid into it, holding a slice of bread while spreading jelly, coloring, or holding a puzzle to place the pieces. Finding a variety of activities to engage the child in the use of this skill is important.

Exposure and engagement in fine motor skills is important. Children experiencing fine motor delays have been found to spend less time on play that requires fine motor skills. Children with more highly developed skills are those who have spent time on play activities that require fine motor skills. For example, a child may prefer to play with large blocks and avoid smaller toys such as Legos. Children should be encouraged to participate in activities that not only address fine motor deficit areas but also are interesting to the child. An example of how this could be done is to use Duplo blocks first and gradually substitute the smaller Legos. In addition, finger plays, as well as manipulative materials such as clay and wax, are valuable to assist with fine motor control.

5.5 Understand the Role Culture Plays in Planning Movement and Musical Activities

It is always important to consider culture when planning lessons on movement concepts and fine and gross motor skills. Each culture has customs and traditions that affect the significance of the skills. Tools that are important to one culture may not be used at all in another culture. For example, some cultures use chopsticks for eating. With a family from China, you might be working at cross purposes by having a child use a fork and spoon. It would be the same trying to teach an American child to use chopsticks. In some cultures, children are given writing materials around the age of 1 year. Most American families, though, prefer to wait until children are able to understand that these tools are to be used on paper, not on walls or clothing.

Another culturally linked family consideration is the importance of play. Diverse groups may view play differently. One group may define play as anything not related to academics. Another culture/family group may view everything a child does as play. Finally, some culture/family groups may place a strong emphasis on play and its related social skills. The reason for these differences can be attributed to lack of appropriate play space and props or toys, and/or to the fact an adult is not always present to serve as a role model and to stimulate play. Some groups may also value fine motor manipulative skills, whereas others may place a higher value on gross motor skills. Often this difference is based on adult role models. Alejandro's father, for instance, is interested in football. He encourages Alejandro to spend playtime kicking and throwing a ball. Across the street from Alejandro's family live Lucas and his family, who like to spend their time reading and building models, and they encourage Lucas to build things with clay and paper.

Children throughout the world share the same movement developmental sequences, reflexes, rudimentary motor skills, and fundamental motor patterns. The child's inherited culture, though, may dictate the pace and sometimes the sequence of progress through the attainment of the skills. The child's culture may encourage mastery of specific movement activities at the game and sport level.

The universal norms used to define ages and stages of motor development were advanced in 1928 with the research of Arnold Gesell and became the stimulus for the Bayley and Denver Scales (Karasik, Adolph, Tamis-LeMonda, 2010). The child-rearing practices of a particular culture may explain the acceleration or the delay of a particular motor milestone (see Table 5.3).

Table 5.3 Child-Rearing Practices and Motor Milestones (Davis, et al., 1998; Hopkins & Westra, 1988; Mei, 1994)

Motor Skill	Country/Region	Intervention	Result	Documentation
Sitting, walking	Africa Caribbean India	Massage and stretching of infant's body	Earlier onset of norms	Hopkins & Westra, 1988
Sitting, crawling, walking	China	Toilet training practice of seating child in sand to provide sensory feedback	Later onset of norms	Mei, 1994
Crawling	United States	Placing infants to sleep on their backs rather than on their stomachs	Later onset of norm	Davis, Moon, Sachs, & Ottolini, 1998

Developmental movement norms are averages based on a sampling of infants and children. There will always be individuals who will accelerate at a motor skill or experience a delayed of the onset of a particular motor skill. It is also important to take into consideration the child-rearing practices of particular cultures that value different postural and locomotor skills (Adolph, Karasik, & Tamis-LeMonda, 2010).

Culture plays a role in the development of concepts and motor skills, particularly fundamental motor patterns and sport mastery skills. American children spend time throwing and catching a ball (baseball and American football); Spanish children spend time practicing kicking a ball (soccer [called football outside the United States]). These choices are based on the dominant sport played in the respective countries.

The environment influences the development of the child because the culture has an impact on the schools, teachers, and families. Children want to model the physical activities they see. Within a culture, families will have a sport or game they value. The result is that their children are encouraged to participate in the desired sport.

The role culture plays in the development of movement skills is important. Once again, it is part of the environment guiding the conscious and unconscious behavior of schools, teachers, and parents.

5.6 *Enhance Family and Community Involvement in Movement and Music*

For the child to develop movement concepts and motor skills, family and community involvement is also very important. Both parent and sibling involvement influence child participation in physical activity. Community engagement allows for maximum use of facilities and creates connections among school, after school, and community engagement.

Healthy People 2020 (2013) objectives call for schools to allow increased access to physical activity spaces outside normal school hours. Information on the website for early and middle childhood includes objectives for increasing the proportion of families who use positive parenting. Evidenced-based resources are provided to promote health literacy, self-discipline, decision making, eating habits, and conflict negotiation. Parents are not only role models on healthy decision making, but they should also include their children in the decision making, explaining why they are making their various choices. This provides children with a feeling of control.

ChangeLab Solutions provides a toolkit for joint use agreements to open school grounds to the community (http://changelabsolutions.org/publications/CA-JUA-toolkit). A community mapping tool is available at KaBoom! Playspace Finder—Community Mapping Tool (http://mapofplay.kaboom.org/?utm_source=psf&utm_medium=se-redirect). The user enters a zip code and the mapping tool finds play spaces in the area. We entered 15221, for example, and identified 12 local areas to play.

The Centers for Disease Control and Prevention (CDC) provides guidelines for engaging families in schools. It recommends that to make a positive connection, parents must be fully engaged in the school. A positive connection helps the parents feel as though they are part of the school and that they are involved with the faculty, staff, and students. To maintain the connection, the schools need to engage the families frequently in a variety of culturally relevant activities, such as "family fun nights." Sustaining parent engagement is critical; families need to feel empowered to make a difference.

Parents should demonstrate their love of movement and music. Dads and moms can make up songs and move to the music as they do their chores. They can engage their children in the movement of the action. Pots and pans make wonderful drums to engage the children and provides a beat to move to. Families should attend community band concerts, parades, sporting events, and even just hikes through the woods to expose their children to a variety of movement and music choices.

Summary

Movement and music are related through expression both in skilled and unskilled movement and through expression of the emotional joy of making music. Coordinated movement has flow and rhythm, as does music. In early learning, movement and music are frequently coupled to provide expression of action. Children move fast with the fast music; they move in unbound flow with free-form music.

Early movement learning is based on learning concepts that include movement and fitness concepts. Movement concepts include body awareness, space awareness, movement qualities, and relationships. Fitness concepts include cardiovascular endurance, muscular strength and endurance, flexibility, and body composition.

Fine motor development of the hands begins with body stabilization and depends on exposure and practice manipulating the fingers and hands. Bimanual control is the coordinated use of the two hands; it can be the hands doing the same thing, such as clapping, or they can be doing two different things, such as rubbing the head while patting the belly.

Culture and family influence the selection and pace of both gross and fine motor development. Therefore, the community should be involved in the encouragement of both movement and music.

Summary Related to Outcomes

Learning Outcomes	Guiding Principles
5.1 Understand the relationship of movement and music	Environment and Curriculum Reciprocated
Movement and music provide multisensory learning. Infants begin life with an innate rhythm. Music can enhance movement learning through rhythm.	

Learning Outcomes	Guiding Principles
5.2 Know the content of developmentally appropriate movement	Environment and Curriculum Reciprocated

The content of developmentally appropriate physical education for children emphasizes the learning of movement and fitness concepts. This provides the language for motor skill development.

Learning Outcomes	Guiding Principles
5.3 Create lessons to enhance understanding of movement concepts	Environment and Curriculum Reciprocated

Movement concepts include body awareness, space awareness, movement qualities, and relationships. Teaching of these concepts should be based on movement education, guided discovery, and inclusion styles of teaching.

Learning Outcomes	Guiding Principles
5.4 Create lessons to enhance development of fine motor skills	Environment and Curriculum Reciprocated

A foundation of gross motor skills is needed to develop fine motor skills. Exposure and practice are important in the development of fine motor skills. Selecting the appropriate size materials to manipulate is critical for the development of the skill.

Learning Outcomes	Guiding Principles
5.5 Understand the role culture plays in planning movement and musical activities	Family and Community Involved

Providing a variety of culturally relevant movement and music is important for developing movement for a lifetime.

Learning Outcomes	Guiding Principles
5.6 Enhance family and community involvement in movement and music	Family and Community Involved

Both parent and sibling involvement influence a child's participation in physical activity and music. Engaging the family in developing movement skills enhances the likelihood that the child and family will meet the physical activity guidelines. The school needs to connect and engage the parents and sustain family involvement.

Demonstrate Your Knowledge, Skills, and Dispositions

Students will demonstrate knowledge, comprehension, analysis, and evaluation of Learning Outcomes related to Guiding Principles.

Learning Outcomes	Guiding Principles
5.1 Understand the relationship of movement and music	Environment and Curriculum Reciprocated

- Select a piece of music that makes you feel happy, and another piece that makes you sad. Play the music and move to the music. Describe the type of movements you made. Play the same music for a classmate and describe the classmate's movements. Are they similar?

Learning Outcomes	Guiding Principles
5.2 Know the content of developmentally appropriate movement	Environment and Curriculum Reciprocated

- One of the children in your class is using too much force when she colors. How would you help the child reduce the force?

Learning Outcomes	Guiding Principles
5.3 Create lessons to enhance understanding of movement concepts	Environment and Curriculum Reciprocated

- Select three movement concepts and find music and songs that enhance understanding these concepts.

Learning Outcomes	Guiding Principles
5.4 Create lessons to enhance development of fine motor skills	Environment and Curriculum Reciprocated

- Give two examples of how music can enhance the development of fine motor skills.

Learning Outcomes	Guiding Principles
5.5 Understand the role culture plays in planning movement and musical activities	Family and Community Involved

- Ask the children if their families like to go to dances (e.g., Greek, contra dancing, square dancing). Discuss the families' participation and have different children demonstrate the dances.

Learning Outcomes	Guiding Principles
5.6 Enhance family and community involvement in movement and music	Family and Community Involved

- Develop a list of activities that will engage the parents in the school.

Planning for Engaging

The following learning activities provide three possibilities or ways to develop a standard taken from the M^2 Movement Standard.

M^2 Movement Standard: The child will develop the concepts of fine motor control by developing finger strength, coordination and eye–hand coordination.

Objective	Objective	Objective
Child will move the fingers individually.	Child will move the fingers individually.	Child will move the fingers individually.
Learning Activity	**Learning Activity**	**Learning Activity**
Ten Little Fingers (Song)	Finger Family	Ten little peas in a pea pod pressed
Tune: "Ten Little Indians"	Finger family up and finger family down	One grew
One little, two little, three little fingers.	Finger family dancing	Two grew
Four little, five little, six little fingers.	All around the town	and so did all the rest

Seven little, eight little, nine little fingers. Ten little fingers on my hand. One little, two little, three little piggy toes, . . . etc. Ten little toes on my feet.	Dance them on your shoulders, Dance them on your head Dance them on your knees and tuck them into bed.	and they grew bigger and Bigger and BIGGER until it POPPED !! Movements: 10 peas, form a fist. One grew—bring one finger out and bring out the others individually. Fingers "grow" and hands clap when the "pod" is popped.
Assessment Observe independent use of fingers.	**Assessment** Observe independent use of fingers.	**Assessment** Observe independent use of fingers.

Now You Try It

Complete the following standard-based learning activity designed to meet various interests and developmental levels. Design two learning possibilities (Possibility Two and Possibility Three) or learning activities to develop the following standard taken from M^2 Movement Standard.

M^2 K–2 Movement Standard: The child will apply an understanding of force absorption to developing a movement skill.		
Possibility One	**Possibility Two**	**Possibility Three**
Landing: Jump up three times. Jump up and land with straight legs. How did that feel? Now jump up and land while bending your legs. How did that feel? How should you land when jumping? With bent legs. Now let's practice jumping. Jump up, jump over, jump off the box, jump on one foot, the other foot. Jump to the music.		
Assessment Listen to the children jumping. You should not hear a heavy sound as they land.	**Assessment**	**Assessment**

References

Abels, K., & Bridges, J. (2010). *Teaching movement education: foundations for active lifestyles.* Champaign, IL: Human Kinetics Publishers.

Adolph, K.E., Karasik, L.B., & Tamis-LeMonda, C. S. (2010). Motor skill. In M. H. Bornstein (Ed.), *Handbook of cultural developmental science* (pp. 61–88). New York: Psychology Press.

Brook, B., Wagenfeld, A., & Thompson, C. (n.d.) *Fingergym fine motor skills.* Samford Valley, Queensland, Australia: Academic Press, http://www.fingergym.info/downloads/ Finemotordevpp1-4.pdf. Accessed June 16, 2013.

Davis, B. E. , Moon, R.Y., Sachs, H.C., and Ottolini, M.C. (1998). Effects of sleep position on infant motor development. *Pediatrics, 102,* 1135–1140.

Greaves, S., Imms, C., Krumlinde-Sundholm, L., Dodd, K., & Eliasson, A.C. (2012). Bimanual behaviours in children aged 8–18 months: A literature review to select toys that elicit the use of two hands. *Research in Developmental Disabilities, 33,* 240–250.

Haywood, K. & Getchell, N. (2009). *Life span motor development* (5th ed). Champaign, IL: Human Kinetics Publishers.

Healthy People 2020. (2013). 2020 Topics & Objectives: Early and middle childhood. http://healthypeople.gov/2020/topicsobjectives2020/overview.aspx?topicId=10.

Hopkins, B. & Westra, T. (1988). Maternal handling and motor development: An intracultural study. *Genetic, Social and General Psychology Monographs, 114,* 379–408.

ICHPER·SD (n.d.) International standards for physical education and sport for school children. http://ichpersd.org/index.php/standards/international-standards.

Karasik, L. B., Adolph, K. E., Tamis-LeMonda, C. S., & Zuckerman, A. L. (2010). Carry on: Spontaneous object carrying in 13-month-old crawling and walking infants. *Developmental Psychology, 48,* 389–397.

Kuhtz-Buschbeck, J., Stolze, H., Boczek-Funcke, A., Joehnk, K., Heinrichs, H., & Illert, M. (1998). Kinematic analysis of prehension movements in children. *Behavioural Brain Research, 93,* 131–141.

Laban, R., & Ullmann, L. (1963) *Modern educational dance* (2nd ed.). London: Macdonald & Evans, Ltd.

Lee, M., Liu, Y., & Newell, K. (2006). Longitudinal expressions of infant's prehension as a function of object properties. *Infant Behavior and Development, 29*(4), 481–493.

Mei, J. (1994). The northern Chinese custom of rearing babies in sandbags: Implications for motor and intellectual development. In J.H.A. van Rossum and J. I. Laszo (Eds.). *Motor development:Aspects of normal and delayed development.* Amsterdam, Netherlands: VU Uitgeverij.

Mosston, M., & Ashworth, S. (2002). *Teaching physical education* (5th Ed.). Boston: Benjamin Cummings.

National Association for Sport and Physical Education (1995). *Looking at physical education from a developmental perspective: A guide to teaching.* Reston, VA: AAHPERD.

National Association for Sport and Physical Education (2004a). *Moving into the future: National standards for physical education* (2nd ed.) Reston, VA: AAHPERD.

National Association for Sport and Physical Education (2004b). *Physical activity for children: A statement of guidelines for children 5–12* (2nd Ed.). Reston, VA: AAHPERD.

National Association for Sport and Physical Education (2006). *Recess for elementary school students*. Reston, VA: AAHPERD.

National Association for Sport and Physical Education (2009). *Active start: A statement of physical activity guidelines for children from birth to age 5* (2nd Ed.). Reston VA: AAHPERD.

National Association for Sport and Physical Education (n.d.) *Appropriate practices in movement programs for children ages 3–5* (3rd Ed.). Reston, VA: AAHPERD.

Phillips-Silver, J., & Trainor, L.J. (2005). Feeling the beat: Movement influences infant rhythm perception. *Science*, 308, 1430. www.sciencemag.org/cgi/content/full/308/5727/1430/DC1.

Pryde, K., Roy, E. & Campbell, K. (1998). Prehension in children and adults: The effects of size. *Human Movement Science*, 17(6), 743–752.

Sievers, B., Polansky, L., Casey, M., & Wheatley, T. (2013). Music and movement share a dynamic structure that supports universal expressions of emotion. *Proceedings of the National Academy of Sciences*, 110(1), 70–75. doi: 10.1073/pnas.1209023110.

Thelen, E., Corbetta, D., Kamm, K., Spencer, J., Schneider, K., & Zernicke, R. (1993). The transition to reaching: Mapping intention and intrinsic dynamics. *Child Development*, 64, 1058–1098.

Wrotniak, B., Epstein, L., Dorn, J., Jones, K. & Kondilis, V. (2006). The relationship between motor proficiency and physical activity in children. *Pediatrics* 118(6), e1758–e1765. doi:10.1542/peds2006-0742.

chapter 6

Dance and Music: A Healthy Lifestyle Partnership

LEARNING OUTCOMES AND GUIDING PRINCIPLES

Students reading this text will be able to demonstrate Learning Outcomes linked to Guiding Principles based on the National Association for the Education of Young Children's *Developmentally Appropriate Practice in Early Childhood Programs Serving Children from Birth through Age 8.*

Learning Outcomes	Guiding Principles
6.1 Determine the importance of dance	Movement and Music Integrated
6.2 Describe dance standards	Standards and Assessment Provide Guidance
6.3 Explain teaching dance	Environment and Curriculum Reciprocated
6.4 Formulate dances	Environment and Curriculum Reciprocated

> ## Making Connections
> ### Power of Dance
>
> The night is dark, scary, and filled with many strange-looking creatures. It is BooZoo! The merry-go-round is going in the opposite direction, zoo staff members are dressed in creepy costumes, and at every turn there is a menacing display designed to delight the little Halloween guests as they grab candy from large plastic jack-o-lanterns. The animals living at the zoo, and the children visiting the zoo, are not concerned. They know it is all fun! Eight-year-old Natalie, who is dressed as Scooby Doo, and her four-year-old brother, Henry, clad as an Angry Bird, are there to enjoy the fun. After visiting exciting and scary booths and displays, they wander into the dancing area where lively music is playing over the loudspeakers. Immediately, Natalie and Henry join the dancing skeletons, witches, pumpkins, and other strange creatures. Natalie moves to the beat of the music, doing robot movements with her arms, legs, and head. Henry moves his weight from one hip to the other until his father encourages him to "shake his tail feathers." This command puts Henry into creative motion, shaking his tail while alternating the movement of his arms in upward thrusting motions. Henry completes his dance with his interpretation of break dancing, hands on the ground and spinning around. What a wonderful time Natalie and Henry had at the BooZoo—Natalie said it was "awesome"!

6.1 *Determine the Importance of Dance*

Dance is "awesome" because it is an art form that enhances physical activity and provides many physiological and psychological benefits important to young children. Dance, a physical activity that improves aerobic capacity, flexibility, balance, and muscle development, uses nonlocomotor and locomotor motor skills to express creative thoughts and experiences. It also crosses over from a physical education activity to the arts area—it is a creative bridge between movement and music.

The majority of people who hear music start to move just like Natalie and Henry did when they heard the music at BooZoo. Ellen DeGeneres, for example, knows how important dance is in uniting an audience, using dance five days a week at the beginning of her talk show to stimulate unifying movements and to excite the audience. Dance is a form of expres-

▲ Grandfather and granddaughters enjoy dancing together.

sion linked to controlled rhythmic movements (Kealiinohomoku, 2001). Weikart (2003, p. 3) states that "rhythmic movement performed to music is one of the most exciting and unifying experiences we can provide for children and adults."

Dance is vital in the lives of young children because it helps them understand and enjoy the movement of their bodies in a fun and creative way. It also provides a way to use music to develop an awareness of the culture and traditions surrounding the child and his or her family and community. In addition, dance activities lead to a physically active and healthy lifestyle.

Dance is one of the four forms of the arts (drama, visual arts, music, and dance) (Ballisti & Haibach, 2011) in the New Zealand early childhood curriculum Te Whāriki. This national curriculum recognizes the importance of both health and physical education, but it also recognizes the arts as an essential learning area that provides opportunities to learn about cultural practices and enhance creativity (Sansom, 2009). In addition, when they dance, children gain control of their bodies while increasing agility, improving coordination, and increasing balance while learning to move in space to a rhythm.

Most children enjoy moving to music in a rhythmic manner. Dance should be done for the pure delight it provides to children and to the adults moving with the children. National standards, as with music, physical education, or academic areas, provide guidance in planning dance movement activities for children.

6.2   *Describe Dance Standards*

The National Dance Association (NDA, 2012) has developed dance standards to provide guidance in engaging children in dance, learning the language of dance, and developing and enhancing motor skills. The seven National Dance Association standards help the teacher provide quality and accountability in the creative dance environment. They offer guidance but are broad enough to encourage educators to adapt the application of the standards to the interests and abilities of the children and teachers, as follows (reprinted with permission from the American Alliance for Health, Physical Education, Recreation and Dance, www.AAHPERD.org):

- *Standard 1:* Identify and demonstrate movement elements and skills in performing dance.
- *Standard 2:* Understand choreographic principles, processes, and structures.
- *Standard 3:* Understand dance as a way to create and communicate meaning.
- *Standard 4:* Apply and demonstrate critical and creative thinking skills in dance.
- *Standard 5:* Demonstrate and understand dance in various cultures and historical periods.
- *Standard 6:* Make connections between dance and healthful living.
- *Standard 7:* Make connections between dance and other disciplines.

The standards outline how the movement of dance combined with music stimulates the creative process and critical thinking, communicates meaning, provides cultural background, and enhances healthful living because of physical activity.

Comparison of Dance, Physical Education, and Music Standards

Dance and physical education standards are similar because dance is an art form that is a physical activity incorporating nonlocomotor and locomotor movements (McGreevy-Nichols, Scheff, & Sprague, 2001). Music is definitely part of a dance program, and the music standards provide similarities and understanding to the dance standards. It is interesting to see how the music, dance, and physical education standards mesh with one another (see Table 6.1).

In Table 6.1, the music and the physical education standards are compared and categorized according to the dance standards. Some deficits in the music and physical education standards are found when they are compared with the dance standards.

The physical education standards do not emphasize creativity, communication, critical thinking, cultures, historical periods, and connection to other disciplines. The music standards do not enforce a healthy lifestyle. Therefore, dance plays an important role in the education of young children because it connects music and physical education and unifies all disciplines in an effort to develop a healthy child.

M² FUN   Dance: Magic Circle

Begin the activity by having all the children form a tight circle, shoulder to shoulder. The teacher is positioned in the center of the circle. As the teacher moves, the circle will also move. The circle can maintain the same position on the floor and rotate direction, or it can move about the room. Once the children have mastered the group movement concept, the large group can be divided into smaller groups moving about the room.

Table 6.1 Comparison of the National Dance, Physical Education, and Music Standards

Dance	Physical Education	Music
Identify and demonstrate movement elements and skills in performing dance.	• Demonstrate competency in motor skill to perform physical activities	• Sing • Perform with musical instruments
Understand choreographic principles, processes, and structures.	• Demonstrate understanding of movement • Exhibit behavior respectful of others in physical activity settings	• Compose and arrange music • Read and notate music
Understand that dance is a way to create and communicate meaning.		• Improvise musical patterns
Apply and demonstrate critical and creative thinking in dance.		• Listen to, analyze, and describe music and performance
Demonstrate and understand dance in various cultures and historical periods.		• Understand the relationship between musical history and culture
Make connections between dance and healthful living.	• Value physical activity for health, enjoyment, challenge, self-expression • Maintain health, enhancing physical fitness • Participate regularly in physical activity	
Make connections between dance and other disciplines.		• Understand the relationships among music, the arts, and other disciplines

(Column 1 and column 2 reprinted with permission from the American Alliance for Health, Physical Education, Recreation and Dance, www.AAHPERD.org. Column 3 summarized from National Association for Music Education (2012).)

Movement Elements in Dance

When presenting dance activities, it is important to remember the four key elements of movement: nonlocomotor, locomotor, integrated, and manipulative (moving with an object) (Weikart, 2003) (see Table 6.2).

Table 6.2 Types of Movement Linked to Dance

Dance Key	Description	Examples
Nonlocomotor movement	Body anchored in space	• Stomp foot on floor • Tap heel and then toe to floor • Kick one leg into the air
Locomotor movement	Body unanchored in space	• Move forward and backward • Move into the center of a circle and back out • Move to the side while facing forward • Turn the body in a circle
Integrated movement	Creative movement	• Move to a steady beat, demonstrating animal movements
Manipulative movement	Using an object to reposition, manipulate, and extend movement	• Move a scarf in circles • Jump over and through a hoop

When dance is viewed as locomotor or nonlocomotor movement, it is easy to feel confident in integrating it into the daily activities of children. Teachers and parents can simply provide a rhythm and have children stomp, kick, walk, and sway to engage in dance.

Dance must be part of every curriculum for young children because it can contribute experiences that will help children develop creativity and critical thinking skill. It can also enhance the understanding of other cultures and historical periods in a relevant and appropriate manner. Finally, dance can enhance learning because of its relationship to multiple intelligences.

Creativity and Critical Thinking Skills

Creativity is undeniably an important part of dance, but it should be valued throughout the entire education system, especially when working with young children. Creativity and imagination are where all new ideas begin. The world of children depends on new ideas in technology, energy, and environment. All children have imaginative and creative thoughts. It is vital that we stimulate children's imagination, curiosity, and creativity so that as they mature, they can continue to make connections to ideas in new and exciting ways.

Teachers should design a learning environment where children are free to express their thoughts without fear of being wrong. Shereen's kindergarten teacher, for instance, had given each child a piece of 8½" × 11" sheet of white paper. The children were instructed to draw the biggest circle they could on the paper. All the children in the class settled in to work, except Shereen—who raised her hand and asked the teacher for a bigger piece of paper! As educators, we cannot place limitations on the creative thought.

Sir Ken Robinson (2006) has stated that we are squandering children's innate imagination and creativity abilities. He also feels that creativity is as important as literacy and should be valued on the same level as literacy. By teaching dance, especially creative or interpretive dance, creativity and innovation skills will be nourished, not diminished.

The early childhood schools of Reggio Emilia, Italy, are built on the philosophy of helping children develop creative connections in understanding a problem through experimentation that later leads to theories (Vecchi, 2010). Arts play an important role in the Reggio Emilia creative educational process and are considered an important part of Reggio Emilia's "one hundred languages of childhood" (Rinaldi, 2006). Children speak to the world in many ways, not just through mathematics and language. The arts, including dance, are a way in which children communicate.

Dance strengthens creativity and offers children a way to communicate feeling and knowledge—for example, ask children to move as if they are happy, sad, or angry and observe the differences in movement for each emotion. It also enforces critical thinking. When children begin to engage in dance, they must *remember* the steps and motions. Next, they need to *understand* the interpretive nature of the movement while *applying* it to rhythmic patterns. Finally, as they become more comfortable with the movement, they will become choreographers who *analyze, evaluate,* and finally *create* new movements for dances. They will be practicing and developing the levels of the revised Bloom's Taxonomy. We must therefore value and teach dance.

Role of Dance in Cultures and History

It is difficult to state when people first began to dance. Archeological finds from primitive groups suggest that people have been dancing for thousands of years (Kealiinohomoku, 2001). People have danced for a wide variety of reasons, such as battle preparations, life ceremonies, and play. Dance has also been used to tell a story. The forms of dance done throughout the world are vast and unique to each culture.

M² FUN   Animal Dance

Children select from a bag of assorted small plastic animals. The assortment should contain farm and zoo animals, as well as some unusual animals or monsters. Each child will select an animal and create the movement, using the entire body, that he or she feels the animal would make. The atypical animals will provide more opportunities for additional creativity.

Differences in dance are due not only to the reason for the dance but also to the physical difference and learned cultural patterns of the people performing the dance (Kealiinohomoku, 2001). Dances should not be viewed as representing one large group of people, such as Native Americans or Africans—there are Iroquois, Kwakiutl, or Hopi dances, not solely one Native American dance (Kealiinohomoku, 2001). Similarly, Africa is composed of many countries; each country has its own dances. Educators should no longer have the children make headbands with paper feathers and have them form a circle, hop on one foot and then the other while singing a chant to represent Native American dance. Instead, the teacher and the children should study the culture and the dance together and develop the dance together. The World Cultural Dance: Discover Folk Dances from Around the World website (see **video** World Dance Culture) provides a way to view different dances throughout the world. This will assist the teacher and the children in developing their own dances. The collective group can decide whether they wish to do a solo dance, a dance with another person, or a group dance (see **video** Jamaican Dancing Kids). Dance is a powerful tool in breaking down prejudices (Sarabhai, 2009).

Certain dances have been more popular at different historical periods in history than in others. The French minuet in the 1700s and the Charleston in the United States in the 1920s are examples of historical period dances. Popular dance styles change from decade to decade. Once,

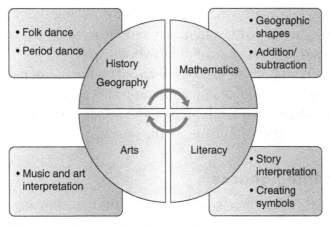

F i g u r e 6.1 Linking dance to the curriculum.

the twist was the dance everyone was doing. Today, the moonwalk or Gangnam Style may be the fad. Children are aware of the popular dances and enjoy doing them (see **video** 2-year-old dancing the paso doble).

Curriculum Integration of Dance

Dance movement can strengthen and provide concrete involvement in many curriculum subjects (see Figure 6.1).

Learning dances associated with a particular historical period or geographic area will help children to understand and appreciate similarities among people throughout the world. Dances with prescribed steps should be simplified for young children. Avoid having children do a group of steps with more than one partner or detailed movement patterns.

Geometric shapes can become concrete by having the children make squares, triangles, and circles with gross movements of the trunk, arms, and legs. Simply grouping children on the dance floor into groups of twos, threes, or fours will provide visual understanding of counting, addition, and subtraction.

Literacy can be enforced by having children select a movement—such as a sway, twirl, or shake—for each character in a familiar story. As the story is read, the children will do the character's movement when the character's name is mentioned. To promote writing skills, children can design a series of symbols to represent dance elements such as a jump or twirl (Logue, Robie, Brown, & Waite, 2008). Asking them to perform a bend, stretch, jump, or twist to depict various words, such as *jello*, *snakes*, *waves*, or *clouds*, can expand children's vocabulary.

Drama, art, and music can be enhanced by the use of dance to stimulate creativity in costume design and sound effects for a dance. In addition to stories, children can interpret famous paintings, sculptures, or tapestries through dance. Dance stimulates all the intelligences.

Multiple Intelligences

Dance strengthens, connects, and complements the following intelligences:

- Musical
- Bodily-kinesthetic
- Logical-mathematical
- Spatial

Music is needed to provide the rhythm for dance movement. Body parts move during dance, resulting in stimulation of the bodily-kinesthetic intelligence. Steps must be counted during movement to the rhythm (logical-mathematical), and an awareness of other dancers while moving will improve spatial intelligence. When children are exposed to the concrete movements of dance, they will begin to develop an understanding of the similarities and differences of movement within and between different cultures and historical time periods. Intelligences will be strengthened and complemented.

M² FUN   Dance and the World

Have the children use basic nonlocomotor and locomotor movements as a warmup. They can shake hands, extend arms overhead and alternate arm movement (climb a ladder), stand on tiptoes, and bend from the waist. Put on music from different countries and just have the children move to the music. When they are done, have them describe how they felt.

Dances are composed of the same basic nonlocomotor and locomotor movements, making dance easy to teach and enjoyable to do.

6.3 *Explain Teaching Dance*

Dance is a powerful tool to use in the learning environment. It has been use to break down prejudices (Sarabhai, 2009). By teaching dances from other countries, we prepare our children for interaction in a world that is growing smaller and smaller as a result of improved communication and technology. We know that dance behaviors can enhance creativity and critical thinking skills and can help children have a healthy life by engaging in physical activity and communicating knowledge, skills, and dispositions. To achieve these advantages and to actively engage children in a dance program, attention must be given to teacher qualities, the environment, and music.

Teacher Qualities

Teachers' beliefs in performing a task shape their competence in teaching. If teachers have high self-efficacy in teaching the arts, they will probably include the arts in the curriculum; conversely, if they have low self-efficacy, they will probably not add the arts into the curriculum (Garvis & Pendergast, 2011). People use their learned self-efficacy beliefs to maintain control over their lives (Bandura, 1997). It has been established that we need to teach dance in the early childhood curriculum for a variety of reasons. Therefore, it is critical that teacher have high self-efficacy to teach dance. To ensure this, teacher preparation programs and teacher professional development programs should include a dance focus (Garvis & Pendergast, 2011). Teachers should recognize the importance of dance. If they have not received formal training in teacher preparation programs or workshops, they can engage in self-study through videos and books. It is also helpful to remember that children are beginners too. Even though some children may eventually develop into famous dancers such as Martha Graham or Mikhail Baryshnikov, no one will be in your classroom to critique how you teach dance and whether you doing every step "correctly." Enjoy movement through dance, and the children will enjoy dance too—it is just about being delighted with movement to music (see **video** Martha Graham's *Appalachian Spring*).

Dance Learning Environment

The environment used to teach dance is important and needs consideration. Most schools are not fortunate enough to have a separate space organized with smooth wood flooring and mirrors. Instead, you may have to move furniture to create an open space. Floors should be smooth and free of obstacles. It is important to review the environment to make sure it is safe and appropriate for the children's developmental level.

Attention must be given to the materials and equipment placed in the dance environment. The equipment should stimulate, extend, or accompany movements of the body (Cone & Cone, 2005). The following are some examples:

- Scarves
- Streamers/ribbons
- Sticks
- Ropes
- Containers (pots, baskets, boxes)
- Hoops

In addition, dance must be linked to strong rhythm patterns, so it is advisable to have the following items in the dance-learning environment:

- Drums
- Buckets (metal and plastic)
- Triangles
- Maracas
- Gongs
- Chimes
- Bells
- Cymbals
- Pot lids

It is not necessary to purchase expensive equipment. The children, teacher, and/or families can make many items. Dollar bargain stores have inexpensive scarves. Cutting plastic rings that are used to hold and transport six-packs of soda or juice into six circles and then tying yellow "caution" tape through the holes will provide each child with a streamer. Rope can be purchased in bulk at hardware or boat supply stores and cut into appropriate sections. Secondhand stores are a good place to find pots and lids to use to for hitting to provide a rhythm for dancing.

Mr. Sebastian is planning a dance activity for his kindergarten class. He reflected back on a ballet class he took as a 5-year-old and remembered that for the recital, the dancers had adult-decorated boxes. Festooned as presents with large bows, the dancers used the boxes to dance around and to extend their reach above their heads and to their sides. Mr. Sebastian decided to use this same idea but in a more child-appropriate manner. The children first decorated a box in whatever manner they wished with paper, material, yarn, and pompons. Once the boxes were completed, the children, with Mr. Sebastian's help, designed a dance using the boxes to dance around, leap over, extend over their bodies and to the sides of their bodies, and pass to other children. All the children had a wonderful time. They decided to decorate more boxes for their families and to invite their parents to a dance party.

Mr. Sebastian was wise enough to design a child-directed activity and to provide each child, and later their parents, with a piece of equipment that enhanced the dance. It is important for teachers to remember to have enough equipment and materials for each child. It is also vital to involve the families—not just as spectators, but also as movers.

Music Selection

Music plays an important role when designing dance activities. Every parent, caregiver, and teacher knows that if music plays, children will move. When selecting music, Weikart (2003) has suggested the following guidelines:

- Use instrumental music without words.
- Select music with a strong underlying beat.

- Employ music with eight- or sixteen-beat distinct phrases.
- Use music having two to three predictable parts.
- Select music of moderate pace or tempo.
- Use music that is familiar to the children.

If the dance music has words, the children may attend to the words rather than the beat (Weikart, 2003). Therefore, it is best to select dance music without words. The selection process should include music with an obvious beat or rhythm. Beat and dance are coupled together when selecting music. Just playing a steady beat on a drum or a plastic bucket will provide the necessary encouragement for young children to dance. A metronome deigned to provide a highly accurate beat simulation could also be purchased. It is also possible to download free software for mobile phones, tablets, and computers from the Internet. By selecting music that has predictable parts and is familiar to children, you will have already tapped into their knowledge base, and it will be easier to expand into new skills associated with the dance movements.

M² FUN Creative Dance Movements

Ask the children whether they have ever engaged in a snowball fight or a pillow fight. Have them describe their movements. Then explain that the class is going to have a pillow fight/snowball fight (children can choose). Explain that the only rule is that the children cannot touch each other—it is a pretend fight. Play Vivaldi's *Four Seasons—Winter* while the children are moving.

It is also helpful to remember that music inspires emotions. Rowen (1994) has made a number of suggestions when selecting music to convey an emotion or mood (see Table 6.3). Musical compositions of a variety of composers inspire emotions and movement when working with young children. It is important for teachers to assist children in recognizing that their movements can reflect their mood—for example, show them that bending over while walking can express the mental state of sadness or depression (Rowen, 1994). Teachers who are motivated to engage each child in their class in at

Table 6.3 Music Conveys Emotion

Emotion	Composer	Music Selection
Happiness or Joy	Sousa	*Washington Post March*
	Tchaikovsky	*Waltz of the Flowers*
	Gershwin	*An American in Paris*
Anger	Dukas	*The Sorcerer's Apprentice*
	Rachmaninoff	*Piano Concerto Number 1*
	Chopin	*Polonaise in A Flat Major*
Fear	Holst	*The Planets*
	Mussorgsky	*Night on Bald Mountain*
Sadness	Brahms	*Piano Concerto Number 2*
	Debussy	*Three Nocturnes*
Excitement	Stravinsky	*Firebird Suite*

least one dance movement activity daily, along with an appropriate dance environment, equipment, and music, set the stage for teaching dance.

Teaching Dance Movement

The early childhood curriculum is the delivery mode for the majority of children to learn dance knowledge, skills, and dispositions. Teachers should be prepared to provide locomotor and nonlocomotor movements to a beat or music. Teachers trained in appropriate motor behaviors and child development, and who possess enthusiasm, will provide children with opportunities for dance and the enjoyment of dance. These are an expansion of movement concepts (language of movement) applied to dance.

Many commercial dance studios offer a variety of dance programs, such as ballet, tap, and jazz, for young children. Such programs may not be practical for every family because of time and financial considerations. It is possible, though, to ask teachers to provide guidance to families about local commercial programs. Families selecting a dance studio should investigate the training the dance teachers have in child development to determine whether the teachers have the appropriate understanding of the

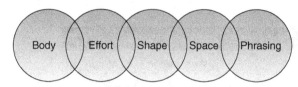

Figure 6.2 Laban's elements of movement analysis.

motor, cognitive, and social emotional stages of young children to ensure that appropriate activities are planned for the young child.

Dance should be integrated into the early childhood curriculum with scheduled periods that are not used as a substitute for recess or free choice time (Stinson, 1988). Early exposure to dance provides children with the tools and the confidence to engage and express themselves through movement (Ballisti & Haibach, 2011). There is a wide variety of dance styles, such as ballet, ballroom, square or folk dances, and street dance, but the style most appropriate for young children is creative or interpretive dance.

Describing how a child can perform nonlocomotor and locomotor movements is helpful in creating dance movements. Rudolf von Laban (1879–1958) was a dancer and scientist of movement who analyzed the elements of movement and provided descriptors for the movement. There are five Laban Movement Analysis (LMA) elements (Rowen, 1994) (see Figure 6.2).

Body. The LMA term *body* describes the movement in relationship to the total physical body. Because the body grows in a proximal–distal manner, it is easier for children to perform the following body movements compared with others (Weikart, 2003):

- Upper body movement rather than movement with weight-bearing parts of their body
- Trunk movements rather than limbs
- Gross motor movements rather than fine motor movements
- Nonlocomotor movements rather than locomotor movements
- Movement without an object rather than with a object
- Symmetrical movements rather than asymmetrical movements
- Single movements rather than sequenced movements
- Managing personal space rather than general space
- Movement timed to the individual's timing rather than external timing

It is important to remember this body information when developing dance movements for young children.

Effort. A description of how the movements are made entails the *effort* element. Is the action done quickly, with strong direct movements of the body, or are the movements slow, light, and indirect? If you ask the child to dance like a butterfly, are the movements in time, weight, and space appropriate to those of a butterfly or more like those of an elephant?

Shape and Space. Bodies take different *shapes* as they move through *space* when dancing. This may be a difficult concept to grasp for young children who are concrete thinkers. Teachers, for example, may hear, "Suzy hit me." Although this may be true, the reality is that Suzy did not realize how her body changed shape in her space around other children. The "hit," though upsetting, was an inadvertent part of the learning process. Such accidents can be avoided by discussing not only personal space when moving, but also how the personal space changes according to body position. Singing "I'm Tall, I'm Small" with appropriate actions will help children understand how shape and space change.

Each child can also be given an elastic loop to stretch or to contract to develop an awareness of how the shape changes size.

Another activity is to give each child a balloon. Tell the children to move the balloon high and then low and to one side and to the other. The additional space consumed by the balloon will help to show children how much space is required around them as they change shape.

Having the children play the "Freeze" game can further enforce shape and space. Play a selection of music or beat a drum or tambourine while the children move around their personal space or room. When the command "Freeze" is spoken and the music or beat stops, the children must freeze individually into a shape. While they are "frozen," ask them to see what body levels they are using and where their bodies are in relation to the shapes of other children. Freeze can also be done in groups—children freeze with other children to make combined shapes.

Phrasing. *Phrasing* will depict how a child will group movements together over a period of time or beat. It is an important element for young children to understand and to use when executing dance movements.

Phrasing forms patterns that, as in music, become familiar to the child, especially when repeated in a dance.

To assist children in understanding the concept of phrasing, begin with a steady eight-count beat on a drum, followed by a series of slower four beats. Repeat this series. Once the children have heard the series in a nonlocomotor position, have them wave their scarves only on the eight-count beats. Once this is mastered, use an instrumental version of the Beatles' song, "Let It Be." Give each child is given a scarf and have the children wave their scarves when they hear a repeating phrase.

Phrasing can also be taught using locomotor movement. For instance, have the children take eight steps and then eight jumps (Weikart, 2003). Phrasing is an import concept in dance and should be emphasized in developmentally appropriate ways.

6.4   *Formulate Dances*

Dance is using the body in nonlocomotor or locomotor movements in isolation or in combination, with or without props. The movement is varied to denote various degrees of effort while using different body shapes in space. The entire process is done in phrases to a steady beat or to music with a steady beat.

Begin by having the children do some stretching in their personal space. This is a good time to teach yoga stretching movements. The children should then do some aerobic movement, such as walking quickly. Ballisti and Haibach (2011) suggest marching in place to move the hips, followed by locomotor movements such as skipping, galloping, jumping, hopping, and turning. Once the children have completed this warmup, they can participate in longer dance movements in which a series of phrases are connected. Stinson (1988) suggests gallop, gallop, gallop, twirl around, and freeze, or curling up slowly and uncurling very fast.

Other ways to engage children in dance movement is to do the following:

- Interpret a painting or sculpture
- Move like animals, real and imaginary

▲ Children moving to music to create a dance.

- Interpret a familiar nursery rhyme or story
- Interpret a theme, such as the seasons of the year or the ocean
- Paint on an imaginary wall using various body parts
- Form letters using the body
- Perform Jaques-Dalcroze's eurhythmics

Although the last item is not considered a dance movement activity, it certainly is a good way to move the body to a beat in nonlocomotor and locomotor movements.

Eurhythmics, as well as all the dance activities mentioned in the preceding list, can be done in a daily dance time period or can be integrated into other subject areas (see **video** Kindergarten Eurythmy).

Older children may enjoy traditional dances, such as folk dances or square dances. The movements can be simplified to match the developmental level of the children. An easy way to motivate older children to dance is to have the children form a circle by holding hands. The circle moves to the right, left, and in and out while listening to a song such as "Oh, Susannah." Remember, younger children will do best in creative, open-ended dances.

Summary

Dance is an important part of the early childhood curriculum because it provides a way for children to move their bodies in a fun and creative manner. It is a tool for communication of emotions and knowledge and serves to encourage a healthy lifestyle. The National Dance Standards developed by the National Dance Association provide guidance when developing curricula for young children. Because dance is such an important part of the early childhood curriculum, teachers and parents are encouraged to view their strengths in teaching dance, not their own perceived weaknesses.

Dance is a combination of nonlocomotor and locomotor movements done in phases with the body in various shapes in a space. The concrete physical movements of dance can be used to enhance and strengthen other curriculum areas.

Summary Related to Outcomes

Learning Outcomes	Guiding Principles
6.1 Determine the importance of dance	Movement and Music Integrated
Dance provides many physiological and psychological benefits. It is a way to integrate the arts into the curriculum.	
6.2 Describe dance standards	Standards and Assessment Provide Guidance
The National Dance Association's seven standards provide curriculum guidance.	
6.3 Explain teaching dance	Environment and Curriculum Reciprocated
Teachers who enjoy movement and who understand child development are ready to teach dance. It is important to have an open and safe environment when engaging in dance activities. Equipment and materials should be present in adequate numbers for each child to enjoy. Music can be obtained from a variety of easy-to-use sources.	
6.4 Formulate dances	Environment and Curriculum Reciprocated
Dance is basic locomotor, nonlocomotor movement to music that can be combined with the manipulation of various objects.	

Demonstrate Your Knowledge, Skills, and Dispositions

Students will demonstrate knowledge, comprehension, analysis, and evaluation of Learning Outcomes related to Guiding Principles.

Learning Outcomes	Guiding Principles
6.1 Determine the importance of dance	Movement and Music Integrated
• What skills do you need to integrate music into the dance curriculum? Describe.	
6.2 Describe dance standards	Standards and Assessment Provide Guidance
• Pick a dance standard and describe how you would use it in your classroom.	
6.3 Explain teaching dance	Environment and Curriculum Reciprocated
• You have a drum. How would you use the drum to teach dance?	
6.4 Formulate dances	Environment and Curriculum Reciprocated
• Describe a dance you would teach. What music and equipment would you need?	

Planning for Engaging

The following learning activities provide three possibilities or ways to develop an M^2 Movement Standard.

M^2 **Movement Standard:** Children will move in a variety of ways (running, jumping, hopping, skipping)		
Possibility One	**Possibility Two**	**Possibility Three**
Children will divide into pairs. Each child in a pair will take turn being the leader. The leader will perform a locomotor movement of his or her choice and the partner must mirror the movement.	Children will divide into groups of two. The children move in locomotor movement over a given distance. Each member of the pair will take different space positions, opposite if possible: • High/low (standing/ kneeling) • Forward/backward • Right side/left side	Make up phrases for children to do to music. • Jump for four beats and walk on knees for four. • Seat-scoot for four beats and run for four beats. • Skip for four beats and crawl for four beats.

Assessment	Assessment	Assessment
The children will be observed as to how well they mirror the movement, length of time they are engaged, and ability to assume leadership and turn taking.	The children will be observed as to how they use critical thinking to solve the movement situations and length of time they are engaged.	The children will be observed as to how they perform various locomotor skills and their position in space.

Now You Try It

Complete the following standard-based learning activity designed to meet various interests and developmental levels. Design three possibilities or learning activities to develop a movement and music standard taken from M^2 Movement Standards.

M^2 **Movement Standard:** The child will demonstrate gross motor control by coordinating movements in the upper and/or lower body.		
Possibility One	**Possibility Two**	**Possibility Three**
Children will make tambourines from two paper plates. Give each child two plates. Decorate plates with markers and other art materials. Put the two plates together and staple around the edge (leave a small opening). Fill through opening with about two tablespoons of rice. Put on a selection of Spanish music (e.g., "Los Pollitos"). Children take their tambourines and move them at their waist, over their heads, and by their ankles. Once movements are mastered, add movements with feet.		
Assessment Observe whether children move their tambourines at the various locations.	**Assessment**	**Assessment**

References

Ballisti, J. & Haibach, P. (2011). Progression through movement: teaching dance to elementary student. *Journal of Physical Education, Recreation, & Dance*, 82(8), 14–16.

Bandura, A. (1997). *Self-efficacy: the exercise of control*. New York, NY: W.H. Freeman.

Cone, T., & Cone, S. (2005). *Teaching children dance*. Champaign, IL: Human Kinetics Publishers.

Ell, S. (2004). Preschool dance. *Journal of Dance Education*, 4(4), 119–121.

Garvis, S., & Pendergast, D. (2011). An investigation of early childhood teacher self-efficacy beliefs in the teaching of arts education. *International Journal of Education*, 12(9), 2–10.

Kealiinohomoku, J. (2001). An anthropologist looks at ballet as a form of ethnic dance. In A. Dils & A. Albright (Eds.). *Moving history/dance culture* (pp. 33–43). Middletown, CT: Wesleyan University Press.

Logue, M.E., Robie, M. Brown, M., & Waite, K. (2008). Read my dance; promoting early writing through dance. *Childhood Education*, 85(4), 216–222.

McGreevy-Nichols, S., Scheff, H., & Sprague, M. (2001). *Building more dances: blueprint for putting movement together*. Champaign, IL: Human Kinetics Publishers.

National Dance Association (2012). National Dance Standards, K–4. http://www.aahperd.org/nda/profDevelopment/standardsk-4.cfm.

Public Schools of North Carolina (2012). Foundations: early learning standards for North Carolina preschoolers. http://www.earlylearning.nc.gov/Foundations/pdf/BW_condensed.pdf.

Rinaldi, C. (2006). *In dialogue with Reggio Emilia: Listening, researching and learning*. Florence, KY: Taylor & Francis Publishers.

Robinson, K. (2006). Schools kill creativity. TED Talk. http://www.ted.com/talks/ken_robinson_says_schools_kill_creativity.html.

Rowen, B. (1994). *Dance and grow: developmental dance activities for three- through eight-year-olds*. Pennington, NJ: Princeton Book Co.

Sansom, A. (2009). Mindful pedagogy in dance: Honoring the life of the child. *Research in Dance Education*, 10(3), 1161–1176.

Sarabhai, M. (2009). Dance to change the world. TED Talk. http://www.ted.com/talks/mallika_sarabhai.html.

Stinson, S. (1988). *Dance for young children: finding the magic in movement*. Reston, VA: National Dance Association, AAHPERD.

Vecchi, V. (2010). *Art and creativity in Reggio Emilia: Exploring the role and potential of atelier in early childhood education*. New York, NY: Routledge.

Weikart, P. (2003). *Teaching movement and dance: A sequential approach to rhythmic movement*. Ypsilanti, MI: High/Scope Press.

chapter 7

Development of Gross Motor Skills for a Lifetime of Movement

LEARNING OUTCOMES AND GUIDING PRINCIPLES

Students reading this text will be able to demonstrate Learning Outcomes linked to Guiding Principles based on the National Association for the Education of Young Children's *Developmentally Appropriate Practice in Early Childhood Programs Serving Children from Birth through Age 8.*

Learning Outcomes	Guiding Principles
7.1 Coordination and balance underlie the development of gross motor skills	Individual Needs Met
7.2 Apply knowledge of movement skill development to lesson planning	Environment and Curriculum Reciprocated
7.3 Apply National Standards for Physical Education to selection of content for learning activities	Environment and Curriculum Reciprocated
7.4 Use music to enhance learning	Movement and Music Integrated
7.5 Provide a learning environment conducive to decision making and building confidence	Individual Needs Met

Making Connections
Motivation for Movement

Micki had difficulty adjusting to kindergarten. She was shy, a little overweight, and had not attended preschool. This was the first time she had been separated from her mother for an extended period of time. She also did not have a great deal of experience interacting with new children. During the first week of school, Micki did not make friends, was always alone, and would cry at various times throughout the day. On the playground during recess, Micki would just stand and watch the other children. She did not move very well. Watching this, Ms. Sokolof knew what she needed to do. She started talking to Micki on the playground and asked her if she wanted to walk with her to the fence and back. They did this several times throughout the week during recess, engaging in conversation and singing some familiar songs. Some of the other children noticed the two of them walking and asked to join. It became a merry scene, with Ms. Sokolof having conversations and singing songs with the children. Micki started to talk to the other children during these walks. As Micki, Ms. Sokolof, and the other children started to increase their speed, they were soon "jogging," not just to the fence but around the playground. Through this activity, Micki developed friends, a sense of belonging, and a love of school. To the delight of all involved, Micki became much more willing and motivated to try new physical activities.

7.1 Coordination and Balance Underlie the Development of Gross Motor Skills

Gross motor skill development is necessary for engagement in physical activity. A foundation of balance and coordination—the ability to combine actions of the muscles to perform a movement—is needed when developing motor skills. Coordination is very important, because lack of coordination causes ineffective movement and fatigue occurs quickly. Using movement concepts, one could describe a mature action as smooth and not jerky. The skill of walking, for instance, requires sequential timing of the muscles that produce a coordinated movement. The action of a mature pattern starts at the hips, with one upper leg moving forward followed by the lower leg, with the heel of the foot striking and then rolling onto the toe. The motion is directed forward as the individual swings the arms contralaterally (opposite) to the legs. If you watch new walkers, they

▲ A child jumping for the enjoyment of the movement.

tend to lock the knee and swing the leg forward as a whole. Their arms are held high at the chest and their forward motion is limited as they move one side followed by the next. Younger children use proportionately more muscle mass and more force than mature walkers.

Balance is related to stability. The initial understanding of balance can include balancing a beanbag on different body parts while standing in self-space and then moving in general space. Children will notice that while standing in self-space, balancing the beanbag on the head is easier than doing so when walking. As children move, they have to be aware of their walking patterns.

M² FUN ▸ **Coordination—Move Like the Animals**

In this activity, the children are performing bilateral coordination, moving arms together, legs together, arm and leg on the same side, or the opposite arm and leg together. The teacher starts the activity by calling out the name of an animal and the children move like the animal. To use arms together and then legs together, the children move like an inchworm. Hands walk out, then feet walk to meet hands. A bear moves the same-side hand and foot to move forward, followed by the hand and foot on the opposite (other) side. A lion uses one hand and the other foot. Animal noises are encouraged!

Balance can be divided into static and dynamic balance. *Static balance* is maintaining a stable position, whereas *dynamic balance* is maintaining

M² FUN   Balance—Tightrope Walker

Find or place a line on the floor—you can use tape, a rope, or your imagination. Ask if the children have been to the circus and have seen the tightrope walker. How do tightrope walkers move? [Slowly] How big are their steps? [Small] How do they use their arms? [Out to the side] Where do they look? [At a specific point ahead of them]

Move forward, backward, heel-toe, and over the line as a tightrope walker would do.

balance while moving. Examples of static balance include standing still, holding a pose, and balancing on one leg (see **video** Balance and Motor Memory). Dynamic balance is required when moving. Balance is important in walking, and the child acquires balance through experience. Xiaohe pulls to a stand while holding onto a table. The first time he lets go of the table, he immediately falls backward on his bottom. As he continues to pull up, he practices balance and is eventually able to stand independently.

Three mechanical principles relate to stability and balance: base of support, center of gravity, and line of gravity. The *base of support* is the body part in contact with the ground. A wide base of support is most stable. A young child learning to stand positions his or her feet wide apart. The *center of gravity* is the point around which the body has half the weight above and half below; if the body were put on a fulcrum, it is the point at which the body would be balanced. The *line of gravity* is where the center of gravity is in relation to the base of support. If a line is dropped from the center of gravity, does it fall inside or outside the base of support? When standing (static balance), the line of gravity falls within the base of support (the feet). As the child starts to walk, the line of gravity moves outside the base of support, but then the child moves a foot forward to maintain a dynamic balanced position. The most stable position has a wide base of support, low center of gravity, and the line of gravity inside the base of support. See Figure 7.1 for a sample lesson on balance.

Objective: The child will understand the concept of base of support.

Activities:

1. What is balance?
   a. Not falling
2. Do the following activities:
   a. Lie down on the ground.
   b. Put two feet and one hand on the ground.
   c. Stand with feet shoulder width apart.
   d. Stand on one foot.
   e. Stand on one foot with eyes closed.
   f. Which activity was hardest, and why?
3. Walk on a line on the floor.
   a. Walk normally.
   b. Walk heel-to-toe.
   c. Which activity was harder, and why?
4. What changed today as we balanced?
   a. What was in contact with the floor?
   b. When was it easier to balance?
      • More in contact with the floor
   c. When was it easier to balance?
      • Less in contact with the floor
   d. This is our base of support
5. Evaluation
   a. Using general space, the children demonstrate easy balance positions and more difficult balance positions.
   b. As the positions become more difficult, ask the children how they can modify the position to make it easier. This can lead into a center of gravity lesson.

Figure 7.1   Sample lesson on balance (this could also be a science lesson)

Concepts that assist in balancing include the following:

■ Holding arms out to side (lowering the center of gravity)

■ Focusing on an object

■ Wider base of support for greater stability

■ Line of gravity within the base of support

■ Balancing on one body part more difficult owing to narrower base of support

M² FUN Balance and Coordination

Obstacle Course Challenge—Follow the Feet

Use footprints for the children to use to follow an obstacle course. The footprints include the whole foot, the ball of the foot, and the heel of the foot. Create a series of pathways that children follow.

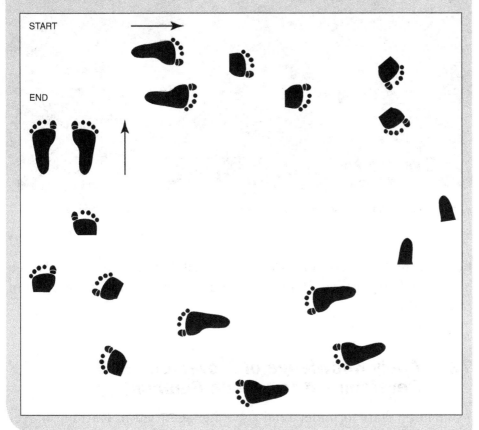

When developing balance skills, it is necessary to include the following:

- Balance at many different levels
- Balance on many different objects
- Balance while holding many different objects
- Moving in different directions while balancing
- Balance while moving with others

▲ Young child using a push toy to assist with balance as she practices walking.

Before a child can perform a gross motor skill they must be in a balanced position whether static or dynamic, and they must have some level of coordination.

7.2 Apply Knowledge of Movement Skill Development to Lesson Planning

As children start to understand the language used in learning movement, they also learn what skills they can do and when to perform these skills (see Figure 7.2). A young child who does not yet have a one-hand overhand throw, for example, cannot use that pattern to throw the ball across the field to her teacher, so she may choose to throw the ball to another child nearby, who then throws the ball to the teacher. Then, as she acquires movement skills, she will also learn when to use a specific skill and how to modify the skill.

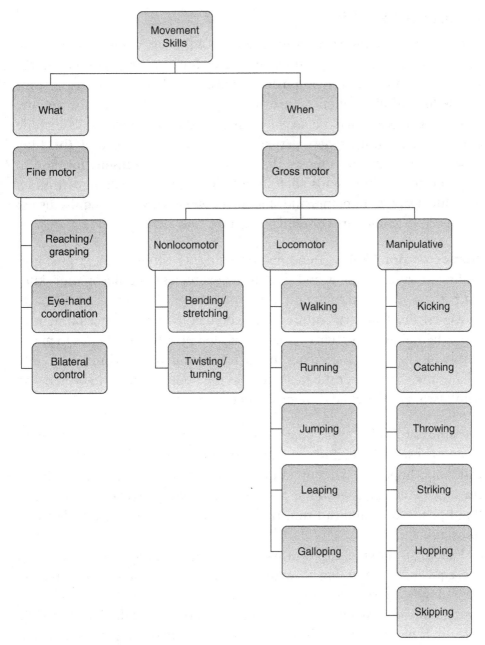

Figure 7.2 Movement skills the child can learn.

Gross Motor Skills

Large muscle groups, such as the muscles of the leg, trunk, and arm, are used in performing gross motor skills, which are categorized into nonlocomotor, locomotor, and manipulative skills. The child first needs to learn the skills and also when to use them. When the body is not moving through general space, *nonlocomotor skills* are used. These skills include bending/stretching, twisting/turning, pushing/pulling, and the like. *Locomotor skills* are movements that move the body from one location to another and include skills such as rolling, crawling, walking, running, jumping, leaping, hopping, and skipping. *Manipulative skills* require use of an object; examples are throwing, catching, and kicking.

Nonlocomotor Skills. Bending/stretching, twisting/turning, pushing/pulling, curling, jumping, and landing are examples of nonlocomotor skills. With these skills, the individual does not move through general space; however, the skills are required for everyday living and development of fundamental motor patterns. A cap is twisted off a jar; one bends to pick a penny off the floor or stretches to reach a banana on the counter. A child pushes the chair under the table or pulls the book toward him or her. The trunk twists as the child develops a mature throw.

Locomotor Skills. The goal of locomotor skills is to move through space. These skills include walking, running, chasing, fleeing, sliding, galloping, hopping, skipping, and so forth. Walking is a prerequisite to running. Running is a similar pattern to walking; however, it includes a flight phase. If a child can run, the child has the strength and balance to jump up.

Sliding is moving sideways with a leading and following foot and is a prerequisite to galloping to gain experience in strength and balance. Galloping is a forward-facing slide, step-close, step-close, that also has a leading and following foot. The gallop is more difficult than the slide because it has a longer flight phase. A child can perform both sliding and galloping with the dominant foot prior to using the nondominant foot.

Hopping has a one-foot takeoff and same-foot landing. If a child has difficulty hopping, he or she can hold onto a support to gain experience in strength and balance. Skipping is a step-hop, step-hop pattern. Singing the cue words (step-hop, step-hop) helps the child develop a rhythm for

Table 7.1 Throwing Sequence

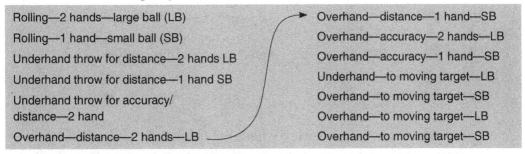

Rolling—2 hands—large ball (LB)	Overhand—distance—1 hand—SB
Rolling—1 hand—small ball (SB)	Overhand—accuracy—2 hands—LB
Underhand throw for distance—2 hands LB	Overhand—accuracy—1 hand—SB
Underhand throw for distance—1 hand SB	Underhand—to moving target—LB
Underhand throw for accuracy/distance—2 hand	Overhand—to moving target—SB
	Overhand—to moving target—LB
Overhand—distance—2 hands—LB	Overhand—to moving target—SB

hopping. If the child's skip is jerky, skipping to music or skipping with another child can help to develop a smooth skip.

> While Oma and Jon were waiting for Kim, Jon's older sister, to finish school for the day, Jon showed Oma that he could skip. Jon, however, was galloping, so Oma took Jon's hand and together they sang "step-hop" to help him learn to skip. When Kim met them, she took Jon's other hand; the three held hands and skipped all the way home.

Manipulative Skills. These are skills that require interaction with an object, typically the hands or feet. Manipulative skills include throwing, catching, kicking, striking, punting, dribbling, and volleying. Key words for the development of throwing, for example, are step (opposite foot), hips (swing forward), shoulders (move forward), arm (follows upper arm). A developmental sequence for throwing starts with rolling a large ball with two hands, then increases in complexity by using one hand with a small ball (see Table 7.1). At this point the child might have difficulty releasing the ball. Aaron looks to see where the ball went after he threw it; surprisingly, he finds it still in his hand. Complexity increases to the use of a two-hand underhand throw for distance with a large ball, followed by a one-hand underhand throw for distance with a small ball. The sequence continues, increasing in complexity by throwing for accuracy/distance. The more complex throw is the overhand throw, first with two hands and a larger ball and then the one-hand overhand throw. The change in the one-hand overhand throw can be observed in the Fundamental Motor Patterns—Throwing **video**.

Developing the skill of catching requires anticipation timing. The child needs to understand the time–space relationship. The levels of the catching skill are observed in the Fundamental Motor Patterns—Catching **video**.

Table 7.2 Developmental Sequence for Catching

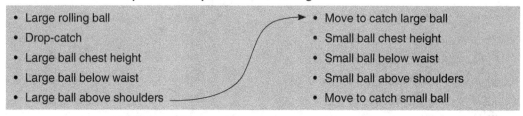

• Large rolling ball	• Move to catch large ball
• Drop-catch	• Small ball chest height
• Large ball chest height	• Small ball below waist
• Large ball below waist	• Small ball above shoulders
• Large ball above shoulders	• Move to catch small ball

Anticipation timing is knowing where the ball will be and when it will get there so the catcher can move his or her hands to that place. Beginning catchers are afraid of being hit with the ball, so it is important to use a large, light ball. Catching develops by first catching a rolling large, light ball, followed by catching the same ball thrown at chest level using a two-hand underhand throw. Key words to help the child catch are "look" (at the ball), "reach" (for the ball), and "give" (absorb the force). The next level of difficulty includes catching a large ball at waist level, followed by a ball thrown above the shoulders (see Table 7.2). Moving to catch a ball increases the difficulty. Catching a small ball is the next level of difficulty and follows throwing to the chest, below waist and then above the shoulders. Moving to catch a small ball is the most difficult. Also, catching an overhand throw is more difficult than catching an underhand throw. Typically, an overhand throw has greater force than an underhand throw.

M² FUN   Improving Catching

The children have had experience rolling a large ball using two hands while sitting, kneeling, and standing. To work on catching, the children create two lines in front of the teacher. The children then face their partners and spread out at arms' length. They then take two giant steps back. The children start rolling the ball to each other and think about "look-reach-give" as they catch. Each time they catch, they scoot back. This is then followed by kneeling while throwing and catching and, finally, two-hand underhand throws to each other. The thrower tries to get the ball to the chest of the catcher (the easiest place to catch). To increase the difficulty, the children then throw within the catcher's self-space but the child has to reach for the ball.

Table 7.3 Developmental Sequence for Kicking

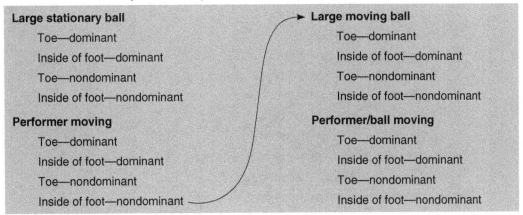

Large stationary ball	Large moving ball
Toe—dominant	Toe—dominant
Inside of foot—dominant	Inside of foot—dominant
Toe—nondominant	Toe—nondominant
Inside of foot—nondominant	Inside of foot—nondominant
Performer moving	**Performer/ball moving**
Toe—dominant	Toe—dominant
Inside of foot—dominant	Inside of foot—dominant
Toe—nondominant	Toe—nondominant
Inside of foot—nondominant	Inside of foot—nondominant

Kicking can include kicking a large stationary ball followed by running to kicking a stationary ball, kicking a moving ball, and finally moving to kick a moving ball (see Table 7.3). Kicking starts with the toe of the dominant foot and moves to the nondominant foot. The inside-of-foot kick follows the toe kick. Kicking a large stationary ball is the first to develop, followed by the child running to kick the ball, followed by the child and the ball both moving. Anticipation timing is required here—the child needs to predict where the ball will be and get to that spot in time to contact the ball with his or her foot.

Striking has many variations. The developmental sequence moves in a proximal/distal direction, from no instrument (hand), to short instrument (paddle), to long instrument (tennis racket, bat). Striking requires anticipation timing—the mover needs to time his or her movement to the action of the ball. The following are the types of striking:

- Sidearm—2 hands (batting)
- Sidearm—1 hand (tennis forehand/backhand)
- Overhand—2 hands (volleyball setup)
- Overhand—1 hand (tennis serve, volleyball strike)
- Underhand—2 hands (setup in volleyball)
- Underhand—1 hand (serve in volleyball)

Table 7.4 Developmental Sequence for Striking

- Stationary ball/2-hand underhand
- Stationary ball/1-hand underhand
- Large rebounding ball/2-hand underhand
- Large light stationary, ball/short paddle, underhanded
- Large rolling ball/short paddle underhand
- Large ball on tee/short paddle side arm
- Small ball suspended, waist high/short paddle
- Small ball suspended, shoulder high/short paddle
- Small ball suspended, overhead/short paddle
- Large ball on tee/plastic bat
- Large ball in one hand/1 hand underhand
- Large rebounding ball, 1 hand underhand
- Large rebounding ball

A developmental sequence for striking is in Table 7.4.

When creating the environment for children to practice and learn the various skills, it is important to follow a developmental sequence. This can be accomplished by reviewing the structural and functional constraints of the child, analyzing the task, and creating an environment to build success.

Following the motor milestones, Abed stood before he walked, walked before he ran, and ran before he jumped. Standing develops the strength and balance needed for walking. Constraints to walking include strength and balance. To match the environment and task to the child, a push toy can be used. Walking increases task difficulty because dynamic balance is required, whereas running increases the strength requirement and balance difficulty due to a flight phase.

Educators must be aware of the gross motor sequences to understand the progress of each child and to design learning activities appropriate to the developmental level of the child. For example, skipping should not be required until the child can step and hop. A child with a visual impairment can catch a ball that has a beeping sound or has beans inserted.

7.3 Apply National Standards for Physical Education to Selection of Content for Learning

The National Association for Sport and Physical Education (NASPE), an association of AAHPERD, has established National Standards for Physical Education (NASPE, 2004). These are content standards (see Table 7.5) that indicate "what students should know and be able to do" (p. vi). For each standard, sample benchmarks are provided. Content standards are provided for kindergarten, second, fourth, sixth, eighth, tenth, and twelfth grades. Within a grade, sample benchmarks and assessment examples are included.

An example for standard 2, "Demonstrates understanding of movement concepts, principles, and tactics as they apply to the learning and performance of physical activities," for kindergarten is for the child to "establish a beginning movement vocabulary (e.g., personal space, high/low levels, fast/slow speeds, light/heavy weights, balance, twist)" (NASPE, 2004, p. 8). A sample benchmark would be to perform locomotor patterns while moving the various directions. Assessment of this action might be to observe the children as they respond to cues to move in various directions. State standards are built from the national standards.

Table 7.5 National Standards for Physical Education (NASPE, 2004)

National Standards for Physical Education

1. Demonstrates competency in motor skills and movement patterns needed to perform a variety of physical activities.

2. Demonstrates understanding of movement concepts, principles, and tactics as they apply to the learning and performance of physical activities.

3. Participates regularly in physical activity.

4. Achieves and maintains a health-enhancing level of physical fitness.

5. Exhibits responsible personal and social behavior that respects self and others in physical activity.

6. Values physical activity for health, enjoyment, challenge, self-expression, and/or social interaction.

(Reprinted with permission from the American Alliance for Health, Physical Education, Recreation and Dance, www.AAHPERD.org.)

Planning Physically Active Lessons

The early childhood physical activity curriculum includes understanding concepts (movement and fitness), development of fundamental motor skills (e.g., running, jumping, catching, throwing) and engagement in moderate to vigorous physical activity. To plan for physically active lessons, NASPE (2009) has prepared a position statement on appropriate practices in movement programs. Although the statement is geared for children ages 3 to 5 years, the guidelines are appropriate for all ages:

1. Children should engage in movement programs designed for their individual developmental levels.
2. Young children learn through interacting with their environment.
3. Young children learn and develop in an integrated fashion.
4. Planned movement experiences enhance play experiences.

   Teachers serve as guides or facilitators for young children. (NASPE, 2009, pp. 4-5; reprinted with permission from the American Alliance for Health, Physical Education, Recreation and Dance, www. AAHPERD.org)

For each of these premises, examples of appropriate and inappropriate practices are given. The learning environment needs to be tailored to young children. An example of an appropriate practice for addressing diversity and equity is for teachers to select activities that represent a culturally diverse environment. Games, sports, and dances from around the world are included. Boys and girls are encouraged and exposed to all types of physical activity; there are no activities for only boys or only girls. Boxers jump rope and football players dance. There are professional football teams for women, and women have been included on college football teams.

Children need to be physically active throughout the time they are engaged in physical activity; they should not be merely standing, listening, and watching. We do not recommend playing "Duck, Duck, Goose," for example, because during this game, most of the children are sitting not moving. Instead, teachers should select activities that keep all the children busy all the time.

Sufficient equipment is needed for all children to be actively engaged. Children should not be selected by other children to form teams. Instead, teams should be preset by the teacher or avoided altogether. Teachers can randomly give out colored paint swatches or pictures of birds to determine teams. Teams can be selected by birthdays, or by odd and even numbers.

Competition is not part of the learning process. Children should not be compared to one another; each child is at his or her own developmental level, and we strive to individualize the lesson to help each child improve. Physical activity should not be used as a punishment. Children should always be permitted to go outside for recess and go to gym. Teachers need to demonstrate enthusiasm for an active lifestyle.

The curriculum facilitates the total development of the child, including movement skills and concepts that foster participation in physical activity that develops health-related fitness. The program should include culturally appropriate movement to music that is expressive and creative.

Practice Environment and Feedback

Early childhood educators need to facilitate maximum practice. Children should be active for the vast majority of the time while learning movement concepts and skills. The environment needs to be structured so all children are moving and are successful. When practicing throwing, each pair of children should have their own ball. This might seem extravagant; however, this can be accomplished at very little expense. For instance, a great ball for catching is an origami (art of paper folding) ball. Use of this ball also adds variability because the child has to be aware of the force used to catch the ball. The children (as young as 5-year-olds) can fold their own ball and improve their fine motor coordination through paper folding. Alternatively, children can stuff paper into a bag; when the opening is closed, the bag makes a good ball. The ball might not be round, in this case; however, this would add variability to the catch and help the child in adapting to the force, speed, and direction of the throw.

When children are engaged in strenuous activity, the educator needs to be aware of a young child's need to rest and hydrate. Children tend to go all out—but then they need to rest. Many children will run at top speed, but then fall on the ground to rest. Because young children do not sweat as older children and adults do, it is important to have several water breaks throughout an activity period.

As children practice movement concepts and skills, the practice environment needs to provide both repetition and variability. Children must learn to practice in a variety of environmental contexts. Providing a variety of ball sizes and weights gives children the opportunity to refine their skills while the tasks increase in difficulty.

The educator not only needs to create a learning environment for children, but also needs to give feedback, or information about how the children can improve their performance. Providing feedback to children serves three main purposes: information, reinforcement, and motivation. Informational feedback provides the individual with knowledge of how he or she is moving. It includes information about what is being done correctly and what is incorrect. It is important that the information helps children understand what they need to change. For younger children, the feedback is very simple and helps to guide the child. When moving in general space, the educator could have the children freeze and then ask the questions, "Are you using good general space? Are there any empty spaces within the boundaries?" and then point to an open space and have some of the children move there. Or, when children are running, the teacher can cup hands behind ears and ask, "What do I hear?" If the children are running flat-footed, you will hear a "herd" running through the room.

When giving feedback to a child or a group of children, the "sandwich" technique should be used. First, reinforce the child, then provide information on how to improve the movement, and finally provide information to motivate the child. For example: "I like the way you are moving in general space—you are moving into open spaces. Remember, sliding is side-step, side-step, while galloping is step-close, step-close. Try facing forward as you gallop."

Reinforcement can be positive or negative. Positive reinforcement evokes warm feelings and increases the likelihood that the individual will perform similarly in the future. Positive reinforcement, such as "you are moving nicely through general space" or "keep up the good work by not touching," helps to keep the child focused and give his or her best effort. The phrases should be short and positive. Negative reinforcement, however, provides unpleasant feelings that the child will want to avoid.

Feedback can also motivate the child to continue to practice. Information on how to correct the movement allows the child to change his or her performance and be successful. Success is addictive—on the other hand, children who are frustrated with their performance are likely to quit.

A variety of ways to provide feedback can be used. Modeling shows the learner what the skill "looks like." Children are excellent at demonstrating skills. Children enjoy seeing themselves perform, so videotaping can also be used to provide feedback. When working with children, not only is it necessary to understand how to provide feedback, but it is also important to understand how to include children with special needs and those who are at different stages of development. (For more information on practice, common problems, and teaching hints, visit https://www.eduweb.vic.gov.au/edulibrary/public/teachlearn/student/phasefmsmod.pdf, Australian Council for Health, Physical Education and Recreation, Victorian Branch, Inc.)

Including Children of Varying Abilities

Throughout the text, we emphasize the concept of being "developmentally appropriate." We believe that the child is not "wrong"; rather, the child is at a specific developmental level. It is the purpose of the educator to figure what the child can do and analyze the task to see the next step the child must take to improve. We believe that a developmentally appropriate curriculum, teaching strategies, and activities should be modified to include all children, not just typically developing children. A child who is visually impaired, for instance, can catch a ball. The teacher can toss a soft, large ball to the child's chest and use the words "listen, reach, and give." If a "sound" ball is available, the teacher can toss that; if not, the teacher can gain the child's attention and time the ball toss to the words so when the teacher ends with the word "reach," the ball contacts the child's hand and then the child "gives" with the catch.

Children with disabilities need to be placed in the least restrictive environment that meets their educational needs. This is important because all children need to be provided the opportunity to develop movement skills and to be physically active for a lifetime. Merely having children who are in wheelchairs keep score is inappropriate.

Inclusive environments are critical for children. Children need to be exposed to other children of varying ability levels. The environment is not competitive, but cooperative. It is important for children to realize that sometimes a child helps others and at other times is the one being helped. The teacher needs to modify the requirements and/or structure the environment to match the child's skill level. Throughout childhood, it is important to focus on the process, not the product. In other words, concentrate on how the child is performing the skill itself, not how far or how fast he or she can run.

Ellis, Lieberman, and LeRoux (2009) provide examples of creating an effective learning environment for all children so they can feel "comfortable, motivated, and successful" (p. 19). Differentiated instruction applies information about the learners to develop goals for the individual children and matches the information available to the children with the strategies the teacher uses. It is important that children be able to demonstrate what they have learned in a variety of ways (Thousand, Villa, & Nevin, 2007).

7.4 Use Music to Enhance Learning

Music plays a significant role in learning motor skills. It can provide a positive learning environment, enhance effort, and provide a guide to movement performance. Music motivates the individual to move.

Music creates a positive learning environment by reducing stress, and regulating energy. If the children are anxious, playing soothing music can calm the children. If they are lethargic, an upbeat tempo can stimulate action. Playing music as children practice motor skills can increase productive practice behavior and decrease nonproductive behavior.

Coordinated movement is an organization of movements coupled to rhythm. The skilled mover uses rhythm in displaying smooth motion, with one part of the movement flowing to the next. Music provides the tempo for movement. Children listening to fast music move fast; when listening to slow music, they reduce their speed.

7.5 Provide a Learning Environment Conducive to Decision Making and Building Confidence

Parents and educators want children to engage in physical play that is safe— this is a primary goal. It is also helpful to develop learning environments that physically and psychologically challenge the child. Children will use their own motor skills to challenge and motivate their physical engagement.

Physical activity behaviors are established during preschool development (Hinkley, Salmon, Okely, Crawford, & Hesketh, 2011). To establish physical activity behaviors, it is important to emphasize competence, autonomy, relationships, and enjoyment (Stuntz & Weiss, 2010).

Feelings of competence are important in the establishment of physical activity behaviors. Children who have higher perceptions of physical competence demonstrate higher levels of physical activity and give more effort and persistence. In the Kinder Kinetics program, 5-year-old Luying would say "I can't" when facing any new movement. Such language is not encouraged in Kinder Kinetics. Instead, Luying was persuaded to say, "I will try." As she was supported by the environment and she tried each new movement, Luying started to develop a feeling of competence. With practice, "I can't" dropped from her vocabulary, she changed her behavior, and even started encouraging other children.

When children feel they are good at an activity, they participate (Barnett, Morgan, van Beurden, & Beard, 2008). Children use several sources of information to determine their competence: social, self-referenced, and outcome (Stuntz & Weiss, 2010). If parents and teachers support children's physical play, they may engage in behaviors that will stimulate their mental and physical attributes. According to the research of Sutton-Smith (2003), neuroscientists suggest that children will seek out uncertainty. This fuels their emotions and provides motivation to continue in an endeavor. This is why children like to be "dizzy" and spin and spin until they fall over laughing and giggling.

Tovey (2007) suggests that environmental risk assessment should shift from removal to planning. What can be done to the environment to offer situations that will provide a challenge or decision making by the child? Perhaps a medicine ball could be part of the ball collection given to toddlers. It will be enjoyable to watch the toddlers handle a ball that is not easy to move, as this encourages problem solving and skill development. They discover which balls can be thrown underhanded, which ones thrown overhanded, and which ones must be pushed on the ground. The topography of the environment can be changed to provide challenges in walking, running, and skipping. Climbing and balance will be tested through the natural exploration of the child. Materials should be movable to provide more opportunities to use a variety of gross motor movements and decision-making skills. Imagination Playgrounds (www.imaginationplayground.com), for example, provide a wonderful way to stimulate the emotional and cognitive response process. Building gardens—especially outdoor musical gardens—is also a wonderful way to increase movement.

Summary

Motor skills are needed to engage in physical activity. Development of motor skills follows a proximal–distal, cephalocaudal, and gross-to-fine motor sequence. When planning lessons, the educator needs to construct a developmental sequence that increases in complexity to challenge the child and create a learning environment that supports the development of the skills. In a learning environment, children need to be physically active most of the time; they should not be left standing, waiting, and listening. It is also important for children to develop competence in the skills and feel as though they can make decisions and are able to develop relationships. This type of a learning environment will create children who love to move—and move for a lifetime.

Summary Related to Outcomes

Learning Outcomes	Guiding Principles
7.1 Coordination and balance underlie the development of gross motor skills	Individual Needs Met
Underlying the development of motor skills is a foundation of balance and coordination, which also increase with the development of movement skills.	

Learning Outcomes	Guiding Principles
7.2 Apply knowledge of movement skill development to lesson planning	Environment and Curriculum Reciprocated

Gross motor skills include nonlocomotor, locomotor, and manipulative movements. Nonlocomotor movements are stationary actions; for locomotor skills, the child moves through space. Manipulative skills include manipulation of an object.

7.3 Apply National Standards for Physical Education to selection of content for learning activities	Environment and Curriculum Reciprocated

To develop lessons for physical activity, the educator needs to use the National Standards for Physical Education to select developmentally appropriate content. The practice environment must be structured to assist the child in attainment of the skill and the children need to be active most of the time. The educator needs to provide appropriate feedback that assists the child in acquiring mastery.

Differentiated instruction provides the educator with strategies to include children of all ability levels in the same class. All children need to be engaged at their level of ability.

7.4 Use music to enhance learning	Movement and Music Integrated

Music provides a positive learning environment while enhancing effort and guiding movement performance.

7.5 Provide a learning environment conducive to decision making and building confidence	Individual Needs Met

To develop a love of movement, children need to feel they can do the skill; they make decisions, develop relationships, and, most of all, have fun.

Demonstrate Your Knowledge, Skills, and Dispositions

Students will demonstrate knowledge, comprehension, analysis, and evaluation of Learning Outcomes related to Guiding Principles.

Learning Outcomes	Guiding Principles
7.1 Coordination and balance underlie the development of gross motor skills	Individual Needs Met

- Why are balance and coordination the foundation of gross motor skills? Do balance and coordination change with practice? Give an example of a skill and describe how balance and coordination are necessary for skill development.

Learning Outcomes	Guiding Principles
7.2 Apply knowledge of movement skill development to lesson planning	Environment and Curriculum Reciprocated
• Select a motor skill, analyze the mature pattern, and determine appropriate cue words to aid in the development of the skill. For example, we gave "look, reach, give" as the cue words for catching.	
7.3 Apply National Standards for Physical Education to selection of content for learning activities	Environment and Curriculum Reciprocated
• Obtain a copy of your state physical education standards. Select a standard and a skill that are developed in that standard. Create an objective to develop a component of the skill and create a learning environment.	
7.4 Use music to enhance learning	Movement and Music Integrated
• Give two examples of how music can enhance the development of gross motor skills.	
7.5 Provide a learning environment conducive to decision making and building confidence	Individual Needs Met
• Explain what you will do as an educator to enhance the motivation of the children in your class to be physically active.	

Planning for Engaging

The following learning activities provide three possibilities or ways to develop an M^2 movement standard.

M^2 Movement Standard: The child will identify the critical elements of fundamental motor patterns.

Possibility One	Possibility Two	Possibility Three
Takeoff and Landing	*Takeoff and Landing*	*Obstacle Course*
What are the ways you can "take off" and what are the ways you can land? • Two feet to two feet (jump up or jump out) • Two feet to one foot • One foot to two feet • One foot to the other foot (leap) • One foot to the same foot (hop)	Draw different hopscotch patterns using the different types of jumps.	Create an obstacle course using the different types of jumps. Leap over a brook, jump up to hit a ball suspended from the ceiling, jump through hoops, jump from two feet onto a small target using one foot, etc.

Assessment	Assessment	Assessment
Observe the patterns to determine which type of jump children are having difficulty performing.	Observe the patterns to determine which type of jump children are having difficulty performing.	Observe the patterns to determine which type of jump children are having difficulty performing.

Now You Try It

Complete the following standard-based learning activity designed to meet various interests and developmental levels. Design two learning possibilities (Possibility Two and Possibility Three) or learning activities to develop M^2 Movement Standards.

M^2 **Movement Standard:** The child will identify the critical elements of fundamental motor patterns.		
Possibility One	**Possibility Two**	**Possibility Three**
Skipping: Identify the critical elements of skipping: step-hop. Children practice step-hop. Increase the tempo of the hop. Skip to music.		
Assessment Determine that the children are skipping and not galloping.	**Assessment**	**Assessment**

References

Barnett, L., Morgan, P., van Beurden, E., & Beard, J. (2008). Perceived sports competence mediates the relationship between childhood motor skill proficiency and adolescent physical activity and fitness: A longitudinal assessment. *International Journal of Behavioral Nutrition and Physical Activity*, 5(40). doi:10.1186/1479-5868-5-40.

Ellis, E., Lieberman, L. & LeRoux, D. (2009). Using differentiated instruction in physical education. *Palaestra*, 24, 19–23.

Hinkley, T, Salmon, J., Okely, A., Crawford, D., & Hesketh, K. (2011). Influences on preschool children's physical activity: Exploration through focus groups. *Family Community Health*, 34(1), 39–50.

National Association for Sport and Physical Education (2004). *Moving into the future: National Standards for Physical Education* (2nd Ed.). Reston, VA: AAHPERD.

National Association for Sport and Physical Education (2009). *Active start: A statement of physical activity guidelines for children from birth to age 5* (2nd Ed.). Reston, VA: AAHPERD.

Stuntz, C. & Weiss, M. (2010). Motivating children and adolescents to sustain a physically active lifestyle. *American Journal of Lifestyle Medicine*, 4, 433–444. doi:10.1177/1559872610368779.

Sutton-Smith, B. (2003). Play as a parody of emotional vulnerability. In J. Roopnarine (Ed.) *Play and educational theory and practice, play and culture studies 5.* Westport, CT: Praeger Publishers.

Thousand, S., Villa, R., & Nevin, A. (2007). *Differentiating instruction.* Thousand Oaks, CA: Corwin Press.

Tovey, H. (2007). *Playing outdoors: spaces and places, risk and challenge.* Maidenhead, UK: McGraw-Hill Open University Press.

c h a p t e r 8

Fitness and Nutrition Create a Healthy Lifestyle

LEARNING OUTCOMES AND GUIDING PRINCIPLES

Students reading this text will be able to demonstrate Learning Outcomes linked to Guiding Principles based on the National Association for the Education of Young Children's *Developmentally Appropriate Practice in Early Childhood Programs Serving Children from Birth through Age 8.*

Learning Outcomes	Guiding Principles
8.1 Develop a physically educated person	Individual Needs Met
8.2 Understand the relationships among physical activity, physical fitness, nutrition, and wellness	Individual Needs Met
8.3 Categorize types of physical fitness	Individual Needs Met
8.4 Explain the components of health-related fitness	Individual Needs Met
8.5 Determine required participation in health-related fitness	Individual Needs Met
8.6 Know the qualities of a physically educated child	Assessment and Standards Provide Guidance
8.7 Determine the role of environment in nutrition	Environment and Curriculum Reciprocated
8.8 Construct a balanced nutritional environment for young children	Individual Needs Met
8.9 Create a culture that promotes physical activity and healthy eating	Family and Community Involved

---

Making Connections
Developing a Healthy Lifestyle During Childhood

As Denise was jogging around the block at 5:30 in the morning, listening to her favorite musical mix on her smartphone, she was reminiscing about her school days. Today was her 50th birthday and her friends had been commenting about how healthy she looked, and how she had not changed since high school. Denise watched what she ate and tried to do something physical every day. One day she might jog, on another day bike with her children, and on some days she played soccer with her family. On days when she was not active, she felt sluggish. Denise also ate healthily. She made sure she began each day with a glass of water and a healthy breakfast. In addition, she did not skip meals, ate lots of vegetables and fruits, and limited her fat, sugar, and salt consumption. Many of her friends, though, had put on weight and did not seem to have much energy.

Reflecting on her school days, Denise was thankful that Mr. Wagner had been one of her elementary school teachers. He taught her the importance of physical activity and the relationships among physical activity, nutrition, and wellness. Mr. Wagner's classes were always fun and helped her develop confidence in her skills and make good eating decisions; she felt this was instrumental in the development of her enjoyment of movement and choices of healthy food. Although she never had the desire to be an athlete, Denise has always enjoyed moving and being a physically educated person.

8.1 *Develop a Physically Educated Person*

Denise is a physically educated person. The American Alliance for Health, Physical Education, Recreation and Dance (AAHPERD) has published a document that defines the physically educated person (Frank, et al., 1991). According to this definition, four aspects relate to a person's being physically educated:

- Is
- Does
- Knows
- Values

▲ Involving the child in preparation of nutritious food encourages healthy eating.

To be physically educated, Denise *is* physically fit, *does* physical activity, and *knows* about physical fitness and how to design appropriate programs for her wellness. Finally, she *values* the feelings attained from achieving fitness and understands the importance of fitness in a healthy lifestyle.

Thanks to her teacher, Mr. Wagner, Denise learned early to value physical activity. She appreciated engaging in physical activity, being physically fit, and experiencing overall wellness.

8.2   *Understand the Relationships Among Physical Activity, Physical Fitness, Nutrition, and Wellness*

Developing physically active children is important because of the relationships among a physically active lifestyle, physical fitness, wellness, and reduced risk factors for cardiovascular disease, among other chronic diseases, such as type 2 diabetes, which is now being diagnosed in increasing numbers of children. To understand the relationship, we first define physical activity, physical fitness, and wellness. Physical activity and physical fitness are frequently used interchangeably, but they are different and have specific implications for health.

According to Caspersen, Powell, and Christenson (1985), *physical activity* is usually defined as "any bodily movement produced by skeletal muscles that results in energy expenditure." *Exercise* is also often interchanged with physical activity; however, exercise refers to a more structured and planned form of physical activity that is done to enhance fitness. A child chasing a dog in the yard is physical activity. A child who is given a ball and asked to run around markers while dribbling the ball with her foot is also doing physical activity, but doing jumping jacks, sit-ups, or push-ups are more exercise related because they are isolated physical movements done solely for the purpose of increasing physical fitness. Both physical activity and exercise have effects on a variety of physiological systems (e.g., heart rate, blood pressure, breathing rate).

Physical fitness comes from achieving a set of skills necessary to perform a physical activity. The relationship between physical activity and fitness is reciprocal. Physical activity influences fitness; increased fitness can, in turn, increase the level of physical activity. As their fitness levels increase, individuals tend to increase their activity levels; the fittest individual tends to be the most active. Physical activity and its consequence of fitness influence health, but being healthy also influences both physical activity and fitness (Bouchard & Shephard 1994). Those who are healthier engage in more physical activity.

Physiological Fitness Indicators

Developing physically active children is important because of the relationship between physically active lifestyles and reduced cardiovascular risk factors. Children's fitness levels are alarming. More than 40 percent of children show one risk factor for cardiovascular disease: obesity, high blood pressure, or high cholesterol levels.

One of the most prevalent health problems among youth today is obesity. It is so significant that we are afraid that this will be the first generation that will not live longer than their parents. In the past 30 years, childhood obesity has more than tripled (CDC, 2012) and in 2008, more than one-third of children and adolescents were considered overweight or obese (National Center for Health Statistics, 2011; Ogden, Carroll, Curtin, Lamb, & Flegal, 2010). The data are particularly alarming for low-income children. The 2009 Pediatric Nutrition Surveillance System (PedNSS) data show that nearly one-third of the 3.7 million low-income children between 2 and 4 years of age in the survey were obese or overweight (Polhamus, Dalenius, Mackintosh, Smith, & Grummer-Strawn, 2011). Comparing data from the period 2003–2006 with data from 2009, the obesity rate from birth to age 4 increased from 12.4 percent to 14.7 percent of children—meaning that one in seven low-income, preschool-aged children was obese (Polhamus, 2011).

Ogden and Carroll (2010) and Ogden, Carroll, Kit, and Flegal (2012) analyzed the change in obesity by comparing data collected between 1988 and 1994 to those collected between 2007 and 2008. The prevalence of obesity increased 5.1 percent for non-Hispanic white boys, 9.1 percent for non-Hispanic black boys, and 12.7 percent for Mexican-American boys. Among girls in the period 2007–2008, non-Hispanic black adolescents were significantly more likely to be obese (12.9 percent) compared with non-Hispanic white adolescents (5.6 percent) and Mexican American girls (4 percent).

In addition to long-term health problems, such as diabetes and heart disease, obesity is also related to problems that include decreased academic performance and social exclusion (Castetbon & Andreyeva, 2012). Obesity results from consuming too many calories from the wrong types of food that spike blood sugar and insulin production (Hyman, 2012) as well as from not engaging in adequate periods of physical activity. It is difficult to treat obesity in children; therefore, it is better to prevent it from occurring in the first place. Eating quality food and maintaining an adequate level of physical activity are important for achieving this goal.

Skilled Movers and Physical Fitness

Being a skilled mover may be one component that contributes to adequate levels of physical activity. The question is: Do children who have better motor skills engage in higher levels of physical activity compared with children who are less skilled? A higher level of energy expenditure, coupled with nutritional changes, will have the result of a lower chance of a child's being overweight or obese. Several authors have noted the importance of developmentally appropriate physical activity and physical education in preschools (Logan, Scrabis-Fletcher, Modlesky, & Getchell, 2011) and schools (Castetbon & Andreyeva, 2012; Cliff, Okely, Morgan, Jones, Steele, & Baur, 2012). The appropriate level of physical activity also needs to be paired with appropriate nutrition.

M² FUN Hot Potato

Give infants and toddlers yard balls and give older children regular balls. Begin by having the children sit and pass the objects back and forth to you or to a partner. The game can be made more difficult by having the children kneel or stand when passing the object back and forth. To increase complexity, speed the passing to play "Hot Potato."

The relationship between obesity, overweight and motor skills seems to be evident at all ages. A strong relationship exists among body mass index (BMI), motor skill proficiency (Logan, et.al., 2011), and body weight (Castetbon & Andreyeva, 2012), even when adjusting for confounding factors (birth, mother, and family characteristics). Children with lower BMIs tend to be more skilled and more physically active, and spend less time in sedentary activity (Wrotniak, Epstein, Dorn, Jones, & Kondilis, 2006). Overweight children had poorer locomotor skills.

Children engaged in physical activity programs aimed at reducing obesity also benefit from the relationship among physical activity, motor skill performance, and obesity. Preadolescent children of normal weight have higher skill levels in locomotor skills such as running, sliding, galloping, and hopping and in the stationary dribble and stationary kick (Cliff, 2012). Children in this age range who demonstrated poor physical control and coordination were more likely to be obese when measured at 33 years of age (Osika & Montgomery, 2008).

Not only is there a relationship between gross motor skill performance and obesity in children, but there also appears to be a relationship between fine motor skill performance and obesity. Poor fine motor skill performance is associated with a higher level of obesity in young children (Castetbon & Andreyeva, 2012; Logan, et al., 2011) and preadolescents (Wrotniak et al., 2006). Children who are obese displayed around 50 percent more errors on a visual–motor drawing task when compared with their normal-weight peers (Petrolini, Iughetti, & Bernasconi, 1995)

When the fine motor task increased in complexity by requiring the child to place pegs in a pegboard under different postural constraints (sitting or standing), fewer differences were evident between normal-weight and overweight children. However, when required to stand and perform the task, the younger children and those children who were overweight performed at a lower level (D'Hondt, Deforche, DeBourdeaudhuij, & Lenoir, 2008).

It is important for parents and teachers to help children develop an enjoyment of movement and a lifetime commitment to being physically active through the development of skilled movement and healthy diet choices.

8.3   *Categorize Types of Physical Fitness*

Physical fitness can be categorized as either skill related or health related. Skill-related fitness is important for enhancing athletic performance, whereas health-related fitness is important for overall wellness.

Skill-Related Fitness

Skill-related fitness is important for sport performance and includes the following:

- Agility
- Reaction time
- Balance
- Coordination
- Speed
- Explosive power

Agility describes how quickly the child can change directions. Using good general space, for example, Sam can move quickly to avoid running into Alicia who is running in his direction.

Reaction time looks at how quickly the child can respond to a given signal. Teachers find reaction time important when playing memory games. Although Shaleah and Shalen reach the answer at the same time, Shaleah presses the button faster because of her quick reaction time.

Balance is the ability to maintain the position of the body in space and includes both *static* and *dynamic* balance. Static balance is used in stationary control (limited movement), whereas dynamic balance is involved when the body is moving. To maintain balance, the vestibular (part of inner ear responsible for balance), visual (eyes), and proprioceptive (awareness of body parts) systems work together. As Carole walks on the beam she is very stable in her movements because of her good balance skills, whereas Marianne has difficulty staying on the beam.

Coordination involves the sequential timing of the muscles to produce a movement based on the feedback from sensory input from the visual and auditory systems. The smooth transition from one muscular contraction to the next produces an efficient action. When Fabio throws the ball, he produces one movement that is smooth without stopping. He steps (with the opposite foot) and uses his hips (twist), shoulders (follow the hips), upper arm (follows the shoulders), and forearm (follows the upper arm). One muscle group follows the next.

Speed is the ability to move in the shortest amount of time required. With practice, Ovande is able to run faster than before.

Explosive power allows the individual to quickly produce a lot of force—as when performing a long jump. Justin runs down a path and explodes to jump over a creek. He knows he cannot land in the water and get his shoes wet.

Health-Related Fitness

Health-related fitness is concerned with the components that lead to the reduction of health-related risk factors and includes the following:

- Cardiovascular endurance
- Muscular strength and endurance

- Flexibility
- Body composition

M² FUN Moving Through the Jungle

This activity involves different types of animals moving through the forest and stopping periodically to rest at a tree. Around the room, scatter carpet squares, beanbags, or something that children can touch—these are the trees. However, the forest needs to have a ranger-check to make sure the trees are not being damaged. Therefore, some children are stationed at cones; these are the forest rangers who watch the trees. The activity starts with children spread around the room touching the trees, or acting as forest rangers in their observation tower. Before starting the music, the teacher tells the children how they are supposed to move around the room and what body part they are supposed to use to touch the tree. When the music stops, the rangers scan the forest to make sure the children are touching the tree with the correct body part. If not, the ranger takes the place of the child at the tree. When the music starts again, all children are open to move and stop at a tree when the music stops.

The teacher can have the children move like animals (e.g., bears, dogs, kangaroos) and have them touch with the animal's body part (e.g., paw, hind leg, tail).

Poor cardiovascular endurance is related to heart disease in adults, whereas limited abdominal strength and endurance, in combination with low flexibility in the back, are related to low back pain. Body composition with high levels of body fat is related to cardiovascular disease.

For adults, increased health-related fitness leads to increase physical fitness as well as the following health benefits:

- Stronger heart and improved cardiovascular fitness
- Lower blood pressure and heart rate
- Reduced risk of heart disease

- Stronger muscles and bones

- Improved flexibility

- More energy for daily activities

- Maintenance of normal body weight (greater lean body mass and lower percentage of fat)

- Greater efficiency for work and play

- Reduced stress and tension

Skill-related fitness is important for older children and adults when playing sports, but it is more important to emphasize health-related fitness for all children, especially young children. We want children to develop a "love of movement" and physical activity habits early in life so they can develop behaviors enabling them to be physically active for a lifetime. Teachers of young children should be concerned with health-related fitness and how to encourage the development of an active lifestyle in young children.

8.4 Explain the Components of Health-Related Fitness

Physical exercise can be divided into two categories: aerobic and anaerobic. This section covers cardiovascular endurance, muscular endurance and strength, flexibility, and body composition. Changes in both aerobic and anaerobic performance are related to physical size and body composition (fat-free mass and fat mass). Each subsection that follows provides a brief overview of the changes in size for the various systems and the physiological changes due to growth and maturation for each health-related fitness component.

Cardiovascular Endurance

Cardiovascular or cardiorespiratory endurance (the terms are used interchangeably in the literature) is a form of muscular endurance. It is the person's ability to transport oxygen to the working muscles and remove waste products, and is also called *aerobic performance*. The body systems related to cardiovascular endurance include the heart and circulatory system and the lungs and the respiratory system.

Maximal oxygen consumption (max VO_2) is the maximum capacity needed by an individual to transport oxygen and use it during exercise. It is used as a measure of the individual's ability to sustain physical work for extended periods of time (i.e., physical fitness). Research has provided clear information about maximum oxygen consumption in older children and adults, but relatively little data exist on children younger than 6 years of age. For children 6 years and older, the data indicate that max VO_2 for boys is constant during childhood and adolescence, with a sharp increase during the adolescent growth spurt, apparently related directly to body size and the rapid growth spurt during adolescence. Girls, on the other hand, are comparable to boys when body weight is accounted for, but experience a decrease in max VO_2 around 10 years of age. Much of this decrease is due to an increase in body fat. Young children are comparable to adults in max VO_2 when body weight is taken into account (relative max VO_2 versus absolute max VO_2).

Gender differences in max VO_2 are minimal in childhood until about 12 years of age. Females do not demonstrate much improvement after 14 years of age, whereas males increase until about 18 years of age (Gabbard, 2011). Maximum oxygen consumption is related to body fat during the adolescent growth spurt. During this period, females increase in percentage of body fat, thus accounting for much of the gender differences.

Muscular Strength and Endurance

Muscular strength is the maximum force that can be generated by a muscle or

▲ Developing strength can be fun.

muscle groups, whereas *muscular endurance* is the capacity of the muscles to continue to work over an extended period of time. Strength is an anaerobic physical activity.

Children increase in muscular strength during childhood and adolescence with minimal gender differences prior to puberty. At puberty, levels of the hormone testosterone increase in males and consequently, males have a sharp increase in muscular strength. This increases to around 40 to 50 percent in adulthood for males. Adult females have only around 60 percent of the muscle mass and force characteristics of males (Gabbard, 2011). Strength increases are due to the cross-sectional size of the muscle; consequently, gender differences relating to strength are due to a size difference, not a difference in the nature of the muscle fiber.

Flexibility

Flexibility refers to the range of motion around a given joint and is joint specific. Flexibility is important for completing daily tasks and preventing injury. Tasks that require flexibility include daily tasks such as tying shoes, rising from a chair, and bending to pick up an object. Flexibility is not related to the length of the limbs and is not restricted by increased muscle strength. Females tend to be more flexible than males.

Fitness tests typically measure flexibility of the back, hip, and hamstring muscles via the sit-and-reach test. Children sit on the floor with their legs in front of them, bend at the waist, and reach for their toes. Flexibility is noted by how far they can reach beyond their feet.

To improve flexibility, individuals must move their joints regularly and systematically through an increasingly larger range of motion. Static (slow and gradual) stretching rather than ballistic (bouncing) stretching is recommended. The stretch should go beyond the typical muscle length but not to the point of pain. Adults should not move a child's limbs through the entire range of motion because they can easily push the child beyond the normal range of motion and cause injury.

Body Composition

Body mass can be divided into lean and adipose tissue. Lean body mass consists of bone, muscle, and organs, whereas adipose tissue is body fat.

Knowing an individual's body composition (percentage of lean body mass and fat) is important because excess fat is related to increased health risk. In addition to influencing health risk, body fat also has an influence on the individual's self-concept. Obesity can negatively contribute to self-concept and make it difficult for the obese child to relate to others. It has been documented that children as young as 3 years of age are aware of the prejudice against obese people (Harriger, Calogero, Witherington, & Smith, 2010; Musher-Eizenman, Holub, Miller, Goldstein, & Edwards-Leeper, 2004). Higher levels of body fat can also affect motor performance. Shirley (1931) discovered that heavy babies demonstrated greater delays in walking than did lighter babies. Jaffe and Kosakov (1982) found that 29 percent of the overweight babies and 36 percent of the obese babies demonstrated motor development delays. Only 9 percent of the normal-weight infants demonstrated motor development delays.

Body weight is not an accurate indication of percentage of body fat. Muscle weighs more than body fat. Two individuals can weigh the same but have very different amounts of lean body mass and body fat. One can have a high percentage of lean body mass and low body fat while the other can have a significantly greater proportion of body fat, yet both may be classified as overweight.

BMI is an estimate of body fat, not a measure of body fat, and is used as a screening tool. Height (inches) and weight (pounds) are measured and put into the formula BMI = [weight/(height × height)] × 703. The BMI score is compared to sex- and age-specific charts and a percentile ranking is obtained. Sex-specific charts at 6-month age intervals estimate percentile rankings. The percentile indicates the relative position of the child in comparison to children of the same sex and age. The categories of BMI are:

- Underweight   <5th percentile
- Healthy weight   5th percentile to <85th percentile
- At risk of overweight   85th percentile to <95th percentile
- Overweight   95th percentile and above

Of concern for early childhood educators is whether overweight children become overweight adults. Tracking research has investigated this issue. Unfortunately, the research shows that overweight children do have a greater risk of becoming overweight adults (Singh, Mulder, Twisk, van Mechelen, & Chinapaw, 2008). Throughout this text, we refer to appropriate nutrition and sufficient physical activity as "healthy" because they help an individual maintain a healthy weight and be physically fit. We want to increase health-related fitness.

8.5 Determine Required Participation in Health-Related Fitness

To improve health-related fitness, the acronym FITT can be used:

- Frequency
- Intensity
- Time
- Type

Frequency should be every day and *intensity* should be moderate-to-vigorous physical activity. Each day, children should be physically active for a *time* period of at least 60 minutes, and the *type* of physical activity should vary. Determining the type of physical activity is important for the child to continue engagement in the activity. During the childhood years, exposure to a variety of physical activities is important; children need to find several activities at which they feel competent.

During the 60 minutes a day of physical activity, children should participate in vigorous physical activity, muscle strengthening and endurance, flexibility, and bone-strengthening activities at least three days per week.

The goal of moderate-to-vigorous physical activity is to improve cardiovascular fitness and muscular endurance that is related to aerobic activities (with oxygen). Muscular strengthening, on the other hand, is increased through anaerobic training. Examples of aerobic activities include skipping, rope jumping, and chasing, whereas anaerobic activities include sprinting (bursts of intense physical activity), vertical jump, and perhaps tug-of-war if the child is exerting maximal force in a short burst of energy.

The difference between moderate and vigorous physical activity can be identified by the heart rate, breathing rate, and amount of sweating. When starting moderate physical activity, there will be a slight but noticeable increase in heart and breathing rate. Brisk walking is an example of moderate physical activity; one can still talk while engaged in moderate physical activity. When doing vigorous physical activity, one will huff and puff and find it difficult to talk. Heart and breathing rates greatly increase, and the person will sweat. Chasing after a child can be an example of vigorous physical activity! Short-term intense bursts of physical activity (such as sprinting) are considered anaerobic.

The early child care educator should allow time for children to run around and be active. Children always love to play tag or be chased. On the playground and in the gross motor skills room, equipment should be set up to encourage large muscle activity. The equipment should be reorganized and changed frequently to keep the environment novel.

Prior to puberty, increased strength does not accompany an increase in muscle size but does lead to improvements in ability to exert force in the intended direction and to activate the contracting and lengthening components of the muscular contraction. The stronger child is better able to isolate the required muscles and not contract two opposing muscles at the same time. Younger children use more muscle mass and more forceful contraction to perform the same movement as an older child who has had experience with the movement. Nicholas, at age 3.5 years, copies his older brother Benjamin to perform a one-legged balance. Although they look the same, Nicholas uses more muscles (contralateral muscles) and more force to perform the same balance position. Nicholas will tire more quickly than his older brother, who has isolated the specific muscles and only uses the force needed.

A major part of determining either aerobic or anaerobic efficiency is in performing the skill. If a child can perform the skill efficiently, then he or she is also conserving energy and will improve the score. For example, when asking a child to jump up, the skilled performer efficiently times muscle contractions and uses appropriate muscle force. The young child, however, contracts more muscles than necessary and uses more force in the muscles. Therefore, this child cannot last as long as an older child can.

Children completing repeated forceful contractions might cause injury to their growing bones. Little League officials, for example, noticed an injury problem in children training extensively in baseball. A pattern of children with elbow problems resulted from damage to growth plates at the elbow. As a result of these injury patterns, Little League officials initiated rules that restricted the numbers of games a child can pitch, the amount of time a child should spend practicing, and the amount of rest required between games. This rule drastically reduced the number of injuries.

Males, at puberty, have a distinct advantage in strength training due to their increased levels of testosterone. However, prior to puberty strength gains are limited. Strength is not a factor in movement and sport for the young child; skill level makes the difference.

Under no circumstances should preadolescent children compete in strength training (American Academy of Pediatrics, 2008). Instead children should be provided with appropriate playground strength opportunities to climb, hang, and push and pull.

Including Fitness Activities

Paralleling the National Standards for Physical Education, NASPE (2012) has also developed a scope and sequence for grade-level fitness standards, The Scope and Sequence of Fitness Education for Pre K–16 Programs, NASPE Fitness Education Project (www.aahperd.org/naspe/publications/upload/Scope-Sequence-of-Fitness-Education-for-PreK-16-Programs.pdf). The following is NASPE's definition of fitness education:

> Fitness education is the instructional and learning process of acquiring values, knowledge and skills; experiencing regular participation in physical activity; and promoting healthy nutrition choices to achieve life-enhancing health-related fitness (p. 5). (Reprinted with permission from the American Alliance for Health, Physical Education, Recreation and Dance, www.AAHPERD.org.)

An example of an age-dependent standard is the technique for developing cardiovascular fitness. For preschool, the standard includes performing cardiovascular activities demonstrating body control. For first and second grade, this changes to including body alignment and control when performing cardiovascular activities.

The standards are used to create a developmental sequence that is then associated with a grade level and increases in difficulty with increasing age. The following example demonstrates the increased requirement for body control: starting with generic control, moving to specific control during skilled movement, and concluding in fifth grade with skilled form and knowing the principles of aerobic training.

Guidelines for infants, toddlers, and young children were revised in 2009 (NASPE, 2009). The following is NASPE's position statement on engagement of infants, toddlers, and young children in physical activity:

> All children from birth to age five should engage daily in physical activity that promotes movement skillfulness and foundations of health-related fitness (p. iv). (Reprinted with permission from the American Alliance for Health, Physical Education, Recreation and Dance, www. AAHPERD.org.)

Throughout the publication, NASPE provides physical activity patterns of infants, toddlers, and young children. For each guideline, there are specific examples of how to increase levels of physical activity so the infant, toddler, or preschooler is physically active for 60 minutes or more per day.

As children engage in moderate to vigorous physical activity, we need to understand how they adapt to the environment. Therefore, next we address issues relate to temperature regulation. Understanding how environmental temperature affects children differently from adults is critical as we develop our lessons. We discuss the issues of children working, playing, and exercising in hot, humid, and cold environments.

Temperature Regulation

Children are exposed to all types of environments, ranging from the hot and humid climates of the south to the extremely cold climates of the north. It is important to understand that children do not respond to hot or cold climates similarly to adults. Children's sweat glands are not fully developed and consequently do not dissipate heat as well as those of adults. Children also dehydrate rapidly. This means that they feel overheated before the teacher does and also lose water faster. In addition, children do not acclimatize to heat as well as adults. When there is a rise in temperature, it takes the child longer to adjust to the hot environment. Consequently, a child can develop heat-related problems much more quickly than an adult.

Children also have a greater problem in colder climates. When exposed to the cold, children, especially young infants, lose their body heat more quickly. Children need to be clothed in layers; as the temperature rises, clothing can be shed so children do not run the risk of overheating.

In cold environments, especially when swimming in cold water, we need to watch and listen to the child. We should not think that just because we are not shivering, the child is fine. We need to look for signs of temperature loss—blue lips and shivering.

Sweating is not a good predictor of exercise intensity or effort for either adults or children. We tend to sweat more in hot and humid climates than on hot, low-humidity days. The evaporation mechanism is what is important. The evaporation of sweat from the skin cools the blood in the capillaries near the skin's surface—which, in turn, helps to maintain an optimal temperature level. If the adult is hot, the child probably feels the heat to a greater degree because the child's sweat glands are not completely developed. Thus, it is extremely important for staff in direct contact with children to allow frequent water breaks and, when necessary, time for the children to rest and cool down in the shade.

Water

Water is needed to survive—we can live longer without food than without water. The adult body is 50 to 60 percent water by weight, and the percentage of body water decreases as age increases (Leeds, 2012). Water functions to transport dissolved nutrients through the blood system and to cool the body and brain. It also helps to cushion the body, regulates body temperature, provides lubrication to eyelids and joints, assists digestion in the gastrointestinal tract, and removes waste from the body. The main source of water to the human body is drinking water. Some foods, particularly fruits and vegetables, contain significant amounts of water, and can be considered when helping children meet the body's need for water. Dehydration can lead to dizziness, fatigue, and lack of concentration.

Because water is so important, adults should encourage children to drink throughout the day, particularly during and after physical activity. Children should have child-accessible sources of water readily available. It is encouraging to see many desks in schools with individual water bottles on them and large canisters of water with individual paper cups available on playgrounds and playing fields. It is important to make sure that children are always hydrated during normal activity periods or during illness. Children should be encouraged by adults to drink water frequently throughout the day. An inadequate consumption of water will cause an imbalance between the interior and exterior of body cells, as well as the loss of electrolytes vital to the health and survival of the cells and systems of the body.

Throughout this section we have presented the research underlying the development of health-related fitness throughout childhood. The next section provides recommendations for helping young children develop an understanding of physical fitness and its importance across the lifespan.

8.6 *Know the Qualities of a Physically Educated Child*

As early childhood educators, we want to instill a love of movement in toddlers, young children, and preadolescents. The National Children and Youth Fitness Study (Dotson & Ross, 1985; Pate & Ross, 1987) attempted to find factors that influence a child's level of physical activity via a fitness test. The study looked at children from 5 to 18 years of age. The results indicated that children who did better on fitness tests tended to participate in more community-based activities, watch less television, have physical education instruction from a specialist, be exposed to more types of activities, and live in families that were more active.

Research indicates that children need to be exposed to physical activity early, and must be able to choose a physical activity at which they feel successful and in which the family can participate together. Teachers and parents need to be good role models. Children need to see their parents engage in physical activity—because the family that participates together stays healthy together!

We need to acknowledge this initial passion for movement so children continue to enjoy a lifetime of physical activity and fitness. In addition, we need to instill a passion for eating healthy vegetables, fruits, whole grains, proteins, and dairy foods.

8.7 Determine the Role of Environment in Nutrition

Mr. Jimenez is preparing the classroom for his kindergarteners after their holiday vacation. By now he is familiar with his children and the conditions in their surroundings (classroom, home, and community) that have an effect on their learning and help frame who they are and their role in the larger community. The daily learning plan that centers on music and movement can be affected by many events over which Mr. Jimenez has little control:

- Will Kasandra be distracted because of her usual breakfast of pancakes made with white flour and chocolate chips and covered with high-fructose corn syrup?

- Will Ramiro not eat any breakfast and be tired and irritable?

- Will Berta forget to sit at the non-peanut lunch table and have an allergic reaction to Carlo's peanut butter sandwich?

- Will Frankie be tired due to lack of sleep because he traveled with his family over the holiday?

- Will the children tease Martha about her weight?

Mr. Jimenez understands that the events, people, and objects that are in the lives of the children have an important effect on the physical and mental health of each child. He knows that Kasandra's diet, which is low in nutrients and high in sugar, is influencing her learning. Her energy levels may have fluctuations due to her consumption of simple-carbohydrate foods. Mr. Jimenez knows that Ramiro's pattern of not eating at regular intervals is affecting his concentration and his long-term health. Berta's allergy attack caused by a protein or chemical toxin may have a devastating and life-threatening reaction on her, and it will also be disruptive to the daily learning of all the children in the classroom. Mr. Jimenez will have to make spontaneous adjustments to his learning plan to accommodate the allergic reaction. Frankie's lack of sleep will affect his energy level and his immune response, which may have long-term repercussions to his health and learning. This will mean Mr. Jimenez will have to send learning activities home for Frankie to work on while he is absent from school. The teasing of Martha about her weight could damage Martha's positive sense of self. In addition, Martha does not always feel comfortable participating in movement activities. Her weight is starting to affect her social development and her physical well-being. Her family and Mr. Jimenez can be understanding and provide guidance.

The behavior habits of families and their children have a tremendous effect on experiencing a healthy lifestyle. Higher rates of overweight and obesity are evident in African American females and Mexican American males (Rand Health, 2004). There is a negative correlation between weight gain and income level and the related educational level. Children from low-income families are more susceptible to obesity (Sherry, Mei, Scanlon, Mokdad, & Grummer-Strawn, 2004). Individuals of lower socioeconomic position consume diets that are higher in fat and lower in fruit and vegetables (Williams, Veitch, & Ball, 2011). Many families would like to purchase better-quality food, but it is expensive to purchase and not always available where they live.

Healthy eating is an important part of physical fitness and well-being; the environments children are associated with in daily activities—such as schools, child care programs, and retail stores in the communities—can influence (positively or negatively) the healthfulness of the children's diets (Story, Kaphingst, Robinson-O'Brian, & Glanz, 2008). Behaviors associated with weight gain (increased sedentary activities and overeating) are learned and need to be replaced with behaviors associated with maintaining a healthy weight (physical activity and healthy eating habits) (Shields, 2009). To maintain a healthy weight, it is important to have a balance between amount of food consumed and the amount of energy expended. It is also important to maintain balance by practicing healthy eating habits. Healthy eating is eating the correct foods in the correct amounts to maintain a sufficient level of energy to match the activity level of the child.

Characteristics of Healthy Eating

To experience a healthy lifestyle, children should be provided with high-quality food that provides energy to be active. Energy is necessary to play, to build body tissue, and to maintain the body temperature at 98.6 degrees Fahrenheit. A *calorie* is a term used to describe the amount of heat produced by the metabolizing of food. High-quality food is necessary for the activity level and growth of children because it contains vital nutrients needed to maintain maximum growth and health. Energy-supplying and non–energy-supplying nutrients are examined next for the roles they play in providing energy to the body (Leeds, 2012).

Energy-supplying nutrients are important because carbohydrates provide energy to the body, aid in the synthesis of substances, and promote normal bowel movements. Fats or lipids, another energy-supplying nutrient, serve as storage for excessive calories, supply a source of fuel, and also provide body insulation. Fats also provide taste and aroma to the foods we eat and are higher in calories than carbohydrates and protein. Finally, proteins are the building blocks of the body. They are required for building and maintaining all body tissues.

The non–energy-supplying nutrients—vitamins, minerals, and water—encourage good health through the building and regulating of body functions, prevention of disease, and the promotion of healing. Carbohydrates, fats, and proteins are found in five food groups: grains, vegetables, fruits, dairy products, and meat and beans. The total calorie amount needed from the five food groups varies according to the age and gender of the child. Older children need more calories than younger children. In addition there is slight gender difference in older children. The Mayo Clinic has provided healthy-eating guidelines for young children(Mayo Clinic, 2012) indicating the importance of eating an age-appropriate amount of food to regulate calories. The proportions of food eaten by a child may contribute to a gain in weight. The amount of food a child eats varies from meal to meal and day to day; however, children should never be encouraged to overeat, and the foods they are given should follow the proper proportions of the five basic food groups.

It is also significant to see the larger amount of vegetables and fruits needed for a healthy diet compared with proteins and grains. The amounts given in the tables will vary according to the growth and activity levels of each child.

We cannot forget that all children also need water to maintain a healthy lifestyle. Children between the ages of 1 and 3 years need to drink four 8-ounce cups of water daily, whereas children between 4 and 8 years of age need to drink five 8-ounce cups of water each day (Consortium to Lower Obesity in Chicago Children, 2013).

Drinks containing caffeine and alcohol act as diuretics and increase urination, depleting the body of water content. Beverages containing caffeine should *not* be given to children to provide the daily requirement of water.

Remember Martha in Mr. Jimenez's class? Her family and her teacher should encourage her to follow the proper nutrient proportions when she eats (see Table 8.1) using the healthy diet guidelines. Of course, they should also support her the drinking at least five cups of water daily and engaging in frequent physical activity.

The healthiest foods listed in Table 8.2 are considered to be nutrient-rich foods high in vitamins, minerals, fiber, and protein (Mateljan, 2007). In addition, the foods are not highly processed and contain only naturally occurring nutrients. Use of the healthiest foods seasoned by herbs (e.g., parsley, basil, cilantro, rosemary) and spices (e.g., turmeric, cinnamon, pepper) promotes the health of the children.

Statistics have shown that children in the United States are facing a dim future because of weight gain. The types of food eaten and the proportions of the foods eaten must be examined. What effect is children's environment having on their diet?

Table 8.1 Proportion Guidelines for a Healthy Diet

Age	Gender	Calories	Protein	Fruits	Vegetables	Grains	Dairy
2–3	Female	1,000–1,400	¼–½ cup	1–1½ cups	1–1½ cups	⅓–⅔ cup	2–2½ cups
2–3	Male	1,000–1,400	¼–½ cup	1–1½ cups	1–1½ cups	⅓–⅔ cup	2–2½ cups
4–8	Female	1,200–1,800	⅓–⅔ cup	1–1½ cups	1½–2½ cups	⅓–¾ cup	2½–3 cups
4–8	Male	1,200–2,000	⅓–⅔ cup	1–2 cups	1½–2½ cups	⅓–¾ cup	2½–3 cups

• Calories and portion sizes will vary according to growth rate and activity level.

Table 8.2 Healthiest Food Recommendations

Food Group	Examples
Dairy	• Whole milk recommended for children 1–2 years • 2% milk recommended for children 2–3 years • 1% milk recommended for children 3 years and older consuming 2 or 3 cups daily • Low-fat yogurt • Low-fat cheese
Vegetables	Spinach, Swiss chard, asparagus, broccoli, kale, tomatoes, Brussels sprouts, green beans, summer and winter squash, bell peppers, cauliflower, green peas, cabbage, carrots, beets, eggplant, cucumbers, onions, sweet potatoes, potatoes, avocados, corn, mushrooms, olives
Fruits	Strawberries, raspberries, cantaloupe, pineapple, kiwifruit, oranges, papaya, watermelon, grapes, blueberries, bananas, plums, apples, pears
Grains	Oats, rye, quinoa, brown rice, wheat, buckwheat
Protein	• Nuts and seeds (sunflower seeds, flaxseeds, sesame seeds, pumpkin seeds, walnuts, almonds, peanuts, cashews) • Lean poultry • Fish • Beans and legumes (soybeans, kidney beans, pinto beans, black beans, garbanzo beans, tofu, navy beans, split peas)

Characteristics of Unhealthy Diets

Children are eating approximately one-third of their calories through meals at restaurants, and these meals tend to be below standard nutritional choices (Crothers, Kehle, Bray, & Theodore, 2009). In addition, families are buying many high-calorie but low-nutritional foods. Advertising by the food industry targets families' need for shortened or no food preparation time by marketing quick-to-prepare but low-nutritional foods. The food industry spends $20 billion a year marketing foods low in nutrition to children (Brownell & Warner, 2009). The cereals most frequently marketed to children—Honey Nut Cheerios, Froot Loops, Lucky Charms, and Pebbles—contain 32 percent to 41 percent sugar (Cereal

F.A.C.T.S., 2012). This type of marketing, typically using cartoons, is engaging and difficult to combat. At a very early age, children learn to eat foods that are not good for them.

The result is that children and adults are eating foods high in sugar, fat, and salt. Observe what children are eating in restaurants, schools, and child care facilities, and you will see many consuming sweetened drinks, cookies, candy, and chips. These types of foods are highly processed and tend to be substandard in nutritional choices. In addition, the proportion sizes of the food served exceed the recommended amounts.

Sugar. Children are drinking excessive calories that provide little nutritional value. Sugar-sweetened drinks and juices should not be given to children except in very limited amounts. Children who drink several servings of sugar-sweetened drinks every day have a higher risk of being overweight (Consortium to Lower Obesity in Chicago Children, 2013). They are consuming more liquid calories without decreasing their solid calorie intake. Sugar has been placed in almost every processed food item, including meat, vegetables, fruit, potatoes, and bread (Kessler, 2013).

Many items sold in restaurants and grocery stores have multiple forms of added sugars, such as sucrose, glucose, and dextrose. When in the grocery store, examine various cans of beans, for example, and observe the amount of sugar added to the vegetables. Also inspect the contents of many popular cereals to see the types of sugars placed in the food. When you see the amount of sugar added to the grains, you will see why they are tasty to so many individuals. The result is that Americans are consuming much more sugar than they did 200 years ago. In the early 1800s, the average person consumed 10 pounds of sugar a year; today the average Americans are eating 150 to 180 pounds per year (Hyman, 2012).

High-fructose corn syrup is a food product made from corn stalks through a chemical process that makes a compound that is sweeter and cheaper to use than cane sugar (sucrose). It is rapidly absorbed into the bloodstream, triggering liver damage and spikes in insulin that can cause metabolic disturbances (Hyman, 2012). In the 1970s, high-fructose corn syrup was not used in processed foods; however, by 2012 about 50 percent of the sugar mixture in foods was high-fructose corn syrup (Ritter, 2012).

Fat. The food industry has added fats to processed foods to improve flavor and to help food enter the digestive tract with less effort. The result is that more food can be eaten in a shorter length of time with less effort. To eat a meal of unprocessed food, each mouthful needs to be chewed 25 times; processed food can be chewed in about 10 chews per mouthful (Kessler, 2013). Many families, for example, select chicken nuggets at a fast food restaurant, thinking it is a healthy choice because it is lean chicken. What children are really eating, though, is chopped chicken pressed with ingredients such as water, sugar, oil, and chemicals and then fried (Kessler, 2013). This is why they come in "cute" shapes, which attracts children.

Salt. Salt is the other food additive that is increasing our desire for food. Originally, the only way to put salt in food was to add it at the cooking stage or at the table. Today most processed foods have salt added. Too much salt increases the likelihood of high blood pressure, osteoporosis, dehydration, and other physical problems. The effects of too much salt consumption by adults are detrimental, but this is especially true for children whose hearts and kidneys are developing. Salt should not be at the table in schools.

The major cause of weight gain today is due to the amount of processed food in our diets. We are eating too many foods to which the food industry has added sugar, fat, and salt (Kessler, 2013). Sadly, these processed foods, high in added sugars, fats, salt, and additional calories, have little or no nutritional value. Our children's health is being placed at risk because of the foods they are eating. It is important to plan healthy meals for children.

8.8 Construct a Balanced Nutritional Environment for Young Children

To ensure that each child develops to his or her fullest potential, it is important to focus and to support the family, the community, and the culture that creates the environment surrounding the child. Children have a right to adequate nutritional and responsible feeding practices. What can families, child care staff, school administrators, teachers, and communities do to ensure that the children have not only adequate but also high-quality nutrition? Use of food guides and food labels, ensuring accessibility to quality foods, involvement in food preparation, and making quality changes to the school lunch programs will help to guarantee quality nutrition for children.

Food Guides

Food guides—such as the "Choose My Plate" visual developed by the federal government (see Figure 8.1)— provide visual representations to assist families in designing daily meals and snacks.

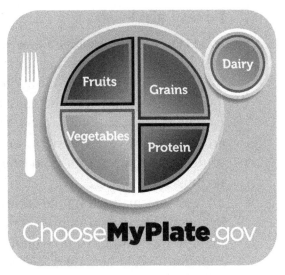

Figure 8.1 "Choose My Plate" (http://www. choosemyplate.gov/print-materials-ordering/ graphic-resources.html)

Choose My Plate uses a dinner plate as a visual to provide a comparison of how much of the five food groups to eat. Half the plate should be fruits and vegetables, with vegetables dominating. The plate visually demonstrates almost equal portions of grains and protein. Half of the grains should be composed of whole grains, entire-grain kernels, and half-refined grains in which the grain kernel is mulled. A variety of foods qualify as proteins (meats, nuts and seeds, seafood, eggs, and soy products). Dairy portions are represented by a cup or circle. Dairy includes milk, cheese, yogurt, and soy milk.

M² FUN   Food Rainbow

Give each child a paper plate and assorted paint swatches (red, purple, yellow, green shades, brown) from your local hardware store. Around the room, position pictures of food displaying a wide variety of color. Have the children design their plate using all the colors. They will create a rainbow of food.

Food Labels

Food labels assist families and caregivers by providing the nutritional content of foods used to meet the recommended allowances. The 1990 Nutritional Labeling and Education Act made food labels user friendly by providing the buyer with the name of the product, its net weight, and the manufacture's name and address. The label lists the ingredients in order of prominence in the food item, and provides the nutrition content per adult-size serving, as well as an evaluation of the nutrition content of each serving (see Figure 8.2).

The information on food labels lists the percentage of calories in the following areas: total calories, fat (saturated, unsaturated), cholesterol, sodium, total carbohydrates (dietary fiber, sugars), and protein. Special attention should be paid to the sodium (salt) content, sugar (carbohydrates), and fat. We know that these items can cause dietary problems. In addition, attention should also be given the number of calories and the

Nutritional Facts

Serving Size 1/2 cup (125g)

Servings Per Container   about 6

Amount Per Serving

Calories 60   Calories from Fat 15

	% Daily Value*
Total Fat 2g	3%
Saturated Fat 0g	0%
Cholesterol 0mg	0%
Sodium 590mg	25%
Total Carbohydrate 9g	3%
Dietary Fiber 3g	12%
Sugar 7g	
Protein 2g	
Vitamin A 13%	Vitamin C 0%
Calcium 6%	Iron 10%

*Percent Daily Values are based on a 2,000 calorie diet

Figure 8.2 Example of a nutrition label.

serving size. Remember, when preparing food for children, that the labeled serving sizes are for adults. Many children are eating serving sizes for adults, which are causing them to consume too many calories.

In addition, it is vital that children do not consume fruits and vegetables contaminated with pesticides. Pesticides may increase the risk of triggering toxic neurological and cancer-causing responses in the human body (Moore, 2003). Fruits and vegetables should be washed to remove pesticides. The Environmental Working Group (EWG) (2013) has identified a listing of fruits and vegetables, referred to as the "Dirty Dozen," that have the highest levels of pesticides; fruits and vegetables that are on the list include apples, potatoes, celery, and others. Buying organic varieties of these fruits and vegetables helps to reduce the exposure. The EWG also lists the "Clean Fifteen," which include mangoes, mushrooms, and onions, among others. (For more information, visit the website of the EWG, http://www.ewg.org.)

Accessibility to Quality Foods

It is important for children and their families to have access to fresh quality foods. Much of the food eaten in the United States is trucked or flown to the purchasers from great distances. This means that many foods are picked early to ensure freshness when packaged, shipped, and distributed. In this journey, food loses not only freshness, but also nutrients. If foods are purchased locally, not only is freshness ensured, but air pollutants are also reduced. Therefore, food should be purchased locally whenever possible. Farmers' markets are growing in number and many schools are now growing cafeteria foods on school grounds. The children are often involved in the process. This movement is even taking place in inner city schools, where vegetables are grown on rooftops and even vertically on walls. View the inspiring story of Stephen Ritz, a teacher in the inner city (see **video** A Teacher Growing Green in the South Bronx).

Food Preparation

The preparation of food is another area in which foods can become contaminated with chemicals (biological and physical) that can cause harm to children and adults. Examples of possible contaminants are shown in Table 8.3 (Idaho Food Protection, 2013).

Table 8.3 Food Contaminants

Food Contaminants		
Physical	**Chemical**	**Pathogenic**
Jewelry	Cleaning agents	Parasites
Glass	Pesticides	Bacteria
Adhesive bandages		Viruses
Staples		
Machinery parts		

Physical contamination can occur when preparing food; an individual may lose rings, earrings, or a chip of a fingernail. Glass containers used in the process may be broken and a small piece may accidentally fall into the food. Nancy was eating a chocolate chip ice cream cone when she discovered a very large "chocolate chip"—a brown piece of plastic, part of the beater that broke off the paddle used to make the ice cream.

Pathogens.   Care should be taken to avoid the spread of pathogens such as *Salmonella* or *E. coli*, *Listeria*, *Norovirus*, and *Shigellosis* because they can cause diarrhea, vomiting, and breathing difficulties. Food is the perfect incubator for the spread of these contaminants.

Hand Washing.   Anyone working with food should make sure his or her hands are washed or wear gloves before handling the food. Hands should be washed with soap and warm running water, rubbing all surfaces, including the front, back, fingers, and nail beds, followed by thoroughly rinsing and drying the hands with a paper towel before using the towel to turn off the water (see Figure 8.3). If cloths or towels are used, the "one use rule" should be followed; this rule also applies to gloves worn in food preparation or any cleanup duty.

Temperatures.   Foods should be thoroughly cooked to destroy parasites, bacteria, and viruses, and stored at appropriate temperatures to avoid the growth of contaminants. Cold foods should be stored at 41 degrees Fahrenheit or colder and cooked foods should be kept at a holding temperature of 135 degrees Fahrenheit or hotter. The temperatures

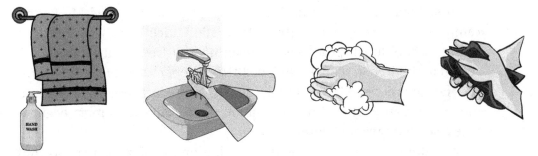

Figure 8.3 Steps in hand washing.

between 41 and 135 are considered the danger zone for foods. The optimal food temperatures must be maintained with anyone—from professionals to children—working with food. Simple hygiene and basic temperatures will certainly help to ensure that foods cooked and given to children are safe.

School Lunch Programs

Many children receive one- to two-thirds of their foods through school lunch programs. The national school lunch program is big business. Approximately 31 million American children ate federally subsidized lunches in the 2008–2009 school year (Julian, 2010). School lunch programs are part of the problem because they have been designed to provide foods that children will eat—pizza and chicken nuggets are popular entrée choices and corn and potatoes (fried) are the major vegetable choices (Julian, 2010). Schools that should be part of the solution have become part of the problem. The U.S. Department of Agriculture's (USDA's) Food and Nutrition Services division administers the nation's school lunch program and agriculture distribution of surplus commodities. The USDA does maintain nutritional regulations. The regulations were changed in 2010 when President Obama signed the Healthy Hunger-Free Kids Act. This act was the first major change in 30 years in the way school lunches were administered (USDA, 2013a). Some of the changes made by the 2010 act were to availability of free potable water during mealtimes, review of nutritional and wellness standards, and encouragement of physical activity for children.

Individuals such as Jamie Oliver (originator of the "Feed Me Better" campaign) and Ann Cooper (the "Renegade Lunch Lady") are trying to change school lunch programs by ensuring that fresh, nutritious food is served to children in schools (Julian, 2010). Cooper (2011) feels we should say "no" to processed foods containing fats, high-fructose corn syrup, hormones, and antibiotics. Children, families, and educators must begin to take a stand on what children are eating.

Children should be exposed to tasting and cooking classes so they broaden their knowledge of foods. In addition, every school, be it rural or inner city, should engage in gardening classes in which children can begin to make the connection to healthy foods. Schools can be part of the solution (see **video** Nutrition: Turning Kids into Healthy Eaters).

Total Environment

It is also important for children to have an environment free of allergens and contaminates. Allergic reactions occur when the protein in the foods produce *antibodies* that may cause breathing problem or hives. Since 1960, the incidence of food allergies in children has increased from 1 in 100 children to 1 in 20 children. Peanuts, milk, eggs, wheat, soy, tree nuts (walnut and almonds), fish, and shellfish can cause allergies (Devoe, 2008).

Allergic reactions affect the quality of life (physically, socially, and emotionally) for the child and the family. Cafeteria staff and teachers involved in food preparations must ensure cleaning procedures to avoid cross contamination. Lists should be kept in every classroom as to what foods need to be avoided to accommodate the children with allergies. Many schools encourage families to give their children's classmates non-food birthday gifts or to order foods for children's birthday parties from a list prepared by the cafeteria staff.

Additional allergic reactions may be caused by chemicals in the environment. Fragrances in the form of air fresheners, scented candles, and perfume can trigger allergic symptoms (Farrow, Taylor, Northstone, & Golding, 2003). Schools, child care facilities, and families who want to ensure children a healthy, chemical-free environment must examine all the possible sources of chemicals in the environment, such as dryer sheets, laundry detergents, soaps, hairspray, and plastic bottles, to name a few.

Plastic bottles can contain the chemical family of *obesogens*. These chemicals have been correlated with the obesity epidemic in 6-month-old infants because they bind to receptors that regulate hormonal control of fat cell development and balance (Erickson, 2010). Fructose found in beverages and foods is an obesogen. Additional obesogens can be found in compounds used in nonstick cookware and some plastic toys.

Child-Rearing Practices

Sleep is very important to the health of every individual for every developmental aspect—physical, cognitive, and social. Children's sleep patterns often reflect child-rearing practice or behaviors. Children should have the required amount of sleep each night, supplemented with appropriate naps, and regulated by consistent bed and nap times. It has been shown that children who slept fewer hours each night (having a later bedtime or earlier rising time) were more likely to be overweight (Crothers, Kehle, Bray, & Theodore, 2009). Based on this fact, experts recommend that infants through school-age children have 10 or 11 hours of sleep each night (Snell, Adam, & Duncan, 2007).

Another child-rearing practice—the first in a child's life involving food—is whether to breast-feed or formula-feed the infant. Breast-feeding has emotional, physiological, and practical advantages for both mother and child. Families and child care staff should encourage and support the breast-feeding mother in her choice. Supplemental water and/or formula or solid foods should not be introduced to the breast-fed infant without the permission of the family. Some mothers and families may choose to use formula. In any case, families should be involved in the decision when to introduce solids into the diet of the infant. The early introduction of solids is linked to rapid weight gain. This gain may have implications for obesity problems later in the life of the child (Sloan, Gildea, Stewart, Sneddon, & Iwaniec, 2007). Pediatricians and nutritionists need to be consulted as to the best time to introduce solids to an infant, which is generally between 4 and 6 months of age.

Clearly, many factors may have an effect on providing children with a healthy environment. The question now is: How we can improve the situation and create an environment where children can reach their full potential? How we can create a balance between a healthy child and a healthy environment?

8.9 *Create a Culture That Promotes Physical Activity and Healthy Eating*

Developing a culture that promotes a physically active lifestyle and healthy eating is important. To do this, the family, school, and community must be involved and work together to create a healthy environment for children.

The family is the most important part of creating a physically active culture and ensuring a diet high in nutritionally dense foods. Mothers who were physically active had children who were two times more likely to be physically active than children of inactive mothers. If both parents were active, the child was 5.8 times more likely to be active (Moore, Lombardi, White, Campbell, Oliveria, & Ellison, 1991). Reasons for the greater level of physical activity of children of active parents include parents as role models and facilitators of physical activity who are involved and provide encouragement (Welk, 1999).

Children will model their parents' behavior; if their parents are active, the children will want to be involved. For children to be physically active, the parents have to facilitate the activity to make participation in physical activity easy. Facilitation includes registering for physical activity classes and providing transportation to the facility. Parents engaged with their children in physical activity are an example of parental involvement. By throwing and catching with their children, or taking walks, or even watching children participate in their own activities, parents become directly involved with their children and demonstrate to the child the importance of physical activity (see **video** Barefoot Running with Kids).

Parents can also model appropriate eating habits and encourage their children to adopt the same eating patterns. When parents provide feedback to their children, parents can influence the children's perception of their competence that directly influences involvement. Parental feedback needs to be not only positive, but also informative.

Not only is parental involvement critical for developing a culture of physical activity, but so is involvement of the early childhood educator. A physical activity culture within the school should be developed. The early childhood educator is also a role model for children, and as such should be involved with the children participating in physical activity, facilitate physical activity, and provide encouragement. Children will watch their teacher's every move. If the teacher is involved in movement activities with the children, the children will also move. Children love to have their teacher play with them—be it playing catch, walking or running around a field, and yes, even chasing. The teacher can facilitate physical activity by including "activity breaks," providing opportunities to be physically active during recess, and incorporating physical activity as a means to learn math, language arts, social studies, and other subjects. Ms. Angelo, a substitute teacher, always carried with her a "fun bag" to supplement the classroom teacher's planned activities. Most of the items (beanbags, paper streamers) in the bag were used to stimulate physical activity. She also carried an electronic device with a variety of downloaded music to promote free movement.

Not all parents are good role models for creating a physically active culture; however, as a teacher, you can assist the family in understanding the importance of physical activity. The Centers for Disease Control and Prevention (CDC) (2011) emphasizes the importance of family and community involvement to develop policies, practices, and programs to develop and implement healthy eating and participation in physical activity. The CDC's strategies (CDC, 2011, p. 42) that are applicable to the early childhood educator include *communication* among schools, families, and community members; *participation* in programs and activities that promote healthy eating and physical activity; and *cultural awareness* in healthy eating and physical activity.

To accomplish these goals, the early childhood educator needs to communicate with parents frequently about the curriculum on healthy eating and physical activity. Feedback and suggestions from families and other community members should be encouraged. You can tell them of your policies on healthy eating and physical activity and get input from them on the policies. You can also provide community and family members with opportunities to volunteer and be involved. Newsletters are a great way to communicate with families.

Family and community participation in promoting healthy eating and physical activity is important. To support involvement, family homework, family nights, and Internet-based programs can actively engage the children and families. For this to work, however, multiple opportunities for families to participate are necessary. These opportunities also need to be offered in a variety of formats to attract high levels of participation. Families will thus be able to choose the opportunities in which they are interested and that will also work with their schedules.

Barriers to family participation in school include scheduling conflicts and lack of transportation. To assist with these barriers, try to schedule events to coordinate with other meetings, such as parent-teacher conferences, PTA meetings, and the like, or perhaps have "family time" for 30 minutes around children's pickup time.

Summary

Participating in physical activity is important for a lifetime of health. Early childhood is an important time to develop intrinsic motivation for children to move. We need to realize, however, that young children are not miniature adults. Children are psychologically and physiologically different from adults. We need to understand the physical changes that occur with age and how these changes affect motor performance and fitness measures. Even within a given age, children are very different. Emphasizing the importance of physical activity, providing time during the day to be physical active, exposing children to a variety of activities, and being a good role model are essential for the promotion of a healthy lifestyle.

As we saw earlier in the chapter, Mr. Jimenez was concerned about various children in his kindergarten class who might not have been ready to learn because of circumstances in their environment. Many educators and parents are faced with the problem of how to improve the children's surrounding so every child will be healthy and ready to learn. In his classroom, Mr. Jimenez must deal with the growing obesity problem. He knows that this problem is connected to both lack of exercise and the amount and types of food children are eating. It is important for developing children to have appropriate amounts of protein, carbohydrates, and fats, as well as vitamins, minerals, and water. Excessive use of sugar, fats, and salt in processed foods, however, is playing a significant role in the quality of children's diets and the increase of obesity. The amount of meals eaten out, industry marketing, school lunch programs, socioeconomic situations, sedentary lifestyle, and environmental conditions all play a role in healthy eating habits and a healthy lifestyle. Choose My Plate and food labels assist educators and families in buying and preparing nutritious meals for children. In addition, attention to avoiding pesticides and other contaminants in foods is important for a healthy diet. Watch the following example of a bilingual nutrition lesson on smelling and tasting (see **video**).

Summary Related to Outcomes

Learning Outcomes	Guiding Principles
8.1 Develop a physically educated person	Individual Needs Met
The obesity epidemic is growing at an alarming rate. It is important that educators, parents, and children understand the problem and work toward increasing physical activity and promoting healthy eating.	
8.2 Understand the relationships among physical activity, physical fitness, nutrition, and wellness	Individual Needs Met
The physical and physiological changes that occur with maturation and development are important in understanding and setting goals for children. A young child who has shorter legs and lower aerobic capacity, for example, cannot be expected to run as far or as fast as an older child with longer legs and greater aerobic capacity. Matching the task to the child's structural and functional constraints is needed.	
8.3 Categorize types of physical fitness	Individual Needs Met
The two types of physical fitness are skill related and health related. Health-related fitness is the type of fitness that we need to be concerned with in school. Health-related fitness includes cardiovascular endurance, muscular strength and endurance, flexibility, body composition, and bone health.	
8.4 Explain the components of health-related fitness	Individual Needs Met
Standards are the guide to developing a physically active lifestyle. The national standards, NASPE standards, and various state standards are interrelated. The national standards are broad, with increasing detail as the standards become more local. These are extremely important in determining the prerequisite skills needed for developmentally appropriate physical activity lessons.	

Learning Outcomes	Guiding Principles
8.5 Determine required participation in health-related fitness	Individual Needs Met

Toddlers to aging adults need to be active for a minimum of 60 minutes per day. Although toddlers and young children are not consciously working at developing fitness, they should engage in moderate to vigorous physical activity for at least an hour a day.

8.6 Know the qualities of a physically educated child	Assessment and Standards Provide Guidance

A physically educated child participates in more community-based activities, watches less television, has a physical education teacher, is exposed to more types of activities, and is a member of a more active family.

8.7 Determine the role of environment in nutrition	Environment and Curriculum Reciprocated

Eating nutritionally dense foods is part of being fit. Families and teachers can be part of the solution to obesity by recognizing the importance of movement and quality food when dealing with a child who has a weight problem. Food provides energy through energy-supplying nutrients. Non–energy-supplying nutrients are also important. Fats, sugar, and salt should be avoided in a healthy lifestyle.

8.8 Construct a balanced nutritional environment for young children	Individual Needs Met

Food guides and food labels can provide assistance in providing a quality diet for young children. It is important that the foods eaten by children be fresh. School lunch programs should be aware of the importance of avoiding fats, sugar, and salt and meeting all food guidelines. The environment surrounding the children should avoid chemicals and other items that may cause allergic reactions.

8.9 Create a culture that promotes physical activity and healthy eating	Family and Community Involved

Creating a culture of physical activity requires the involvement of the family, community, and early childhood educators. Families who subscribe to a physically active lifestyle and healthy eating behaviors assist their children in participation in physical activity for a lifetime. The early childhood educator needs to develop a culture of engagement in physical activity and eating foods from the five food groups and, through working with the family, can assist in establishing a physical activity culture at home.

Demonstrate Your Knowledge, Skills, and Dispositions

Students will demonstrate knowledge, comprehension, analysis, and evaluation of Learning Outcomes related to Guiding Principles.

Learning Outcomes	Guiding Principles
8.1 Develop a physically educated person	Individual Needs Met

- Observe children for 30 minutes in a classroom, on the playground, and during lunch. What is the activity level of the children in the classroom and on the playground? What do they eat for lunch? How does your observation relate to the factors discussed in this section?

8.2 Understand the relationships among physical activity, physical fitness, nutrition, and wellness	Individual Needs Met

- What are the components of a culture that promotes a physical active lifestyle?

8.3 Categorize types of physical fitness	Individual Needs Met

- What is the difference between skill-related and health-related fitness? Which one is more important for lifetime health, and why?

8.4 Explain the components of health-related fitness	Individual Needs Met

- Create activities for young children that will enhance each of the components of health-related fitness.

8.5 Determine required participation in health-related fitness	Individual Needs Met

- Observe a group of children for a morning or afternoon. Describe their level of participation in physical activity. Did the class meet the recommended level of participation in physical activity?

8.6 Know the qualities of a physically educated child	Assessment and Standards Provide Guidance

- Explain the factors that are barriers to participation in physical activity. How can these barriers be overcome?

8.7 Determine the role of environment in nutrition	Environment and Curriculum Reciprocated

- Name three changes you would make to your kindergarten classroom to accommodate a healthy eating curriculum. Explain why you would make these changes.

8.8 Construct a balanced nutritional environment for young children	Individual Needs Met

- You are teaching your children about healthy eating and would like to have a series of cooking classes. Present a plan on how you would do this.

8.9 Create a culture that promotes physical activity and healthy eating	Family and Community Involved

Describe the components of a culture that promotes a physically active lifestyle.

Planning for Engaging

The following learning activities provide three possibilities or ways to develop an M² Standard

M² Standard: Children develop knowledge and skills related to healthy habits. Child tries a variety of nutritious foods and knows the differences between healthful foods and those of little nutritional value.		
Possibility One	**Possibility Two**	**Possibility Three**
Children will be shown a puppet with a very large mouth and a container filled with a variety of plastic food familiar to the children. Children will feed the puppet quality foods. Foods determined not healthy will be placed in a garbage can.	Children will plan a healthy lunch menu using knowledge of food labels.	Children will shop, prepare, and cook the planned menu. Families will be invited to participate at all levels.
Assessment Observation of the percentage of correct choices made.	**Assessment** Observation of foods selected using "Choose My Plate" as a guide.	**Assessment** Observation of the quantities foods eaten by the child.

Now You Try It

Complete the following standard-based learning activity designed to meet various interests and developmental levels. Designed two possibilities or learning activities to develop an **M² Standard.**

M² Standard: Children will develop knowledge and skills related to healthy habits. Child tries a variety of nutritious foods and knows the difference between healthful foods and those with little nutritional value.		
Possibility One	**Possibility Two**	**Possibility Three**
Purchase lettuce and kale seeds. Have children plant seeds in three plastic storage containers. Keep one container watered and in the light. Do not water another container, and do not keep the third container in the light. Ask the children to compare the results.		

Assessment	Assessment	Assessment
Determine the detail of their observation of the three containers.		

References

American Academy of Pediatrics (2008). Strength training by children and adolescents: Council on sports medicine and fitness. *Pediatrics*, (121), 833. doi: 10.1542/peds.2007-3790.

Bouchard, C & Shephard, T. (1994). *Physical activity, fitness, and health: International proceedings and consensus statement*. Champaign, IL: Human Kinetics Publishers.

Brownell, K. D. & Warner, K. E. (2009). The perils of ignoring history: big tobacco played dirty and millions died. How similar is big food? *The Millbank Quarterly*, 87(1), 259–294.

Caspersen, C., Powell, K. & Christenson, G. (1985). Physical activity, exercise and physical fitness: Definitions and distinctions for health-related research. *Public Health Reports*, 100(2), 126–131.

Castetbon, K., & Andreyeva, T. (2012). Obesity and motor skills among 4- to 6-year-old children in the United States: Nationally representative surveys. *BMC Pediatrics*, 12:28, 1–9.

Centers for Disease Control and Prevention. (2011). School health guidelines to promote healthy eating and physical activity. *Morbidity and Mortality Weekly Report*, 60(5).

Centers for Disease Control and Prevention. (2012). Childhood obesity facts. http://www.cdc.gov/healthyyouth/obesity/facts.htm.

Cereal F.A.C.T.S. (2012). Food advertising to children and teens score. Retrieved from http://www.cerealfacts.org/cereal_nutrition_advanced_search.aspx?l=tHy.

Cliff, D., Okely, A., Morgan, P., Jones, R., Steele, J., & Baur, L. (2012). Proficiency deficiency: Mastery of fundamental movement skills and components in overweight and obese children. *Pediatric Obesity*, 20, 1024-1933, doi: 10.1038/oby.2011.241.

Consortium to Lower Obesity in Chicago Children (2013). Water intake for children fact sheet. http://www.clocc.net/partners/54321Go/WaterIntake05-07.pdf.

Cooper, A. (2011). Lunch lessons. *Educational Leadership*, 68(8), 75.

Cooper, A. (2013). Chef Ann's healthy kid's meal wheel. Retrieved from http://www.chefann.com/html/tools-links/meal-wheel.html.

Crothers, L., Kehle, T., Bray, M., & Theodore, L.A. (2009). Correlates and suspected causes of obesity in children. *Psychology in the Schools*, 46(8), 787–796.

D'Hondt, E., Deforche, B., DeBourdeaudhuij, I., Lenoir, M. (2008). Childhood obesity affects fine motor skill performance under different postural constraints. *Neuroscience Letters*, 440, 72–75.

Devoe, J.J. (2008). Addressing food: Clear procedures help K12 administrators deal with this escalating problem in schools. District Administration Solutions for School District Management. http://www.districtadministration.com/article/addressing-food-allergies.

Dotson, C., & Ross, J. (1985). Relationships between activity patterns and fitness. *Journal of Physical Education, Recreation, and Dance*, 56, 86–89.

Erickson, B.E. (2010). Fetal origins of disease. *Chemical Engineering News*, 88(45), 40–43.

Farrow, A., Taylor, H., Northstone, K., & Golding, J. (2003). Symptoms of mothers and infants related to total volatile organic compounds in house hold products. *Archives of Environmental Health,* 58(10), 633–641.

Frank, M., Graham, G., Lawson, H., Loughrey, T., Ritson, R., Sanborn, M., & Seefledt, V. (1991). *Physical education outcomes: A project of the National Association for Sport and Physical Education* Reston, VA: National Association for Sport and Physical Education.

Gabbard, C. (2011) *Lifelong Motor Development* (6th Ed.) San Francisco, CA: Pearson—Benjamin Cummings.

Harriger, J.A., Calogero, R.M., Witherington, D.C., & Smith, J.E. (2010). Body size stereotyping and internalization of the thin ideal in preschool girls. *Sex Roles,* 63,609–620. doi: 10.1007/sI1199-010-9868-1.

Hyman, M. (2012). *The blood sugar solution: The ultra healthy program for losing weight, preventing disease, and feeling great now.* New York, NY: Little, Brown and Company.

Idaho Food Protection (2013). Keep it healthy! Food safety employee guide. http://www.healthandwelfare.idaho.gov/Portals/0/Health/FoodProtection/Employees%20Guide%20to%20Food%20Safety.pdf.

Jaffe, M., & Kosakov, C. (1982). The motor development of fat babies. *Clinical Pediatrics,* 21, 619–621.

Julian, L. (2010). Why school lunch is "nasty"! *Policy Review,* 163, 43-53.

Kessler, D. (2013). *Your food is fooling you: How your brain is hijacked by sugar, fat, and salt.* New York, NY: Roaring Brook Press.

Leeds, M. J. (2012). Nutrition for health course packet. Slippery Rock, PA: Slippery Rock University.

Logan, S., Scrabis-Fletcher, K., Modlesky, C., & Getchell, N. (2011). The relationship between motor skill proficiency and body mass index in preschool children. *Research Quarterly for Exercise and Sport,* 82(3), 442–448.

Lyn, R., Maalouf, J., Evers, S., Davis, J., & Griffin, M. (2013). Nutrition and physical activity in child care centers: the Impact of a wellness policy initiative on environment and policy assessment and observation outcomes, 2011. *Preventing Chronic Disease: Public Health Research, Practice, and Policy,* 10. doi: http://dx.doi.org/10.5888/pcd10.120231.

Mateljan, G. (2007). *The world's healthiest foods.* Seattle, WA: George Mateljan Foundation.

Mayo Clinic. (2012). Nutrition for kids: Guidelines for a healthy diet. http://www.mayoclinic.com/health/nutrition-for-kids/NU00606.

Moore, C. (2003). *Silent scourge: children, pollution and why scientists disagree.* New York, NY: Oxford University Press.

Moore, L., Lombardi, D., White, M., Campbell, J., Oliveria, S., & Ellison, R. (1991). Influence of parents' physical activity levels on activity levels of young children. *Journal of Pediatrics,* 118(2), 215–219.

Musher-Eizenman, D., Holub, S., Miller, A., Goldstein, S., & Edwards-Leeper, L. (2004). Body size stigmatization in preschool children: The role of control attributions. *Journal of Pediatric Psychology,* 29(8), 613–620. doi:10.1093/jpepsy/jsh063

National Association for Sport and Physical Education. (2004). *Physical activity for children: a statement of guidelines for children 5–12,* 2nd Ed. Reston, VA: AAHPERD.

National Association for Sport and Physical Education. (2009). *Active start: A statement of physical activity guidelines for children from birth to age 5,* 2nd Ed. http://www.aahperd.org/naspe/standards/nationalGuidelines/ActiveStart.cfm.

National Association for Sport and Physical Education. (2012). *The scope and sequence of fitness education for preK–16 programs.* Reston VA; AAHPERD.

National Center for Health Statistics. (2011.) *Health, United States, 2010: With special features on death and dying.* Hyattsville, MD: U.S. Department of Health and Human Services.

Ogden, C., & Carroll, M. (2010). Centers for Disease Control and Prevention. Prevalence of obesity among children and adolescents: United States, trends 1963–1965 through 2007–2008. http://www.cdc.gov/nchs/data/hestat/obesity_child_07_08/obesity_child_07_08.htm.

Ogden, C., Carroll, M., Curtin, L., Lamb, M., & Flegal, K. (2010). Prevalence of high body mass index in US children and adolescents, 2007–2008. *Journal of the American Medical Association, 303*(3), 242–249.

Ogden, C, Carroll, M, Kit, B., & Flegal, K. (2012). Prevalence of obesity and trends in body mass index among US children and adolescents, 1999–2010. *Journal of the American Medical Association, 307,* 483–490.

Osika, W., & Montgomery, S. (2008). Physical control and coordination in childhood and adult obesity: Longitudinal birth cohort study. *BMJ, 337:a699.* doi:10.1136/bmja699.

Pate, R., & Ross, J. (1987). Factors associated with health related fitness. *Journal of Physical Education, Recreation, and Dance, 58,* 71–73.

Petrolini, N., Iughetti, L., & Bernasconi, S. (1995). Difficulty in visual motor coordination as a possible cause of sedentary behavior in obese children. *International Journal of Obesity Related Metabolic Disorders, 19*(12), 928.

Polhamus, B., Dalenius, K., Borland, E., Mackintosh, H., Smith, R., & Grummer-Strawn, L. (2009). *Pediatric nutrition surveillance 2007 report.* Atlanta, GA: U.S. Department of Health and Human Services, Centers for Disease Control and Prevention.

Polhamus, B., Dalenius, K., Mackintosh, H., Smith, B., Grummer-Strawn, L. (2011). *Pediatric nutrition surveillance 2009 report.* Atlanta, GA: U.S. Department of Health and Human Services, Centers for Disease Control and Prevention.

Rand Health (2004). *Obesity and disability.* Santa Monica, CA: Rand Corp.

Ritter, S. (2012). The bitter side of sugars: Improving our health could hinge on saying good-bye to added sugars. *Chemical and Engineering News, 90*(29), 43–44.

Sherry, B., Mei, Z. Scanlon, K.S., Mokdad, A.H., & Grummer-Strawn, L.M. (2004). Trend in state-specific prevalence of overweigh and underweight in 2- through 4-year-old children from low-income families from 1989 through 2000. *Archives of Pediatric and Adolescent Medicine, 158,* 1116–1124.

Shields, T. (2009). Examination of the obesity epidemic from a behavioral perspective. *International Journal of Behavioral Consultation and Therapy, 5*(1), 142–158.

Shirley, M. (1931). *The first two years: A study of twenty-five babies.* Minneapolis, MN: University of Minnesota Press.

Singh, A., Mulder, C., Twisk, J., van Mechelen, W., & Chinapaw, M. (2008). Tracking of childhood overweight into adulthood: A systematic review of the literature. *Obesity Reviews, 9,* 474–488.

Sloan, S., Gildea, A., Stewart, M., Sneddon, H., & Iwaniec, D. (2007). Early weaning in related to weight and rate of weight gain in infancy. *Child Care, Health and Development, 34,* 59–64.

Snell, E., Adam, E., & Duncan, G. (2007). Sleep and the body mass index and overweight status of children and adolescents. *Child Development, 78,* 309–323.

Story, M., Kaphingst, K. Robinson-O'Brian, R., & Glanz, K. (2008). Creating healthy food and eating environments: Policy and environmental approaches. *Annual Review of Public Health*, 29, 253–272.

USDA Department of Food and Nutritional Services (2013a). Healthy Hunger-Free Act of 2010. http://www.fns.usda.gov/cnd/governance/legislation/cnr_2010.htm.

USDA Department of Food and Nutritional Services (2013b). Nutritional standards for school meals. http://www.fns.usda.gov/cnd/governance/legislation/nutritionstandards.htm.

Welk, G. (1999). Promoting physical activity in children: Parental influences. *ERIC Digest*, ED436480 1999-10-00, http://www.eric.ed.gov/PDFS/ED436480.pdf\.

Williams, L., Veitch, J., & Ball, K. (2011). What helps children eat well? A qualitative exploration of resilience among disadvantaged families. *Health Education Research*, 26(2), 296–307.

Wrotniak, B., Epstein, L., Dorn, J., Jones, K. & Kondilis, V. (2006). The relationship between motor proficiency and physical activity in children. *Pediatrics*, 118(6), e1758–e1765. doi:10.1542/peds2006-0742.

chapter 9

Movement and Music Broaden Learning

LEARNING OUTCOMES AND GUIDING PRINCIPLES

Students reading this text will be able to demonstrate Learning Outcomes linked to Guiding Principles based on the National Association for the Education of Young Children's *Developmentally Appropriate Practice in Early Childhood Programs Serving Children from Birth through Age 8.*

Learning Outcomes	Guiding Principles
9.1 Understand the mind–body connections	Individual Needs Met
9.2 Discuss factors that affect brain health	Individual Needs Met
9.3 Apply the relationships among academic performance and physical activity, exercise, and fitness to planning academic lessons	Environment and Curriculum Reciprocated
9.4 Apply the relationship between academic performance and music to planning academic lessons	Environment and Curriculum Reciprocated
9.5 Employ movement and music as a means to learn	Movement and Music Integrated
9.6 Create 10-minute physical activity/music breaks	Environment and Curriculum Reciprocated

9.1 *Understand the Mind–Body Connections*

The link between the mind and body is not new. Beginning in the Greco-Roman period, the mind–body connection referred to the relationship between the mind and a healthy body. The belief even then was that thoughts and emotions, as well as social and behavioral factors, affected the body and learning. The Greco-Roman culture emphasized the importance of physical exercise for the development of a sound mind. Plato's writing included the relationships among the body, mind, and psyche with the importance of physical exercise.

Within the past few decades, the research on the mind–body connection has expanded to examine the factors that foster children's academic achievement. We know that memory and learning involve the various parts of the brain; thus, we are concerned with brain health and the factors that influence brain health, which in turn affects memory and learning. We also need to understand how children acquire information and master the learning of the information. Music and movement are two factors that enhance learning.

A review of Howard Gardner's multiple intelligences theory will enhance our understanding of the connection between the intelligences and learning.

▲ A fun way to practice math is by playing hopscotch—and instead of landing on the numbers in order, the child jump or hops out the answer to the problem.

Multiple Intelligences

Intelligence should not be restricted to a certain category of behavior or performance, such as linguistic or mathematical abilities that are valued by the American culture (Gardner, 2011). Each child has a unique way of gathering knowledge and skills and mastering the gathered knowledge and skills. In addition, characteristics of the learning environment and the teachers can enhance or discourage learning. Gardner's intelligences—linguistic, musical, logical-mathematical, spatial, bodily-kinesthetic, and personal—can be viewed separately, but can also function together and complement each other. Therefore, using one of the intelligences to enrich learning in another intelligence is advantageous.

The children in Mr. Hassan's classroom were having fun practicing counting and other mathematic skills (logical-mathematical). They were socializing with friends, emotionally involved and making connections while learning (personal). Jumping, hopping, and throwing (bodily-kinesthetic) skills were used to heighten learning in logical-mathematical intelligence. The use of rhythm instruments and singing (musical) strengthen learning. Finally, each child used spatial intelligence to negotiate the room and to move to the various stations. The children were active and learning in an environment that enhanced various intelligences or personal modes to gather and master knowledge and skills.

Recent research has investigated the relationship between physical activity, exercise, and fitness and brain health and academic performance. Initial research investigated older adults and found that regular physical activity had a positive effect on learning and memory and also maintained cognitive functions and brain health.

In this chapter we cover brain health, how music and movement relate to academic performance, how we can use movement to broaden and learn academic concepts valued by a culture, and the importance of physical activity breaks.

9.2 Discuss Factors That Affect Brain Health

Brain-based learning (Jensen, 2007) links learning and memory to the interaction among the emotions, movement, and cognition and discusses the connection between brain development and the environment. Just reading this section, this chapter, and this book has changed your brain. We used to think that we did not grow new neurons, but neuroscientists have found that new neurons are continually being created, and they link to memory, mood, and learning (Jensen, 2007).

For learning and development, we want to enhance *neurogenesis* (development of new brain cells). Exercise, complex environments, new learning, social engagement, nutrition, and low stress enhance the development of new brain cells. Conversely, the process is reduced by inactivity, boredom,

▲ Connection of the body, mind, and spirit through physical activity develops the healthy child.

lack of socialization, poor nutrition, stress, and depression. Brain development responds to movement and novelty. As we learn, neural connections develop through concrete experience and emotions. Social–environmental interaction assists neurogenesis and strengthens connections between brain cells. We want a brain with thousands and thousands of connections (see **video** Run, Jump, and Learn: How exercise can transform our schools, by John Ratey).

Ratey (2008) found that physical activity improves brain function at every age level. The benefits of physical activity to brain health include the following:

- Increase in cerebral blood flow
- Changes in neurotransmitters

- Increases in norepinephrine and serotonin (hormones that influence and elevate mood)

- Permanent structural changes (Ratey, 2008)

Increased cerebral blood flow provides more nutrients and oxygen to the brain. Physical activity enables the cells in the brain to function at an optimal level; it helps to maintain and improve brain functioning, and therefore gives us the ability to learn and focus (see video Brain Gain).

The brain can also rewire and remap itself through the process of *neuroplasticity*. Draganski et al. (2006) hypothesize that plasticity is the result of the nervous system evolving from coping with changes in the environment. The brain has to adapt to new environments. Although it is important to be consistent when working with children, it is also important to provide variety in the curriculum, learning environments, and the materials and equipment, to promote growth of the nervous system. Outdoor spaces for children should have uneven terrain, for example, to encourage adaptations in walking and running.

Social conditions also influence the brain. Social experiences and school behaviors become encoded in our brain through our various experiences. Children are more affected by these experiences than we previously knew (Jensen, 2008). The classroom provides social–environmental interaction and needs to be considered in fostering brain development. Copple and Bredekamp (2009) state that the teachers' continual interactions with the child are the most important determinant of learning outcomes and development, even more so than the curriculum. We therefore need to be

M² FUN Mathematical-Logical, Bodily-Kinesthetic, Musical Activity

Numbers (1, 2, 3, . . .) are written on cards and positioned around the room. A rope or tape is laid on the floor. When the music starts, each child gets a unique number card and places it in correct numerical order on the rope or tape. Once the number is placed, the child repeats the process.

more involved in managing the social environment of students to strengthen prosocial conditions. Children master information in a variety of ways, and teachers and peers provide valuable support in the process.

> Carla and Eugene went to the same early childhood program and were great friends. The learning environment at the program was open and the children were always engaging and helping each other during the day. When they moved to kindergarten at a different school, their expectation was to continue the same easy and supportive exchange. The class had been instructed to engage in a paper-and-pencil math activity. Eugene was having problems with the activity; he called out to Carla, seated at a desk across the room, for assistance. Eugene was used to social support from his peer. Unfortunately, this was not acceptable in the new classroom and the teacher frowned on the verbal exchange.

New research is demonstrating that nutrition might enhance the effects of physical activity on the brain. Praag (2009) suggests that eating natural products such as omega fatty acids and plant polyphenols (found in edible wild plants, walnuts, olive oil, fish, fruits, and vegetables) affects neurogenesis and synaptic plasticity, which are thought to be central to memory and learning. When food shopping, it is helpful to circle the outside rows of the grocery store. By doing this, fresh fruits, vegetables, meats, and dairy products will have priority for selection by the buyer.

Overweight adolescents who do not have type 2 diabetes but do have obesity-related *metabolic syndrome* (a group of risk factors that occur together and increase the risk for coronary artery disease, stroke, and type 2 diabetes) have been found to show reductions in cognitive function and structural integrity of the brain (Yau, Castro, Tagani, Tsui, & Convit, 2012). These results provide additional support for the importance of reduction of obesity.

Play, recess, and physical education are critical for brain development and learning (Jensen, 2007). Jensen summarizes the research and suggests that physical activity benefits children in multiple ways:

- Learners can make mistakes without negative consequences.
- Individual learning is enhanced.

- Children learn to handle "stress" in the gym and the classroom (indoor and outdoor).

- Proteins that aid the neurons' ability to communicate with one another are released.

- Social skills, emotional intelligence, and conflict resolution ability are enhanced.

- Brain chemicals that energize and elevate mood are increased.

In summary, physical activity, exercise, and physical fitness can have beneficial effects on brain development in addition to their other health-enhancing benefits. According to several researchers (Hillman, Castelli, & Buck, 2005; Hollmann & Struder, 1996; Ploughman, 2008; Trudeau & Shephard, 2010), when the brain is activated during physical activity, existing brain cells are rejuvenated and new ones are stimulated. Specifically, during physical activity there is an increase in cerebral blood flow, enhancement of arousal level, changing hormone secretions, and enhanced nutrient intake.

9.3 *Apply the Relationships Among Academic Performance and Physical Activity, Exercise, and Fitness to Planning Academic Lessons*

The terms *physical activity*, *exercise*, and *fitness* have been used interchangeably in the literature: however, each concept has a different focus. Physical activity is defined as any bodily movement, whereas exercise is planned physical activity to enhance fitness. Health-related fitness (related to cardiovascular endurance, muscular strength and endurance, flexibility, body composition) is an indicator of the level of healthy functioning of the various body systems. Physical activity, exercise, and fitness level have all been related to academic performance and cognitive functions.

Studies have used a variety of measures of cognitive functioning (i.e., attention, executive function, intelligence, cognition, academic achievement, memory, spatial perception, perceptual skills, intelligence quotient, achievement, verbal tests, mathematics tests, developmental level, and academic readiness) and a variety of measures of physical activity (i.e., exercise, cardiovascular and muscular endurance, and BMI), and have drawn the following major conclusions (Trost, 2009): More time spent in physical activity with less time in academic practice does not hurt academic performance—and increased levels of movement typically help academic performance. Furthermore, higher levels of physical fitness are related to better academic performance and physical activity breaks though out the day improve attention, academic performance, and behavior.

Therefore, it is important to design a curriculum that has music and movement incorporated throughout every content area (see video Yoga and ABCs).

9.4 Apply the Relationship Between Academic Performance and Music to Planning Academic Lessons

Music is important in the development of the child. In a review of the benefits of music to children, Crncec, Wilson, and Prior (2006) state that music is innate for infants and toddlers—they seek musical interactions with others and maternal singing captures their attention more than maternal speech. Music can calm or arouse the child.

The effects of music on academic performance and other abilities have been investigated, with conclusions paralleling those of physical activity—the results are mixed, but never negative. The research can be divided into the "Mozart effect" (music education) and background music.

The *Mozart effect* states that by listening to a Mozart piano sonata or similar complex music (Crncec, Wilson, & Prior, 2006), spatiotemporal reasoning is improved. *Spatiotemporal reasoning* is the ability to visualize a spatial pattern and see how it can be manipulated and how the parts fit together. The spatiotemporal process is important in tasks that require combining several objects into a whole to match a mental image (Rauscher & Zupan, 2000). An example of spatiotemporal reasoning (or spatial intelligence) is seeing how puzzle pieces fit together or thinking several moves ahead in chess. Research on the Mozart effect has had mixed results, with some researchers supporting the finding (Rauscher & Hinton, 2006) and others not (Crncec, Wilson, & Prior, 2006).

M² FUN   Emotion Motion

Position large paper faces around the room (in safe general space, to prevent bumping) depicting various emotions (happy, sad, angry, bored, tired, worried, surprised). Play different types of music and ask the children to move to the face that depicts how the music makes them feel. How they move (hop, skip, jump, run) should be determined with each music selection.

Research on music instruction has investigated the impact of music instruction on other intelligences: spatiotemporal performance (spatial), mathematics (logical-mathematic), reading (linguistic), and IQ. Music instruction has been found to enhance spatiotemporal performance in children and might have the biggest impact on children between 3 and 5 years of age (Crncec, Wilson, & Prior, 2006).

A link between music and literacy and music and math has been documented. Watch a video of a teacher using music to teach math (see video).

McEwing (2011) builds the case that music and singing are critical to the development of phonological and phonemic awareness. In addition, moving to and playing with rhymes and stories builds vocabulary, comprehension, and narrative skills (see video Music and Dance Drive Academic Achievement).

Both music and literacy rely on the development of the auditory processes. Hansen, Bernstorf, and Stuber (2004) describe some of the auditory elements of literacy related to music, including the following:

- Phoneme awareness
- Discrimination between similar auditory elements
- Speech signals
- Auditory memory

When learning how sounds come together to form words (phoneme awareness), music translates sounds into pitches to form a musical melody (see video Music and Phonological Awareness). Auditory elements of communication require discrimination between sounds. Practice in music

M² FUN   Inside/Outside Count

Place several large refrigerator boxes or tape circles around the room, one base for each group of two or three children. All children stand outside the base. Give the children various commands:

All stand inside the base.

One child step outside the base. How many are left?

All stand inside the base.

Two children step outside the base. How many are left?

One child join the child inside the base. How many are inside the base?

class also requires discrimination between keys and individual pitches. Knowledge of speech signals, such as vocal inflection, volume, and stress, is important to gain meaning from verbal communication.

Auditory signals are significant in music. Children learn to distinguish between high and low registers and to make music loud and soft. These are concepts in creative movement: high, low; loud, soft. Being able to put these elements together on a regular basis forms auditory memory for literacy and music. Tarbert (2012) suggests that music can take auditory memory a step further when the child memorizes several songs for a concert. Seldom is a young child asked to memorize a lengthy passage, but even at a young age, children are able to sing long songs.

Daniel's mom loves music and frequently listens to music with Daniel. Amazingly, three-year-old Daniel knows most of the songs by the Beatles, Bob Dylan, and Adele, among others. Development of auditory skills is an important part of literacy development that is reinforced and enhanced with exposure to music.

Another important process in literacy is visual decoding. Similar elements in music and literacy include knowledge of letters, words, and sentences; visual focus; and visual memory (Hansen, Bernstorf, & Stuber, 2004). Given knowledge of letters, words, and sentences, children understand what to do with the letters and how to put them together to make

M² FUN　**Moving Like the Animals**

Baby Bunny

Baby bunny bounces high; [jump high]

Baby bunny bounces low; [jump low]

Baby bunny blinks his eye; [blink eyes]

Baby bunny waves good-bye. [wave good-bye]

Inchworm

Five inchworms inching up a tree, [wiggle five fingers]

Five insects invited them to see [hold up the other hand]

An iguana inside the tree. [place one hand inside other hand]

Use your imagination and you will see [point index finger to head]

All 10 having fun in a tree! [wiggle all 10 fingers]

words, which they then group to form sentences. When engaged in music, notes are the words. The children read the notes as they read the letters, then combine the notes in duration and pitch to create measures and phrases of music (Tarbert, 2012).

Visual focus is important for music and literacy. *Focus* is attention to visual information without distraction and can also include following a line while reading a sentence in a book. This requires eye coordination for all literacy skills (Tarbert, 2012).

M² FUN　**Musical Creation**

Put rows of tape on the floor to resemble a musical staff. Divide the children into groups and give each group four or eight circles, representing musical notes. Have a group place their circles on the staff. The children will then hum or sing their composition. This activity can be varied by having each child in the group stand on a line of the staff.

The effects of background music in the classroom have also been investigated. Studies of whether the effects of background music enhance cognitive and academic performance have had mixed results (Crncec, Wilson, & Prior, 2006). However, "soothing" background music does appear to provide positive results in special education classrooms by helping children focus and reducing arousal levels and stimulation.

Both music and physical activity have an effect on academic performance. We also know that movement and music are enjoyable, so independent of their effects on academic performance, we can use movement and music as a means to teach academic skills.

M² FUN   Follow the Light

Ask the children to sit on the floor. Darken the room. Use your "magic wand" (flashlight) to make shapes and designs on the walls and ceiling. Ask the children to follow the light movement with their eyes.

9.5 Employ Movement and Music as a Means to Learn

Teachers can use movement and music as a means to learn academic skills. The brain learns best when concrete examples, movement, social engagement, interaction with the environment, and emotions are involved (Kuczala, 2013). Movement is a way to engage children in the content. Children's interest levels in an area can have an effect on attention span. When studying at home, Mateo was always moving. If he sat down to read, he would fidget. If his mother asked him to sit and do the work, he could not concentrate on the task. His mother decided to take advantage of his movement: She would call out spelling words, and he would spell the words as he did cartwheels. In addition, she would call out addition/subtraction problems, and he would hop the answer. Moving and learning assisted in Mateo's selective attention to the task at hand. Taking this one step further, many contestants competing in spelling bees use their finger to write the words in their hands.

Hillman, Pontifex, Raine, Castelli, Hall, and Kramer (2009) found that children are better able to allocate attention resources while walking on a treadmill. They have also found improvement in reading, spelling, and math achievement scores following vigorous exercise.

Marian Volmer, a first- and second-grade teacher, is aware of the relationship among music, movement, and phonemic awareness. She has created "Rev-Up to Read" (Volmer, 2011), an activity she uses as a warmup for primary reading skills. The warmup uses stories, motions, songs, and recitation to build phonic skills. While singing lyrics to "Old MacDonald," for example, the children pound their fists as they sing the vowels. This is a motivational tool that helps get the children "pumped" to learn.

Academic Lessons Using Movement and Music

Using movement and music to teach academic concepts provides hands-on, concrete experiences that assist learning and memory of the concepts. Before integrating movement into teaching practice, educators should understand the following (Elliott, Belcher, & Weikle, 2012):

- Physical education and music content standards
- Aspects of health-related fitness
- Developmentally appropriate practice
- Safety of the learning environment
- Active learning using all the senses

These concepts have been reviewed throughout the text; thus, you are ready to begin active lessons.

When using movement and music to teach concepts, the teacher needs to consider the following (Elliott, Belcher, & Weikle, 2012): full participation by every child, developmentally appropriate activities to enhance success rate, a variety of difficulty levels included, children not singled out—and *fun*.

A	J	P	D			1	0	6	3	2
	T	W	U	G		4	7	2	0	1
Q	B		H	N		8	3	5	4	3
Z	E	O	M	X		7	4	9	8	6
F		R	C	K		8	6	2	0	5
Y	I	L	V	S		3	5	1	7	9

F i g u r e 9.1 Matrix of letters or numbers to incorporate physical activity into academic learning.

Math and language arts practice, for example, can be fun by putting mats with a grid of letters/numbers on the floor. The children can recognize letters, spell words, count, add, and subtract by hopping on the letters, jumping on the answer to an addition problem, or throwing beanbags to spell a word (see Figure 9.1).

The first step in planning an active lesson is to review the curriculum goals and objectives. An age-appropriate academic standard (physical education standard and/or a music standard) should be selected based on similar concepts or components. Discriminating pathways, shapes, and letter or number identification, for instance, can be taught together. As an example, we chose literacy for kindergarten children. The M^2 Literacy Standard is Phonological Awareness: The child will demonstrate understanding of spoken sounds, syllables and words and produce rhyming words.

An M^2 movement standard is:

- The child will develop motor skills to engage in a variety of physical activities.
  - The child will demonstrate an initial level of performance of the locomotor skills.

A M^2 music standard for kindergarten is:

- The child will develop current international and interdisciplinary connections with music.
  - The child will recognize the similarities of music and other disciplinary concepts.

The objective of the lesson is to differentiate rhyming words from non-rhyming words. The teacher gives an example of rhyming words (cat, sat, hat, mat, rat, bat). One word is put on one paper plate, and its rhyming partner is put on a second paper plate.

One set of plates is handed to the children and the other set is spread around the room. On a signal, the children are given a locomotor skill (skip, hop, jump), and they have to use the skill as they find the paper plate that rhymes with their word. When they turn over a word that matches, they start to walk around the room until all the children find their match. The teacher collects the plates, spreads one set around the room and gives the other set to the children. This time they might have to use a different skill to move around the room to retrieve the plates. On some trials, children might be asked to find a word that does not rhyme with their word. This can be changed so that the children carry all the plates and one child needs to find the child with the matching word.

The next rhyming task is to teach the song/rhyme "A-Hunting We Will Go" (by Thomas Arne; public domain)

A-hunting we will go, a-hunting we will go,

Heigh-ho, the dairy-o, a-hunting we will go.

We'll catch a FOX and put him in a BOX,

And then we'll let him go.

Different rhyming words can be used:

- Cat/hat
- Snake/cake
- Goat/boat

As the children learn the rhyme, they change the wording of the song: "We'll catch a _____, and make him _____, and then we'll let him go."

To assess the children, everyone could be side-sliding around the room as the teacher calls out rhyming words. When the teacher calls a word that doesn't rhyme, the children could sit down.

Other Examples

Children should be exposed to a variety of content areas besides language arts, such as mathematics, science, social studies, and visual arts. Using movement and music can enhance learning in all the content areas (see Table 9.1).

Interdisciplinary Learning

Cone, Werner, Cone, and Woods (1998) promote *interdisciplinary learning*, in which two or more subject areas are integrated with the purpose of enhancing both subject areas. The content of each subject area is recognized, yet a greater depth of learning can be gained by integrating the subjects. Through interdisciplinary learning, students apply their knowledge instead of concentrating on mastering facts alone. The children are engaged in higher-order critical thinking as they pose questions and solve problems.

Advantages of interdisciplinary learning include relevance, concrete examples and practical, active learning experiences. The abstract concepts are applied to hands-on real-world examples. Children's play is an example of interdisciplinary learning. As several children "play house," they are practicing a variety of socioeconomic disciplines. They use math as they go to the grocery store to buy food and subsequently use measuring cups to cook the food. They use language arts as they engage in discussions about the role playing, and use health to make healthy food choices.

Table 9.1 Ways to Integrate Physical Activity and Music

Content Area	Music	Movement
Mathematics	Sing counting songs, such as "Alice the Camel": Alice the camel has five humps, Alice the camel has five humps, Alice the camel has five humps, So ride, Alice, ride, boom, boom, boom.	Make beanbags in shapes (circle, triangle, square). Place small plastic buckets in a row. The buckets are labeled with a picture of a shape and/or a word. Children will throw matching beanbags into appropriate bucket.
	Give all the children a set of rhythm sticks. The children will match patterns the teacher counts or beats on a drum.	Children will count how many times they can throw or kick and hit a target with a ball.
Science	Review the stage of the life of a butterfly. Play the overture to *Madama Butterfly* by Giacomo Puccini. Have children interpret the life stages of a butterfly through dance.	Have the children make a large paper sun. One child holds the sun and moves around the room. The rest of the children are plants; they grow from a low to high level as they bend and twist toward the sun.
	Moving to music, children with a scarf in hand act out rain, sun, tornado, and snow.	Children pretend to be molecules. They can move any way they want but cannot touch each other (represents gases). Make the space smaller and continue movement (represents liquid). Once again make the area very small for movement (represents solid).
Social Studies	Listen to folk music from a particular culture. Provide background information on the culture.	Teach a folk dance. Provide background information on the culture.
	Children write a chant or song to use before going outside to the playground.	Children will practice map skills by drawing a map of the playground.
Visual Art	Play music with a variety of different tempos while the children paint.	Have children paint with different body parts.
	Project a picture of a piece of art on a wall. Play various types of music. Ask the children to listen and to determine what music matches the art best.	While the children work with clay, play classical, folk, and jazz music. Discuss how the music made them pinch, roll, or pound the clay.

Table 9.1 (*Continued*)

Content Area	Music	Movement
Language Arts	Read a story to the children. Have them provide sound effects with rhythm instruments.	Read a story to the children and have them act out the story.
	Say a chant and have the children beat or clap to the words.	Make several cards with roots such as *an* and *at*. Make other cards with single letters in them, such as *c, p, b*. One set of children has the root letter and the remainder of the children have the single letters. This group must hop, skip, or jump to the root to make a word.
Nutrition	Chant a finger play, such as "Green Grapes": Five green grapes growing on a vine. I picked one cause it looked so fine! Four green grapes growing on a vine I picked another for my valentine! Three green grapes growing on a vine. I ate another, I couldn't decline! Two green grapes growing on a vine. I ate another in the sunshine. One green grape growing on a vine. I ate it too, cause they were all mine!	Mark 25 cards with five vegetables, five fruits, five meat and fish, five grains, and five dairy. Divide the class into groups of five. Give each group a number. Place five numbered paper plates (1, 2, 3, 4, 5) around the floor. Lay the cards randomly around the room. Each group will select five cards. The object is for the children to move throughout the room to get one vegetable, one fruit, one meat and fish, one grain, and one dairy and place them on their plate.
	Listen to Mexican music while the children make salsa.	Move like a carrot, a tomato, a banana, or a piece of bread.

Interdisciplinary learning is multisensory. It includes visual, auditory, and tactile-kinesthetic modalities as the children interact with the environment. In early development, movement is a means of expression; however, as the child develops, other sensory systems are integrated and vision becomes dominant.

The criticism of interdisciplinary learning is that the identity of each discipline is lost therefore important content is not taught. Not all content needs to be interdisciplinary. Interdisciplinary teaching should only occur when the integration provides enhanced learning.

Cone et al. (1998) developed three models of interdisciplinary teaching that move from simple to more complex. The simplest model is the *connected* model, the second is *shared*, and the most complex is *partnership*. The connected model has one teacher who connects content from two subject areas. In kindergarten, for example, the teacher might integrate knowledge of letters in literacy and shapes from movement. Using a rope, children can create letters out of the shapes they explore in movement.

Teaching third grade, for example, Ms. Royal taught the muscles of the body by integrating movement to identify the muscles (see Figure 9.2).

The shared model of interdisciplinary teaching includes two or more teachers and links similar concepts from two or more subject areas. The teachers collaborate to integrate the lessons, but the teachers teach independently. For example, when learning about a country, the games or dances from that country are taught during physical education while the social studies teacher engages the children in a discussion about the culture of the country.

The most complex model of interdisciplinary teaching is the partnership model—the teachers' team-teach as they attempt to unify the subject area content. For example, the teachers plan and team-teach about a country, including cultural traditions, foods, games, music, and dances.

Cone et al. (1998) provide an example of a shared model, "Alphabet Gymnastics," for children in kindergarten/first grade. Language arts and physical education are the focus of the lesson, with the ultimate objective to create a sequence of movements using three letters. After a short aerobic warmup, students are assigned to a mat, and they create both capital and small letters as the teachers guide them through the shapes; the teachers ask what letter the children made (recognition of the letter). The children go to the chalkboard and different children write letters on the board. The teacher then asks how they can make the letter with their bodies (creating the letter). Children return to their mats and, as one child makes a letter, several others sharing their mat are asked to recognize the letter. Assessment could include identification of the parts of the body that are used to make the different parts of the letter. Games that could be played with this lesson include alphabet freeze tag, in which, when tagged, the child freezes in the shape of a letter. Letter target is another game, in which the child has to throw a ball or beanbag to the target grid of letters and spell a word (see Figure 9.1).

**Identifying the Muscles Used in the Inchworm Science Lesson Plan
Using Physical Activity to Learn**

Grade Level: 3rd grade	**Time Allotted:** 15–30 minutes	**Theme:** N/A

Learning Objective: To understand the importance of muscles and how they work.

Objectives for Students: Students will learn about the different types of muscles, how muscles work, and why they are important.

Objectives for Teacher: Teacher will observe the students' understanding of muscles and determine whether the students can tell what muscles they are working when doing the inchworm activity.

Competencies:

Competency Goal—Science:

M^2 Science Standard for 3rd grade: Structure and Function of Living Organisms

Understand the systems of the human body and their function for supporting life.

Compare and contrast the functions of the muscular and skeletal system.

Materials: Tape, names of muscles written out on paper (to label different muscles), floor space

Procedure:

Teacher says: "Muscles make parts of your body move. They work by making themselves shorter, so that they pull things together. When the muscles on the front of your upper arm get shorter, it pulls up your forearm. That means your muscles are squished together as you pull something up. Biceps are up top and triceps are down here [points to arm]."

-**The students will participate in the inchworm activity. In the inchworm activity, the students literally will imitate the motions and movements of an inchworm. To move like an inchworm, students need to start in a ^ position. Then they walk down into a plank and then down to a push-up and, finally, reverse.**

Inchworm activity

Do you know what muscles this works?

Label muscles as students say them/ask if they felt it in the _____ muscle.

- Arm muscles → biceps, triceps
- Shoulders
- Hamstrings
- Back muscles

(continued)

Figure 9.2 Ms. Royal's third-grade lesson plan.

Reprinted with permission from Ms. Barrett Royal.

If they didn't feel it in these places, have them do the activity again.

Teacher asks "Did you feel it in your abdomen, arms, back?" [If students need scaffolding.] "Do you see all of the muscles we used when we acted like an inchworm? There are a lot of different muscles in your body, and you will learn about them later on."

Assessment:

Teacher will do a check sheet to determine whether the students understand how muscles work and why muscles work, and whether they participate during the discussion.

Differentiation:

- Have students with vision or attention disabilities sit closer to the front.
- Make sure you continually call on all students to give them opportunity and to keep them engaged.
- Have visual resources available for students who may get frustrated trying to illustrate their words and handouts that children can look at more closely if they need to.
- Push your gifted students to find particularly unique ways that their muscles are working, or have them describe what their muscles are doing while they are participating in the inchworm activity.

References:

How to do the inchworm exercise. http://healthyliving.azcentral.com/inchworm-exercise-14442.html.

10 best exercises you never heard of. http://www.livestrong.com/article/550190-10-best-exercises-you-never-heard-of/.

Figure 9.2 (*Continued*)

Using a shared model of interdisciplinary teaching, the movement concept of pathways (straight, curved, zigzag) can be integrated with the academic concepts of shapes, numbers, and letters. The children move their bodies through straight, curved, and zigzag, pathways to help understand the concepts of shapes, numbers, and letters. The three pathways—straight, curved, and zigzag—are used to form shapes, numbers, and letters, which are introduced by the classroom teachers. Children can form letters and numbers with a rope, with their bodies, and even with a partner. Each letter is made up by either a straight (l), curved (C), or zigzag (M) path. For additional examples of learning through movement view the PE Central website.

9.6 *Create 10-Minute Physical Activity/Music Breaks*

A variety of programs have been developed to provide a break in the academics to allow children to release energy; some have included integration of the physical activity with academic concepts. Teachers have found that activity breaks benefit the children's learning (see video).

Brain breaks are 10 minutes of physical activity used to take a break from the academic component and refresh the mind and body. Energizers, TAKE10!, and Active Academics also include 10 minutes of physical activity integrated with academic concepts.

Energizers (Mahar, Murphy, Rowe, Golden, Shields, & Raedeke, 2006) are 10-minute physical activities that apply academic concepts developed by students and faculty at East Carolina University; they increase both daily in-school physical activity and on-task behavior. Integrating Energizers into kindergarten through fourth grade, Mahar et al. (2006) found that teacher-led Energizer activities that involved an integrated grade-appropriate academic content with movement improved on-task behavior by 20 percent.

An example of an Energizer (Eat Smart, Move More NC, 2006) is "Inches, Feet, and Yards, Oh My!" Inches, feet and yards are measured by the children's feet. An "inch" is moving forward by the toes moving forward, whereas "feet" is one foot moving ahead of the other. A "yard" is a giant step. The teacher or another child calls out measurements, such as "two feet forward, one inch to the left, and a yard forward." This ties in to a math concept of understanding alternative forms of measurement. A real-life example of alternative measurement is determining the area of a room by putting one foot in front of the other and counting the steps. Or, to measure material, rope, or string, we can measure a yard by holding the arm out and stretching the material to the nose. (To find a set of elementary school Energizers, visit Energizers at www.eatsmartmovemorenc.com/Energizers/Elementary.html.)

TAKE 10! (http://www.take10.net/) is a program that integrates movement and academics in elementary school classrooms. Kibbe et al. (2011), in a review of 19 research articles evaluating the TAKE 10! program for children between the ages of 5 and 11 years, found that the program could be successfully implemented by the classroom teacher by helping the children focus on learning while also improving physical activity levels. There is a minimal charge for the activity kits.

Active Academics® was developed by Eloise Elliott and her colleagues as part of a grant from the West Virginia Bureau for Public Health, which, in turn, was part of a grant from the Centers for Disease Control and Prevention in 2005–2006. The website (http://www.activeacademics. org/#Home%20Page) provides lesson plans using physical activity to engage the children in math, reading/language arts, health/nutrition, and physical education for kindergarten through fifth grade. They also provide a variety of "classroom energizers" and "moving breaks." Teachers can submit ideas at this site as well.

An example of an Active Academics lesson for pre-K and K grade levels is Morning Movement. The teacher has the letters of the alphabet displayed throughout the room. The children stand in general space and do a movement as they say the alphabet. For example, they can jump, hop, or touch their toes when each letter is read. The months of the year can also be used.

A second-grade math example from the website is Card Play. The teacher removes the aces, kings, queens, and jacks from the deck and then gives each child two cards. On the "go" signal, the children walk around the room. The teacher will say "freeze," and state a number. The children are to find another person with a card so that, by adding or subtracting the two numbers, they arrive at the number the teacher called out. After a short time, the children start walking again as they wait for another number to be called. Using music as the children walk and then stopping the music as a signal to freeze is recommended.

Brain Breaks is a concept developed by teacher education students from Albion College, Concordia University, and the University of Michigan to help increase the number of physical activities implemented into the elementary classroom (Action for Healthy Kids, 2013).

An example of a Brain Break that we have had our college students do is move to the music of the 1950s and 1960s—songs featuring dances such as the Swim, Mashed Potato, Pony, and Twist. All these songs can be found on YouTube. Other examples of Brain Breaks include 10 minutes of activities such as yoga poses, strength development activities such as wall push-ups, and isometric exercises. Even coordination activities such as rubbing the belly and patting the head are fun and a stress reliever.

Summary

The connection between the mind and body has been discussed for centuries. Today's research has found connections among the mind, movement, and music. Movement and music enhance academic performance. It is important that the early childhood educator understand the connection and provide a variety of movement and music experiences to enhance learning and performance. Physical activity and music can also provide a break to the intensity of the academic learning time.

Summary Related to Outcomes

Learning Outcomes	Guiding Principles
9.1 Understand the mind–body connections	Individual Needs Met
The link between the mind and body is not a new concept. The past decade has produced research that demonstrates the relationship among physical activity, exercise, health-related fitness, and academic performance for individuals of varying age.	
9.2 Discuss factors that affect brain health	Individual Needs Met
Physical activity enhances brain health by increasing neurons, providing increased blood flow to the brain, increasing cerebral blood flow, promoting changes in neurotransmitters, increasing brain chemicals to enhance mood, and creating permanent structural changes.	
9.3 Apply the relationships among academic performance and physical activity, exercise, and fitness to planning academic lessons	Environment and Curriculum Reciprocated
Spending more time in physical activity and less in academic practice does not have a negative impact on academic performance. Those who engage in more physical activity and exercise, or have higher levels of health-related fitness, tend to perform better academically.	

Learning Outcomes	Guiding Principles
9.4 Apply the relationship between academic performance and music to planning academic lessons	Environment and Curriculum Reciprocated

Research on the relationship between music and academic performance has focused on the Mozart effect, music education, and background music. The results relating to the Mozart effect are mixed. A relationship between music and academic performance has been found. Many results demonstrate a close relationship between the concepts. For example, the visual focus on reading words and reading music are the same—the eyes move across the page in a left-to-right direction. Smooth coordination of the eyes is important. Background music appears to assist children with special needs to focus and reduce arousal.

Learning Outcomes	Guiding Principles
9.5 Employ movement and music as a means to learn	Movement and Music Integrated

Movement and music can enhance the learning of academic concepts. Through interdisciplinary learning, the children gain a greater integration of knowledge and depth of understanding than when the concepts are taught alone.

Learning Outcomes	Guiding Principles
9.6 Create 10-minute physical activity/music breaks	Environment and Curriculum Reciprocated

Physical activity breaks are important for maintaining focus and can also be used to practice the academic concepts.

Demonstrate Your Knowledge, Skills, and Dispositions

Students will demonstrate knowledge, comprehension, analysis, and evaluation of Learning Outcomes related to Guiding Principles.

Learning Outcomes	Guiding Principles
9.1 Understand the mind–body connections	Individual Needs Met

- Completing a group class assignment, spend one class period learning about movement and music but do not leave your seats. Spend another class period where you experience 10-minute activity breaks. After each class, take a test on the content. Were there differences in the test scores? Explain your answer. How did you feel during and after each lesson, and why?

Learning Outcomes	Guiding Principles
9.2 Discuss factors that affect brain health	Individual Needs Met

- Create a brochure to give to families that explain the factors that affect brain health. Include ideas on what they can do at home to improve brain health.

Learning Outcomes	Guiding Principles
9.3 Apply the relationships among academic performance and physical activity, exercise, and fitness to planning academic lessons	Environment and Curriculum Reciprocated
• Select an academic standard for a specific grade and develop a lesson that uses movement to enhance learning of the concept. Explain how the music assists learning of the standard.	
9.4 Apply the relationship between academic performance and music to planning academic lessons	Environment and Curriculum Reciprocated
• Select an academic standard for a specific grade and develop a lesson that uses music to enhance learning of the concept. Explain how the music assists learning of the standard.	
9.5 Employ movement and music as a means to learn	Movement and Music Integrated
• Create an interdisciplinary lesson integrating movement, music, and an academic standard for a specific grade.	
9.6 Create 10-minute physical activity/ music breaks	Environment and Curriculum Reciprocated
• Create a 10-minute activity break using movement and music the incorporates moderate to vigorous physical activity. Teach it to the class.	

Planning for Engaging

The following learning activities provide three possibilities or ways to develop a standard taken from M^2 Movement Standards.

M^2 Movement Standard.

The child will exhibit a physically active lifestyle by

a. Identifying activities that enhance cardiovascular endurance and are enjoyable

b. Engaging in moderate to vigorous physical activity

Possibility One	Possibility Two	Possibility Three
What is the difference between moderate and vigorous aerobic physical activity?	What muscular strength/ endurance activity requires the most strength?	Match the activity to whether it needs strength or endurance.

Five stations are set up around the gym. Each station includes a variety of cardiovascular endurance activities: dancing to fast music, skipping around the room with a partner, playing hopscotch, jumping rope, running. The children are active at each station for 5 minutes.	Five stations are set up around the gym. Each station includes a variety of muscular strength/ endurance activities: tug-of-war, yoga, animal walks (bear, inchworm, crab, seal), ball squeeze, wall sit. The children are active at each station for 5 minutes.	Five stations are set up around the gym. Each station involves a variety of activities that require more muscular strength/ endurance or cardiovascular endurance. The stations are picking up weights, tag, crab soccer, skipping as fast as possible, and inchworm. Before they move to the next station, the child determines whether it is a muscular strength/ endurance or cardiovascular activity.
After the children have rotated through the stations, they answer the following questions: Which station was the most vigorous? Which was the least? What was different about the stations? Which did you have the most fun at? Which would you do in the future?	After the children have rotated through the stations, they answer the following questions: Which station required the most muscle? Which required the least? What was different about the stations? Which did you have the most fun at? Which would you do in the future?	
Assessment	**Assessment**	**Assessment**
Were the children active at the stations? Why or why not? Discuss the answers.	Were the children active at the stations? Why or why not? Discuss the answers.	Were the children active at the stations? Why or why not? Discuss the answers.

Now You Try It

Complete the following standard basic learning activities designed to meet various interests and developmental levels by designing two possibilities/ learning activities (Possibility Two and Possibility Three) to develop a movement and music standard taken from the M^2 Science Standards.

M^2 Science Standard: The child will identify and apply concepts and principles of force as applied to movement.		
Possibility One	**Possibility Two**	**Possibility Three**
What do I need to do to move through space? What are the different examples of motion? What happens to the motion when you use more force?		

Learning Activity	Learning Activity	Learning Activity
Which movement requires more force? Why?		

References

Action for Healthy Kids (2013). Retrieved from http://www.actionforhealthykids.org/component/content/article/39-step-3-challenges/640-brain-breaks-instant-recess-and-energizers

Cone, T., Werner, P., Cone, S., & Woods, A. (1998). *Interdisciplinary teaching through physical education.* Champaign, IL: Human Kinetics Publishers.

Copple, C., & Bredekamp, S. (2009). *Developmentally appropriate practice in early childhood programs serving children from birth through age 8* (3rd ed.) Washington, DC: NAEYC.

Crncec, R., Wilson, S., & Prior, M. (2006). The cognitive and academic benefits of music to children: Facts and fiction. *Educational Psychology, 26*(4), 579–594.

Draganski, B., Gaser, C., Kempermann, G., Kuhn, H.G., Winkler, J., Buchel, C., & May, A. (2006). Temporal and spatial dynamics of brain structure changes during extensive learning. *Journal of Neuroscience, 26,* 6314–6137.

Eat Smart, Move More, NC. (2006). Energizers. Retrieved from http://www.eatsmartmovemorenc.com/Energizers/Texts/K-5-Energizers.pdf.

Elliott, E., Belcher, D., & Weikle, M. (2012). Active Academics: Getting kids "moving more in school." Presentation at American Alliance for Health, Physical Education, Recreation, and Dance. Retrieved from http://www.activeacademics.org/.

Gardner, H. (2011). *Frames of mind: The theory of multiple intelligences.* New York, NY: Basic Books.

Hansen, D., Bernstorf, E., & Stuber, G.M. (2004). *The music and literacy connection.* Reston, VA: MENC: The National Association for Music Education.

Hillman, C., Castelli, D., & Buck, S. (2005). Aerobic fitness and neurocognitive function in healthy preadolescent children. *Medicine & Science in Sports & Exercise, 37*(11), 1967–1974.

Hillman, C., Pontifex, M., Raine, R., Castelli, D. , Hall, E. & Kramer, A. (2009) The effect of acute treadmill walking on cognitive control and academic achievement in preadolescent children. *Neuroscience, 159,* 1044–1054.

Hollmann, W., & Struder, H. (1996). Exercise, physical activity, nutrition, and the brain. *Nutrition Reviews, 54*(4), S37–S43.

Instructional Support Tools (2012a). Physical education. http://www.ncpublicschools.org/docs/acre/standards/support-tools/unpacking/health/k-2-pe.pdf.

Instructional Support Tools. (2012b). Music. http://www.ncpublicschools.org/docs/acre/standards/support-tools/unpacking/health/k-2-pe.pdf.

Jensen, E. (2007). *Teaching with the brain in mind* (2nd Ed.). Alexandria, VA: Association for Supervision and Curriculum Development.

Jensen, E. (2008). Eric P. Jensen Brain-based education: A fresh look at brain-based education. *Phi Delta Kappan, 89*(6), 408–417.

Kibbe, D., Hackett, J., Hurley, M., McFarland, A., Schubert, K., Schultz, A., & Harris, S. (2011). Ten years of TAKE 10!: Integrating physical activity with academic concepts in elementary school classrooms. *Preventive Medicine*, 52, s43–s50. doi:10.1016/j.ypmed.2011.01.025.

Kuczala, M. (2013). The kinesthetic classroom: Teaching and learning through movement. Paper presented at the American Association of Health, Physical Education, Recreation and Dance.

Lengel, T., & Kuczala, M. (2010). *The kinesthetic classroom: Teaching and learning.* Thousand Oaks CA: Corwin Press.

Mahar, M., Murphy, S., Rowe, D., Golden, J., Shields, T., & Raedeke, T. (2006). Effects of a classroom-based program on physical activity and on-task behavior. *Medicine & Science in Sport and Exercise*, 38(12), 2086–2094.

McEwing, H. (2011). Music, movement, and early literacy: A best practices primer for "Gotta Move!" *Children and Libraries*, Summer/Fall, 29–35.

Ploughman, M. (2008). Exercise is brain food: The effects of physical activity on cognitive function. *Developmental Neurorehabilitation*, 11(3), 236–240.

Praag, H. (2009). Exercise and the brain: Something to chew on. *Trends in Neuroscience*, 32(5), 283–290. doi:10.1016/j.tins.2008.12.007.

Ratey, John J. (2008). *SPARK: The revolutionary new science of exercise and the brain.* New York, NY: Little, Brown and Co.

Rauscher, F., & Hinton, S. (2006). The Mozart effect: Music listening is not music instruction. *Educational Psychologist*, 4(4), 233-238.

Rauscher, F., & Zupan, M., (2000). Classroom keyboard instruction improves kindergarten children's spatial-temporal performance: A field experiment. *Early Childhood Research Quarterly*, 15(2), 215–228.

Tarbert, K. (2012). Learning literacy through music. *Oneota Reading Journal.* http://oneotareadingjournal.com/2012/learning-literacy-through-music/.

Trost S. (2009). *Active education: Physical education, physical activity and academic performance. A research brief.* Princeton, NJ: Active Living Research, a National Program of the Robert Wood Johnson Foundation, summer 2009. Available from http://activelivingresearch.org.

Trudeau, F., & Shephard, R.J. (2010). Relationships of physical activity to brain health and the academic performance of school children. *American Journal of Lifestyle Medicine*, 4(2), 138–150.

Volmer, M. (2011). *Rev-Up to Read.* http://phonicsaerobics.com.

Yau, P., Castro, M., Tagani, A., Tsui, W., & Convit, A. (2012). Obesity and metabolic syndrome and functional and structural brain impairments in adolescence. *Pediatrics*, 130:e856–e886.

chapter 10

Assessment, Evaluation, and Engagement

LEARNING OUTCOMES AND GUIDING PRINCIPLES

Students reading this text will be able to demonstrate Learning Outcomes linked to Guiding Principles based on the National Association for the Education of Young Children's *Developmentally Appropriate Practice in Early Childhood Programs Serving Children from Birth through Age 8.*

Learning Outcomes	Guiding Principles
10.1 Understand the purpose of assessment	Individual Needs Met
10.2 Apply the NAEYC and NAAECS/SDE position statement on assessment	Standards and Assessment Provide Guidance
10.3 Apply ethical conduct to assessment of children	Individual Needs Met
10.4 Create different types of assessment in movement and music	Standards and Assessment Provide Guidance
10.5 Apply assessment to incorporating the Guiding Principles in program development	Guiding Principles: • Individual Needs Met • Environment and Curriculum Reciprocated • Movement and Music Integrated • Family and Community Involved • Standards and Assessment Provide Guidance
10.6 Assessment provides emotional well-being and a high level of involvement	Individual Needs Met

Making Connections
Appropriate Use of Assessment and Evaluation

Aziza is in third grade; her class is getting ready for a weeklong standardized testing program. The 8-year-old is worrying about the tests for several reasons. She is afraid she will not be familiar with the material and will not do well. In addition, she is experiencing stress because she is afraid that her scores will have a detrimental effect on her grades, as the test counts for 15 percent of her yearly grade. She had trouble sleeping the Sunday night prior to the beginning of the test week.

Breon's parents, who are university professors, have opted out for him to take the state's high-stakes testing to determine whether schools are making adequate yearly progress because of the amount of anxiety the tests were causing him and his parents. Throughout the year, Breon's parents were helping him with his test preparation homework. Six weeks prior to the testing, all special classes (music, art, and physical education) were curtailed and the children spent that time in test preparation. At times, both parents and son got upset, and even angry because of the pressure of doing well on the test, Breon had come to hate reading. Once the pressure of the test was removed, though, Breon once again developed a love of reading.

Charlene loved school every day; she knew her teachers were there to help her learn, and they included physical activity and music throughout the day. Each spring, she had to take the state standardized assessment, but her teachers did not emphasize the importance of the test. Prior to the test, her school day did not change. She still enjoyed music and physical activity time. On the day of the test, Charlene did not feel any different than she did on other days.

10.1 Understand the Purpose of Assessment

High-stakes testing can cause stress in many children, as it did for Aziza and Breon. The stress of one test being 15 percent of the grade or a reflection of proficiency can have an impact on performance. The children and families at Aziza's school call the test "Torture at Public School Testing Week"! If, instead, we use the assessment in a positive way, as Charlene's school did—to help the child learn and to have an impact on future learning—the stress is reduced and performance is not negatively affected.

Assessment is defined as an act of gathering data to make decisions; it is an important part of any educational program. Before we conduct assessments, however, we need to consider the following: "Why is this assessment being done? What purpose does it have? Is this particular assessment optimal for meeting that purpose?" (Snow & Van Hemel, 2008, p. 27).

Assessment is a major part of learning. If used to assist children in developing knowledge and skills, assessment enhances not only the child's motivation but also that of the teachers. When children think about their own learning, review experiences, see what did and did not work and what made sense and what did not, their learning, critical thinking, and a deeper understanding are enhanced (Manitoba Education, Citizenship and Youth, 2006).

▲ How strong am I? Authentic assessment can be fun!

The National Association for the Education of Young Children (NAEYC) and the National Association of Early Childhood Specialists in State Departments of Education (NAECS/SDE) have developed a joint position statement on curriculum, assessment, and program evaluation. They state that the following are the purposes of assessment (NAEYC, 2009b, p. 2):

❶ Making sound decisions about teaching and learning

❷ Identifying significant concerns that may require focused intervention for individual children

❸ Helping programs improve their educational and developmental interventions (excerpted from NAEYC, "Early Childhood Curriculum, Assessments, and Program Evaluation, Position Statement" (Washington, CD: NAEYC, 2003). Copyright @ 2003 NAEYC. Reprinted with permission. Full text of this position statement is available at www.naeyc.org/files/naeyc/file/positions/CAPEexpand.pdf.)

The purpose of this chapter is not only to understand the purpose of assessment, but also to review NAEYC's position statement on assessment, ethical conduct, how to develop assessment tools for learning, and program review. We feel strongly about incorporating the Guiding Principles used throughout these chapters; thus we provide you with an evaluation of their effect on your thinking. Finally, we discuss emotional well-being and level of involvement, as they play an important role in development and learning.

10.2   Apply the NAEYC and NAAECS/SDE Position Statement on Assessment

Appropriate assessments are related to the developmental level of the child and are used for skill and knowledge improvement. All programs need to incorporate assessment that is appropriate, valid, and reliable.

A *valid* assessment measures what it is meant to measure. In addition, the assessment must be appropriate for the intended use. A 50-yard dash, for example, cannot be used as a test to measure cardiovascular endurance—because endurance is aerobic, the activity must be long enough to require the full involvement of the cardiovascular system. Furthermore, a reliable test is repeatable—you get the same answer if you give the test a second time.

The strengths of the children, their progress, and their needs should be assessed in a developmentally appropriate, culturally and linguistically responsive manner using authentic assessment activities. The assessment should be related to the children's daily activities and, ideally, should be part of natural daily activities. Aziza's testing, conversely, was not part of her daily routine—her daily and weekly routine was interrupted to make way for a standardized series of tests.

Assessment needs to be culturally and linguistically responsive and inclusive of families. The diversity of the classroom is increasing; therefore, understanding cultural differences is important. By 2030, it is estimated that 40 percent of school-age children will have a home language other than English (NAEYC, 2009b). Assessment should to be appropriate to the culture and language of the child. Families need to understand the purpose of assessment and meet the needs of the family.

It is important for families to understand the purposes of assessment, which are:

- To determine the individual needs of the child
- To understand how the child's progression of learning can be guided by instruction
- To provide program accountability for teachers and families (Snow & Van Hemel, 2008).

Two additional indicators of learning that need to be assessed are emotional well-being and level of involvement. However, these two indicators are not typically evaluated (Laevers, 2003).

Program Evaluation and Accountability

Regular evaluation of early childhood programs is an important goal for improvement. The program itself, not the children, needs to be held accountable for children's learning (HighScope, 2013). NAEYC (2003) suggests indicators of effectiveness for program evaluation. The purpose of program evaluation is for continuous improvement, and measuring attainment of the goals is important. The goals need to include child-oriented goals as well as those related to families, teachers, staff, and the community related to development and learning outcomes. The evaluations need to be valid and reliable, and multiple sources of data taken over time must be used. Those who conduct the evaluations need to be well trained and unbiased.

The analysis needs to be systematic and analyzed to determine the extent to which the program meets the goals. Finally, the evaluation needs to be publicly available. We apply this to assessing the movement and music part of the curriculum, which should be integrated throughout the day. The following sections are specific components of the program that need to be reviewed and included in program assessment related not only to the overall curriculum, but specifically to movement and music.

10.3 *Apply Ethical Conduct to Assessment of Children*

Ethical conduct is critical when working with children. NAEYC (2011) developed a position statement, *NAEYC Code of Ethical Conduct and Statement of Commitment*, on ethical conduct when working with children. Conduct is divided into responsibilities to the following:

- Children
- Families
- Colleagues (co-workers, employers)
- Community and society

We discuss ethical conduct when working with children, specifically the codes related to children and families and assessment. A major theme throughout all the assessment instruments and strategies is that they must be developmentally appropriate. Each section includes guiding ideals and principles. *Ideals* are the ultimate goals of the teachers, whereas *principles* guide ethical decision making.

Ideals

Five ideals from NAEYC's (2011, p. 2, 4) ethical standards relate to assessment:

- I.1.6—To use assessment instruments and strategies that are appropriate for the children to be assessed, that are used only for the purposes for which they were designed, and that have the potential to benefit children.

- I.1.7—To use assessment information to understand and support children's development and learning, to support instruction, and to identify children who may need additional services.

- I.1.9—To advocate for and ensure that all children, including those with special needs, have access to the support services needed to be successful.

- I.1.10—To ensure that each child's culture, language, ethnicity, and family structure are recognized and valued in the program.

- I.2.8—We shall treat child assessment information confidentially and share this information only when there is a legitimate need for it.

Assessment instruments can be used only for the stated purpose, and they must benefit the children. The assessment tools need to be meaningful and provide guidance for both the teacher and the child about the next steps in the learning process. Assessment of a child without a specific goal in mind is inappropriate. Other inappropriate uses of assessment include assessment that is not multifaceted and is based on only a single score, occurs only as content for grading, and is focused on isolated skills that are not applicable. An example of an inappropriate assessment based on isolated skills would be a child dribbling a ball through cones instead of in general space as children are moving, or asking a child to match the pitch of an isolated musical note.

Development and learning are an important part of the assessment process. The assessments are a valuable part of the learning process because they provide feedback to the child, teacher, and family. As a screening tool, they identify children who need more extensive evaluation and/or assistance. Measuring BMI is an example of this ideal, as this measure screens for overweight and obesity. Children deemed at risk of overweight or overweight are given additional assessment and interventions if needed.

Assessment needs to account for the child's culture, language, ethnicity, and family structure. Using an assessment that is based in English for a child who does not speak English is not valid; an alternative assessment needs to be identified. In addition, assessments must be explained to the family to enhance their understanding and the development of their skills as parents.

Principles

Principles help guide the early childhood educator in appropriate conduct and resolution of ethical problems. Five NAEYC (2011, p. 3, 4) principles are relevant to assessment:

- P.1.1—Above all, we shall not harm children. We shall not participate in practices that are emotionally damaging, physically harmful, disrespectful, degrading, dangerous, exploitative, or intimidating to children. This principle has precedence over all others in this Code.

- P.1.1.5—We shall use appropriate assessment systems, which include multiple sources of information, to provide information on children's learning and development.

- P.1.1.6—We shall strive to ensure that decisions such as those related to enrollment, retention, or assignment to special education services, will be based on multiple sources of information and will never be based on a single assessment, such as a test score or a single observation.

- P.2.7—We shall inform families about the nature and purpose of the program's child assessments and how data about their child will be used.

- P.2.8—We shall treat child assessment information confidentially and share this information only when there is a legitimate need for it.

We do not engage in practices that are "emotionally damaging, physically harmful, disrespectful, degrading, dangerous, exploitative, or intimidating" (NAEYC, 2011, p. 3) to children in any way. High-stakes testing can harm children. When under extreme stress, children do not perform up to their capabilities, which can lead to inappropriate labeling and/or placement. It can also harm a child's self-concept and cause him or her to stop trying.

To assess a child correctly, the child should be evaluated on multiple occasions with different assessments. We all perform differently at different

M² ASSESSMENT FUN   Body Parts in Motion

After the children demonstrate various fundamental motor patterns, give them a drawing of a body and have them circle which body parts were involved in that activity.

For the underhand throw, for example, they would circle the feet and the arms.

times; thus, a single assessment is not a good indicator of performance. This is compounded for children. We know that children are variable. One day they perform expertly, but on the next day it is as if they have never performed the skill. A single assessment is not a valid picture of the child's capabilities.

For placement decisions such as enrollment, retention, or assignment to special education services, multiple sources of information must be used. A decision should not be based on one piece of data. Once the results of the assessment are compiled, an individual educational plan can be developed.

Assessment relates to the families of the children. It is important that families understand the purpose of the tests, and how the tests are used.

Any assessment needs to be held in the strictest confidentiality. The information should be shared only when there is a legitimate need. Teachers need to be careful about confidentiality even with children. Ms. Polkis, a first grade teacher, asked Travis to return tests to the children. When Travis went home, his mother asked how he did on the test. He said that he had the third highest grade in the class. Travis then proceeded to tell his mother the results of

▲ When asking a child to show you how high he can count, he might show you by standing on tiptoe and reaching to the sky and saying one, two, three. . . . Children interpret questions differently—thus, the importance of authentic assessment.

all the children in the class. He was a quick learner and had memorized the scores of all the children as he was handing the tests back to the children. Teachers need to be sensitive to other children returning tests, even if they do not memorize all the test scores. They will still see the tests and will remember some of the scores. If the teacher wants to give a child the responsibility of returning tests, the tests could be folded in half with the child's name on the outside so the child returning the tests cannot see the scores.

10.4 Create Different Types of Assessment in Movement and Music

Assessment is a critical component of any curriculum and every content area to ensure effective learning. Assessment can be summative or formative and process or product oriented. *Summative* and *formative* refer to the time at which testing occurs, whereas *process* and *product* testing addresses the type of testing conducted. Any test can be given in a formative or summative manner.

When assessing children, we use both summative and formative assessment. Throughout the learning experience, we use formative assessment to determine what the child has learned and what the child needs to learn—thus, it occurs frequently. Summative assessment is used at specific time points—typically at the end of a unit or series of lessons. It describes where the child is at that specific point in time. Teachers use both types of assessment. Formative assessment guides learning, whereas summative assessment describes the individual at a specific point in time. Summative assessment can be used to determine physical growth (height, weight, body fat) and physical fitness (cardiovascular endurance, muscular strength and endurance, and flexibility) to determine whether the child is within normal bounds. Formative assessment is used to determine whether the child is reaching the expected learning goals and objectives. It is also used to determine what the child is ready to learn, or where the child is in the learning hierarchy to tailor the lessons to the child's knowledge and skills. Formative assessment also helps teachers evaluate and modify their lessons. We use formative assessment to develop the criteria for the summative assessment.

In movement and music, formative assessment is used to measure concepts, skills, attitudes, and values. The first component that needs to be evaluated is a knowledge of concepts. Measuring the child's understanding of the concept of self- and general space can be completed by use of the task sheet (see Figure 10.1). Moving the fish to general space shows the child's knowledge of appropriate use of space. Drawing a line around a group of flowers that use good general space provides an insight into what the child understands. In addition to the cognitive assessment, the child's behavior needs to be measured both during the learning time, and later on to see how the child applies the concept to other areas. For example, the teacher can see if the children understand self- and general space as they move in the gym—are they spread out, moving in a variety of directions, or they clumped together and moving as a unit? Observation by the teachers is a wonderful assessment tool. Applying self- and general space to other areas, the teacher can evaluate children when they are lining up. Do the children push and shove, or are they using their limited space appropriately?

The second component that needs to be evaluated includes skills. Measuring movement or music skills can be completed by product or process assessment, also referred to as quantitative or qualitative testing. *Product assessment* measures outcome—how far, how fast, or how many. *Process assessment* evaluates form. Did the child use a step and a hop when performing a skip, or the correct position of the feet when throwing? Factors that can influence quantitative performance (product) of individuals are developmental factors such as weight, strength, motivation, maturation, and physique. Rey can throw the ball farther than Alonna, not because Rey has better form but because he is bigger, stronger, and more maturationally advanced than Alonna.

We use process testing to develop the movement and music skill criteria. For instructional purposes, qualitative assessment (process) is more appropriate because it not only indicates the instructional sequence, but also provides feedback for both the teacher and the learner. After the child reaches a mature form, quantitative measures may then be used to chart a child's progress.

M² ASSESSMENT FUN   Ringing the Bells

When assessing the vertical jump, hang clappers (bells) at various heights, either from the ceiling or on a rope strung from standards. This gives the children a goal to reach—and they will also enjoy making noise when they attain the goal.

General Space

Find a good spot for the fish to go. Draw a line from the fish to the best 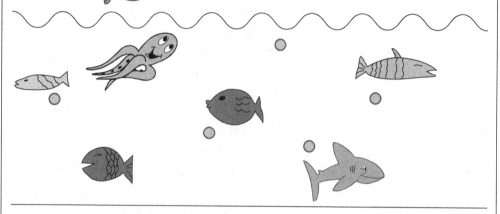 spot.

Circle the flowers using general space correctly. Put an X on the flowers that are too close.

Figure 10.1 Example of a formative assessment for general and self-space.

Authentic Assessment and Rubrics

Authentic assessment uses "real-world" tasks to determine how children are able to use their skills in everyday life and thereby reduces the stress of the formal testing environment. The validity of authentic assessments is high, as they are used in everyday situations.

Authentic assessment can include the following:

- Individual and/or group journals
- Parental reports
- Interviews
- Peer observation
- Self-assessment
- Portfolio
- Role playing
- Observation
- Teacher/student rubrics

A variety of assessment techniques can be used. It is important, especially with young children, that we obtain a true measure of their skills. For example, we can formally test 4-year-old Robert by asking him to jump as high as he can. In this situation, he brings his feet up to his buttocks. However, when we put Robert under balloons strung at different heights, we see that he is able to jump much higher using a more advanced skill level to reach the balloons. Thus, we recommend that testing be completed unobtrusively in an environment that encourages higher levels of skill performance.

For authentic assessment to be valid and reliable, criteria for skilled performance need to be established (we cover development of rubrics later in this chapter). Authentic assessment also needs to frequently use self-testing and peer evaluation; this forces children to evaluate their own skills, which helps to develop mindful movement. Check sheets, task sheets, and exit slips are excellent ways to engage the children.

Check sheets or tally sheets are used to collect data on the number completed, distance, active time, and frequency of the occurrence (see Table 10.1). Task sheets are designed to provide data from a specific requirement—for

Table 10.1 Check Sheets to Evaluate Creative Movement and Fundamental Motor Patterns in 3- to 4-Year-Old Children

CREATIVE MOVEMENT, 3–4 YEAR OLDS

Name_____ Instructor _____

_____ Quick balanced stops on signal
_____ Firmly held freezes
_____ Quick starts on signal
_____ Purposeful movement to solve problems (does child understand problems?)
_____ Uses a variety of movements to solve problems
_____ Listens while moving
_____ Continuous exploratory movement from start/stop signal
_____ Demonstrates understanding of self-space
_____ Controls body parts while moving
_____ Demonstrates understanding of one's own areas of high, medium, low

_____ Moves near to and far from others without collisions
_____ Demonstrates knowledge of names of all large/small body parts
_____ Accurate meeting and parting of specific body parts
_____ Thinking and moving simultaneously
_____ Twisting the body in a variety of ways
_____ Demonstrates ability to change speed of movements abruptly
_____ Duplicates an imposed speed of beat in movements
_____ Moves in wide variety of ways to a moderate pulse beat
_____ Creates new movement responses that h fit the beat

MOTOR DEVELOPMENT, 3–4 YEAR OLDS

Name_____ Instructor _____

JUMPING
_____ Two feet to two feet
_____ Control with soft landing
_____ One foot to two feet
_____ Over obstacles
_____ Run and jump

THROWING
_____ To self
_____ Step with opposite foot
_____ Uses body parts to increase force
_____ Follow-through
_____ To stationary target
_____ To partner

CATCHING
_____ To self at different heights
_____ Bounce to self and catch
_____ From a partner

_____ At various levels
_____ Look, reach, give
_____ Catch yarn ball/scoop

KICKING
_____ Stationary ball
_____ Stationary ball on run
_____ Ball rolled by someone
_____ Kicking at a target
_____ Dribbling the ball
_____ Different parts of the foot

BALANCING
_____ One leg
_____ Different body shapes
_____ Walk on low beam
_____ Variety of tilt boards

Key: * = Proficient = Control
      + = Improving (Pre-Control)

example, hopping on the musical beat. Finally, exit slips are designed to provide feedback from a posed question at the end of a learning activity. The answer does not need to be words; drawings can also be useful.

From the description of authentic assessment, it appears that we are suggesting that assessment is required for everything we do. That is not the case, however; we are suggesting a sampling of behavior, not continual assessment.

Development of assessment starts with the curriculum and weaves throughout the lessons. Assessment is important in knowing what the child can do, selecting the curriculum, determining what the child is learning, and moving to the next level of difficulty.

Designing a Rubric

A *rubric* is a descriptive scheme to evaluate the process or product of the child's knowledge and skills and distinguish among levels of proficiency. Rubric design should begin with a set of criteria taken from curriculum objectives or state standards. The first step is to determine what knowledge and skills need to be assessed. For example, in developing a lesson to teach long rope jumping, the teacher first needs to evaluate the child's skill of rope turning in each hand and jump-bounce (see Table 10.2, left column). Step two includes a graduated scale or performance ratings with words and/or numbers used (see Table 10.2, first row). For this skill we use "needs improvement," "novice," and "competent." Step three adds performance descriptions (Table 10.2, columns 2 through 4). The child must be able to turn the rope with a partner so the jumper can jump (the rope must hit the

Table 10.2 Example of a Rubric for Long Rope Jumping

	Needs Improvement	Novice	Competent
Rope Turning	Children's hands not turning together	Children coordinating the rope turn but rope not high enough or not hitting the ground	Children's hands display bimanual coordination, rope going over head and hitting ground
Jump-Bounce	Jumping with feet too high and/or hitting ground without bending knees	Jumping without a rhythm to the jump-bounce	Rhythmic jump-bounce and can adapt to a change in speed of the rope

ground and go over the child's head). The child also needs to be able to perform a rhythmical jump-bounce. Anyone can jump the long rope if they can perform a rhythmical jump-bounce. The rope turners, however, must be skilled enough to turn the rope to the rhythm of the jumper.

An example of a rubric for singing a song from memory and clapping to the beat is given in Table 10.3. We break the task into the components of singing the words of the song, clapping, clapping in rhythm, clapping and singing simultaneously, and singing and clapping the complete song

Table 10.3 Example of a Rubric for an M^2 Standard to Clap to the Beat while Singing a Song

M^2 Music Standard: The child will recognize the rhythm of a familiar song and clap to the beat while singing the song.				
	Performance Ratings			
Criteria	Needs Improvement	Satisfactory	Good	Excellent
Sing the words	Does not know words or melody	Aware of words and melody but needs assistance	Knows melody and majority of words	Independently knows the melody and all words to the song
Clap	Does not match hands	Brings full hands to the midline but they do not match	Matches full hands together	Claps full hand together at body midline
Clap in rhythm to the song	Does not match clapping to the rhythm of song	Clapping matches rhythm periodically	Clapping matches rhythm of song majority of time	Clapping matches rhythm of song
Clap and sing simultaneously	Needs assistance with words, melody, and matching clapping	Knows melody and majority of words with assistance and matches clap rhythm majority of time	Knows melody and majority of words while clapping hands	Independently sings song while clapping
Effort	Does not engage in singing or clapping	Spends part of time engaged in other activities	Engaged in singing and clapping majority of time	Totally engaged in singing and clapping for entire length of song

smoothly and without effort. Notice that this is also a developmental sequence for performing the skill. The child first needs to know the words of the song and he or she must have developed the skill of clapping. Next, the child needs to clap to a rhythm and then combine the clapping while singing. These are highly coordinated skills for young children.

An example of a children's rubric for throwing is in Figure 10.2. The rubric does not have the same design as that used by the teacher, but it can provide valuable feedback for the children on what they need to focus when performing the skill. The children assess partners or themselves. In this rubric, the first task is one-hand underhand throwing; underhand throwing skill precedes one-hand overhand throwing. The child has practiced the cue words, "step-swing," and has had practice using the cue words to guide his or her performance. For this practice, the child or a partner marks whether the child steps and swings the arm. A smiley/frowny face can be used in place of the words. The one-hand overhand throw is more complex, and the cue words are "step" with the opposite foot to throwing hand, rotate the "hips" forward, "elbow" leads (forearm untwists), and finally the forearm follows ("throw").

Rubrics should also be used to measure learning over time. Assessment of individual learning provides a profile useful in designing a developmental pathway. One such pathway may be musical knowledge and skills. The rubric in Table 10.4 can be used or adapted to provided an assessment of musical knowledge and skills over time.

M² ASSESSMENT FUN **How Long Can I Move?**

To determine the children's aerobic fitness level, play a game of tag. Instead of the children being "frozen," they stay in the game when tagged, but switch to a different locomotor movement. Determine how long the children can maintain the game.

10.5 Apply Assessment to Incorporating the Guiding Principles in Program Development

We feel that the Guiding Principles used throughout this book are important in the assessment of program success. Therefore we have developed a rubric that you can use to evaluate your inclusion of the principles. The rubric is also helpful in evaluating other programs.

Underhand Throw

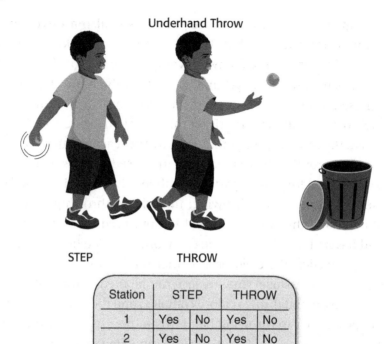

STEP   THROW

Station	STEP		THROW	
1	Yes	No	Yes	No
2	Yes	No	Yes	No
3	Yes	No	Yes	No

Overhand Throw

STEP   HIP   ELBOW   THROW

STEP	HIPS	ELBOW	THROW	Station
Yes	Yes	Yes	Yes	1
No	No	No	No	
Yes	Yes	Yes	Yes	2
No	Yes	No	No	

Figure 10.2 Example of an authentic formative assessment for underhand and overhand throwing.

Table 10.4 Rubric to Measure Musical Skills over Time

Musical Skill	Beginning 1	Developing 3	Accomplished 5
Pitch (high/low)	Needs assistance to recognize pitch	Beginning to recognize pitch with some assistance	Can always recognize difference between high and low pitches
Dynamics (soft/loud)	Needs assistance to recognize difference between loud and soft	Beginning to recognize loud and soft with some assistance	Can always recognize difference between loud and soft
Beat or rhythm pattern	Beginning to make a rhythmic pattern with assistance	Can make a rhythm pattern most of the time	Can always compose a rhythmic pattern
Beat or rhythm echo	Beginning to echo a pattern with assistance	Can echo a rhythmic pattern most of the time	Can always echo a rhythmic pattern
Sing	Beginning to sing a simple melody	Can sing a simple melody most of the time	Can sing a simple melody
Listen (recognize a simple melody)	Beginning to recognize a simple melody with assistance	Can recognize a simple melody most of the time	Can always recognize a known simple melody
Play an instrument	Beginning to use rhythm instruments with assistance	Can use rhythm instruments appropriately most of the time	Can always use rhythm instruments appropriately
Attentiveness	Can be engaged and attentive with assistance	Is engaged and attentive most of the time	Is always engaged and paying attention

Each of the Guiding Principles (Individual Needs Met, Environment and Curriculum Reciprocated, Movement and Music Integrated, Family and Community Involved, and Standards and Assessment Provide Guidance) is discussed in relation to evaluation of the plans for teaching movement and music. For example, how do you know that you met the individual needs of the children or that you structured the environment to enhance the child's learning?

The rubric to determine whether you are including the guiding principles uses the criteria of the guiding principles, which can include "does not meet expectations," "meets expectations," and "exceeds expectations" (see Table 10.5).

Table 10.5 Rubric for Evaluating Use of Guiding Principles in Program Design

	Does Not Meet Expectations	Meets Expectations	Exceeds Expectations
Individual Needs Met	The lessons do not include individual choices of varying abilities and skill levels. Majority of the children are not learning.	The lessons include some choices of varying abilities and skill levels. Majority of the children are learning.	The lessons are individualized to all the children in the class. All children are working at their own pace.
Environment and Curriculum Reciprocated	The environment is not structured to enhance the learning of the curriculum.	The environment is structured to enhance learning of the curriculum	The environment is closely linked to the curriculum to support successful attainment.
Movement and Music Integrated	Movement and music are taught separately.	Movement and music are integrated so that similar concepts are demonstrated by both movement and music.	Movement and music are taught in partnership.
Family and Community Involved	Family and community are not involved in the school.	Family and community are included for specific events throughout the year.	Family and community are involved on an ongoing basis through involvement in planning, providing information, and special events.
Standards and Assessment Provide Guidance	Standards do not guide assessment. Assessment is based on standardized testing and not individual abilities, skills, and knowledge.	Standards guide assessment.	Assessment are based on the guidelines and individualized to the child.

Individual Needs Met

To determine what to teach the children, individual needs must be considered. Initially, the individuals are evaluated for both structural and functional constraints. Structurally, we need to screen children for height, weight, and body fat to determine whether each child is increasing in

M² ASSESSMENT FUN Are You Listening?

Measure children's listening skills and ability to move quickly, by occasionally saying STOP instead of saying GO. Or start counting when they move to get equipment and see how long it takes to return to their self-space—with no running of course.

height and weight and BMI, and whether they are within normal bounds. This is typically completed by the school nurse.

We also need to evaluate fitness, concept understanding, and motor skill development of the individual children. For younger children, we do not need to use standardized testing such as the Presidential Youth Fitness Program (2010); rather, we need to observe the children's movements to make sure they are able to participate in moderate to vigorous physical activity for extended periods of time and that they sweat and do not get out of breath. In addition, we should notice whether their muscular strength and endurance are within normal bounds. BMI can be used to screen for overweight. Those greater than the 85th percentile for BMI should be observed more closely as they engage in physical activity to determine whether additional evaluation is needed.

Structural constraints such as height and weight are slow to change and need to be evaluated on a yearly basis. Functional constraints, on the other hand, are quick to change and are measured continually via formative evaluation, mainly through process testing. Functional constraints include the children's motivation to move and their music and movement performance. Motivation is important to learning and performance. By formative evaluation of movement and music concepts and skills, the child can become successful at his or her own level, and these increases in skill serve as motivation for the child to continue to improve. If the child fails, however, his or her motivation declines. Understanding of the child's level of skill development must be authentic and can be done by observation with use of a checklist and/or rubrics to guide observation. Other forms of authentic assessment include task sheets, projects, logs, and journals.

> ## M² ASSESSMENT FUN
>
> After learning a concept, skill, song, or dance, try speeding up the request to perform. If the skill is well learned, the child will be able to switch speeds quickly; if the child hesitates, he or she has not learned the skill to a level at which he or she can perform automatically.

Environment and Curriculum Reciprocated

Learning by the child is a reciprocal and active process between the explorations of the educator-designed environment and the curriculum-planned activities. An understanding of the environmental and task constraints is important to provide developmentally appropriate instruction. Once the ability, skills, and knowledge of the children are understood, the environment and task are analyzed to determine what the child is ready to learn next. Because younger children are variable in their performance—skilled one minute and less so the next—a variety of levels of performance need to be available in each lesson. For example, if the child catches a ball successfully, she takes a step away from her partner; if she misses, she steps forward as she works on her form. Distance increases task complexity and increases the challenge for the child. Greater force is needed to throw the ball a greater distance, and thus increased force is absorbed. Different size balls, as well as softer and harder balls, also need to be available. Initially, a large ball is easier to catch but, with skill, children need to be able to increase the complexity of the task and choose smaller balls. When practicing jumping over a brook, children can choose the distance that they will jump—the brook is narrow in some parts and wide in other parts.

When education systems talk about assessments, they usually focus on the system obtaining information on each child's curriculum knowledge and skills development. It is also important, however, to assess how the children are being taught. The checklist in Table 10.6 can be used for self-evaluation to improve learning and opportunities for a healthy lifestyle.

Movement and Music Integrated

The early education environment and the curriculum should integrate movement and music development throughout the day to enhance the

Table 10.6 Self-Evaluation of Teacher Engaging Music and Movement

Category	Majority of Time 4–5 Days	Most of the Time 2–3 Days	Rarely Make Time 0–1 Days
Teach music			
Teach movement			
Provide opportunities for music play and exploration			
Provide opportunities for movement play and exploration for 30 minutes or more			
Provide opportunities for creative dance			
Provide opportunities for outside movement play and exploration for 30 minutes or more			
Provide movement and music learning activities appropriate for all developmental levels			
Integrate movement and music into curriculum			
Provide developmentally appropriate music and movement			
Model healthy eating habits			

development of a healthy child who is ready to learn. This needs not only to include concepts within movement, but also to ensure that movement and music concepts are integrated. Words normally used to notify children of activity transition periods might be sung, as in the following:

"Our time at catching is done,

We have had some fun,

Clean up and play in the sun."

Family and Community Involved

Family and community involvement is important in all aspects of the design of the learning environment and implementation of the curriculum to enhance learning. A formal assessment of family and community involvement is not required; however, ensuring that the family is engaged in the curriculum and that the community is involved in the school is important. Awareness of how often the family and community are engaged in the school should be noted and evaluated. Families and community members can be surveyed on their availability to engage in the school.

One simple way to ensure family involvement is to share assessment results with the parents. A simple report can be sent to parents explaining the child's progress in topic areas of tonal development, rhythmic development, and movement development (Marshall, 2009). Parents enjoy learning about their child's progress and are usually anxious to provide guidance at home once they are aware of the developmental focus.

Standards and Assessment Provide Guidance

Based on standards, assessment—both formal and informal—must document the child's growth in developmental areas (physical, cognitive, language, and socioemotional). Educational assessment must have a purpose—and that purpose needs to be communicated to the family. No harm should be done to children. Assessment done inappropriately can cause great harm to children, both emotionally and physically.

The curriculum for children's programs needs to be based on the individual needs of the children, value the cultural background of the children, and base programming on socioemotional needs. Assessment must be used to motivate and engage children. We need to ensure that emotional well-being and involvement are fostered.

10.6 Assessment Provides Emotional Well-Being and a High Level of Involvement

Assessment can enhance motivation for learning. Doing well on a test is exciting—but using the results of the test to direct improvement can be motivating. Assessment can enhance student motivation in many ways. It provides feedback to the children, letting them know what they can do and assisting them in determining what to do next, while also scaffolding the learning. This emphasizes progress in obtaining the goal, and enhances success. Being in control of their own learning also builds children's confidence, and they learn to take risks without punishment for failure.

Assessment of academic and movement and music content is important to assist in and to increase learning. Emotional well-being and involvement guide the child's learning and should not be ignored. Well-being is related to how "at home" children feel in the environment—are they at ease, spontaneous, energetic, and self-confident? A challenging environment enhances individual involvement.

Well-being and involvement are related to self-concept of the child and allows for engagement in the activity. Both well-being and involvement result in concentration and what is termed "flow" in sport psychology, in which the individual is completely absorbed in the activity. To maintain flow, the activity needs to increase in complexity, thus increasing the challenge (Nakamura & Csikszentmihalyi, 2009). Flow is between anxiety on one side and boredom on the other, and is related to mindfulness (Kee & Wang, 2008). With mindfulness, there tends to be more attentional control, emotional control, goal setting, imagery, and self-talk strategies. We all need to be mindful of what we are doing.

Laevers designed a five-point scale that looks at the involvement and well-being of the child in the educational environment (Lewis, 2011). On one end of the scale is *extremely low*, in which the child is crying, screaming, sad, angry, or not responding to the environment. A *low* level indicates the child is not at ease, whereas at a *moderate* level, he or she is neutral or has no emotion. At a *high* level, there are signs of satisfaction but not consistently so. The child who looks consistently happy and cheerful indicates an *extremely high* level of well-being and involvement.

Five-year-old Katie is at the local ice skating rink. This is her second visit, and she has learned the basics. Katie skates around and around for two hours without stopping. Her socioemotional indicator is *extremely high*.

Felipe, 4 years old, is taking swimming lessons at the local pool. He is huddled next to his mother and is crying. Felipe's indicator is at the *extremely low* level. Adjustments need to be made to the learning environment to improve Felipe's well-being and involvement. The environment needs to be rearranged. Felipe's teacher fills a bucket with water and gives him some toys to use in the bucket. Gradually, he gains confidence and is able to leave his mother's side and enter the water.

Other changes to enhance emotional well-being and increase involvement include design of more challenging activities, use of new and unconventional materials and activities, review of relationships between children and the teacher, and, finally, assisting children with emotional or developmental problems.

Summary

Assessment is an integral part of the learning process. It needs to be appropriate, valid, and reliable and occur in a developmentally appropriate and culturally and linguistically responsive environment, using authentic assessment. Multiple assessments are needed to make decisions guiding the child's learning. Following ethical ideals and principles allows for the protection of children so that the assessment does no harm to children. Creating authentic assessment tools is critical to a quality program.

Summary Related to Outcomes

Learning Outcomes	Guiding Principles
10.1 Understand the purpose of assessment	Individual Needs Met
Assessment involves the process of acquiring data to make decisions about learning and instruction. A main focus of assessment is to motivate learning. If children are improving their knowledge or skills, they are motivated to continue. If they are not improving, they lose motivation and do not continue with the task. Assessment is used to identify concerns about the children and the instructional process to assist with program improvement to educate children effectively and efficiently.	
10.2 Apply the NAEYC and NAAECS/SDE position statement on assessment	Standards and Assessment Provide Guidance
The position statement focuses on developmentally appropriate assessment that is valid and reliable. The assessment should evaluate what the child *can* do, not what the child *cannot* do. Assessment also needs to be both culturally and linguistically responsive and authentic. Program evaluation investigates whether there is continuous improvement of children over time and the guiding principles are followed. It is important that the program meet the goals of the families, teachers, staff, and community.	

Learning Outcomes	Guiding Principles
10.3 Apply ethical conduct to assessment of children	Individual Needs Met
An ethical code of conduct is important when working with children. NAEYC's code includes responsibilities to children, families, colleagues, and the community. Ideals are the ultimate goals of the teachers, whereas principles guide ethical decision making.	
10.4 Create different types of assessment in movement and music	Assessment and Standards Provide Guidance
Assessment can be formative or summative, and evaluate process or product. Formative assessment, which evaluates process, guides the learning process. The information shows what the child can do, which leads to the next step in learning. Authentic assessment is important. It evaluates knowledge and skills in "real-life" tasks and includes journals, parental reports, interviews, peer observation, self-assessment, group projects, portfolios, role-playing, rubrics, and the like. Rubrics assist the teacher in evaluating the criteria required to perform the task.	
10.5 Apply assessment to incorporate the Guiding Principles in program development	Guiding Principles: • Individual Needs Met • Environment and Curriculum Reciprocated • Movement and Music Integrated • Family and Community Involved • Standards and Assessment Provide Guidance
We have included Guiding Principles in this book—beliefs that we feel need to be part of every class, school, and district. Teachers need to periodically assess themselves to determine whether they are including the Guiding Principles in their classroom.	
10.6 Assessment provides emotional well-being and a high level of involvement	Individual Needs Met
Children need to feel comfortable and involved in the classroom, which helps to develop self-confidence. Involvement requires successful performance and a challenging environment where the child continually moves to the next level of performance.	

Demonstrate Your Knowledge, Skills, and Dispositions

Students will demonstrate knowledge, comprehension, analysis, and evaluation of Learning Outcomes related to Guiding Principles.

Learning Outcomes	Guiding Principles
10.1 Understand the purpose of assessment	Individual Needs Met
• What is your assessment philosophy?	
10.2 Apply the NAEYC and NAAECS/SDE position statement on assessment	Standards and Assessment Provide Guidance
• Give an example of an appropriate and an inappropriate assessment of children in movement or music. Explain the differences between the appropriate and inappropriate assessments.	
10.3 Apply ethical conduct to assessment of children	Individual Needs Met
• Describe how assessment and testing can harm children.	
10.4 Create different types of assessment in movement and music	Standards and Assessment Provide Guidance
• Select a movement or music concept or skill and create an authentic assessment for it.	
10.5 Apply assessment to incorporating the Guiding Principles in program development	Standards and Assessment Provide Guidance
• Give an example of each of the Guiding Principles and explain why they are critical to early childhood education.	
10.6 Assessment provides emotional well-being and a high level of involvement	Individual Needs Met
• Observe a class of children in a movement and/or music lesson. At random, choose two children and determine their level of emotional well-being and involvement. Support your analysis of the children's engagement. What would you do to ensure continuation of a high level or to increase the level of emotional well-being and involvement?	

Planning for Engaging

The following learning activities provide three possibilities to assess the concept of self-space.

M² Movement Standard: The child will apply an understanding scientific concepts and principles to analyze and improve fundamental motor pattern performance.		
Possibility One	**Possibility Two**	**Possibility Three**
Force production and absorption—catching	Force production and absorption—jumping	Force production and absorption—stopping a rolling ball with the foot

Learning Activity	Learning Activity	Learning Activity
Throw a ball at the wall; what happens? Throw the ball at a mat hanging on the wall; what happens to the ball with each? The mat gives and absorbs force; what you need to do when catching is absorb force. How do we absorb force when catching? *Look* for the ball, *reach* for the ball, *give*.	Jump up and land. Were your legs bent or straight? How did it feel? Everyone jump up and land with straight legs. Now jump up and bend your knees when you land. Which way felt better, and why?	What do you think we need to do to stop a rolling ball? When you caught the ball with your hands, you bent at the elbow and absorbed the force over distance. This time, you absorbed the force by reaching with your leg and bringing the ball into your self-space.
Assessment	**Assessment**	**Assessment**
Children stand in parallel lines facing a partner. They take two steps back. Throwing and catching with each other, as they step back, they catch the ball. If they are successful, they step back; if not, they step forward. The teacher observes the distance between the children and specifically provides feedback to those who remain close together.	Children complete a peer-assessment task sheet that evaluates jumping from different heights and the depth of the knee bend. Discussion of greater height means greater knee bend.	Working with a partner, children complete a self-assessment task sheet that shows kicks from different distances. The task sheet evaluates *reach* with the leg and *give* with the leg.

Now You Try It

Complete the following standard-based learning activity designed to meet various interests and developmental levels by designing two possibilities/learning activities to develop a movement and music standard taken from M^2 Movement Standards.

M^2 **Movement Standard:** The child will move to a rhythm using a variety of nonlocomotor, locomotor, and manipulative movement skills.		
Possibility One	**Possibility Two**	**Possibility Three**
Music leading movement	Music leading movement	Music leading movement

Learning Activity	Learning Activity	Learning Activity
Select different locomotor patterns and different types of music. Play a piece of music and observe what the children do. How does the music tell you to move, which music tells you to run, walk, skip, and so on?		
Assessment	Assessment	Assessment

References

HighScope. (2013). Program assessment. http://www.highscope.org/Content. asp?ContentId=79.

Kee, Y., & Wang, C. (2008). Relationships between mindfulness, flow dispositions and mental skills adoption: A cluster analytic approach. *Psychology of Sport and Exercise*, 393–411.

Laevers, F. (2003) Experiential education: Making care and education more effective through well-being and involvement. In F. Laevers & L. Heylen (Eds.). *Involvement of children and teacher style: Insights from an international study on experiential education.* Leuven, Belgium: Leuven University Press.

Lewis, K. (2011). Ferre Laevers emotional well being and involvement scales. Retrieved from http://www.earlylearninghq.org.uk/earlylearninghq-blog/the-leuven-well-being-and-involvement-scales/.

Manitoba Education, Citizenship and Youth (2006) Rethinking classroom assessment with purpose in mind : assessment for learning, assessment as learning, assessment of learning. http://www.edu.gov.mb.ca/ks4/assess/index.html.

Marshall, H. (2009). Observing and communicating early childhood music and movement development. *Perspectives: Journal of the Early Childhood Music & Movement Association*, 4(2), 14–20.

Nakamura, J., & Csikszentmihalyi, M. (2009). Flow theory and research. In C. Snyder & S. Lopez (Eds.). *Oxford handbook of positive psychology*. New York: Oxford University Press, pp. 195–206.

National Association for the Education of Young Children. (2003). *Early childhood curriculum, assessment and program evaluation: Building an effective, accountable system in programs for children from birth through Age 8.* http://www.naeyc.org/files/naeyc/file/positions/pscape.pdf.

National Association for the Education of Young Children (2009a). *Developmentally appropriate practice in early childhood programs serving children from birth through age 8.* Washington, DC: NAEYC.

National Association for the Education of Young Children (2009b). *Where we stand, NAEYC and NAECS/SDE: On curriculum, assessment, and program evaluation.* Washington, DC: NAEYC.

National Association for the Education of Young Children (2011). *NAEYC Code of Ethical Conduct and Statement of Commitment.* Washington, DC: NAEYC.

Presidential Youth Fitness Program Physical Educator Resource Guide. Retrieved from http://www.presidentialyouthfitnessprogram.org/resources/index.shtml.

Snow, C., & S. Van Hemel. (2008). *Early childhood assessment: Why, what and how.* Research Council of the National Academies, http://www.nap.edu/catalog.php?record_id=12446.

name index

subject index